'DEAR FRIEND, YOU MUST CHANGE YOUR LIFE'

ALSO AVAILABLE FROM BLOOMSBURY

Becoming Beauvoir: A Life, Kate Kirkpatrick
Wittgenstein's Family Letters: Corresponding with Ludwig,
ed. Brian McGuinness
Seneca Letters: A Selection, Eliot Maunder
Luis Buñuel: A Life in Letters, ed. Jo Evans and Breixo Viejo
Diaries and Selected Letters, Mikhail Bulgakov (trans. Roger Cockrell)

'DEAR FRIEND, YOU MUST CHANGE YOUR LIFE'

The Letters of Great Thinkers

Edited by Ada Bronowski

BLOOMSBURY ACADEMIC
LONDON • NEW YORK • OXFORD • NEW DELHI • SYDNEY

BLOOMSBURY ACADEMIC
Bloomsbury Publishing Plc
50 Bedford Square, London, WC1B 3DP, UK
1385 Broadway, New York, NY 10018, USA

BLOOMSBURY, BLOOMSBURY ACADEMIC and the Diana logo are trademarks of Bloomsbury Publishing Plc

First published in Great Britain 2020

Copyright © Ada Bronowski and Contributors, 2020

Ada Bronowski has asserted her right under the Copyright, Designs and Patents Act, 1988, to be identified as Editor of this work.

Cover image © Patrice Cartier/Bridgeman Images

All rights reserved. No part of this publication may be reproduced or transmitted in any form or by any means, electronic or mechanical, including photocopying, recording, or any information storage or retrieval system, without prior permission in writing from the publishers.

Bloomsbury Publishing Plc does not have any control over, or responsibility for, any third-party websites referred to or in this book. All internet addresses given in this book were correct at the time of going to press. The author and publisher regret any inconvenience caused if addresses have changed or sites have ceased to exist but can accept no responsibility for any such changes.

A catalogue record for this book is available from the British Library.

A catalog record for this book is available from the Library of Congress.

ISBN: HB: 978-1-3500-8918-1
PB: 978-1-3500-8919-8
ePDF: 978-1-3500-8917-4
eBook: 978-1-3500-8920-4

Typeset by RefineCatch Limited, Bungay, Suffolk

To find out more about our authors and books visit www.bloomsbury.com and sign up for our newsletters.

CONTENTS

Introduction   1
Ada Bronowski

1 Be Present!   7
Ada Bronowski
Epicurus to Menoeceus, 3rd century BC   14

2 The Price of Time   19
Christelle Veillard
Seneca to Lucilius, AD 63–64   25

3 The Self-Punishing Student of a Doting Teacher   27
Ada Bronowski and Gweltaz Guyomarc'h
Marcus Aurelius to Fronto, AD 146–147   34

4 A Philosophy for the Poor from a Cynical God   37
Alberto Camerotto
Kronus to Me, from Lucian of Samosata's *Satumalia*,
a December between AD 160 and 175   44

5 Real Philosophy for Real People   47
Delphine Antoine-Mahut and Marie-Frédérique Pellegrin
René Descartes to Princess Elisabeth of Bohemia, Egmond,
1 September 1645   51

6 Good Intentions and the Resistance of Reality   57
Delphine Antoine-Mahut and Marie-Frédérique Pellegrin

Princess Elisabeth to René Descartes, The Hague, 13 September 1645   62

7 'No. Colours are real.'   65
Sarah Hutton

Anne Conway to Henry More, 3 December 1651   70

8 A Philosopher-Empress in a Revolutionary World   73
Kelsey Rubin-Detlev

Catherine the Great to Prince Charles-Joseph de Ligne, Peterhof, 30 June 1791   80

9 From Exile with Love   85
Catriona Seth

Germaine de Staël to Madame de Tessé, Auxerre, 30 June 1806   89

10 Erotic Affinities   91
Katherine Harloe

Johann Joachim Winckelmann to Leonhard Usteri, Rome, 14 September 1763   94

11 Rational Empiricism?   97
Dalia Nassar

Friedrich Schiller to Johann Wolfgang von Goethe, Jena, 19 January 1798   104

12 'What then is Happiness, My Dear Friend?'   109
Luigi Capitano

Giacomo Leopardi to André Jacopssen, Recanati, 23 June 1823   115

13 A Philosophy of Love 119
Máire Fedelma Cross
Flora Tristan to Charles Fillieu, Paris, 30 July 1843   124

14 Just the Magnificence of Reality 127
Rick Anthony Furtak
Henry David Thoreau to Harrison G.O. Blake, 3 April 1850   131

15 *De Profundis*: A Philosophical Letter 135
Stefano Evangelista
Oscar Wilde to Lord Alfred Douglas, Reading Gaol, January–March 1897   142

16 A Correspondence Theory of Truth 149
Nicholas J. Owen
Mohandas K. Gandhi to Maganlal Gandhi, 2 April 1910   157

17 Dispelling the Tower of Fear 163
Charlie Louth
Rainer Maria Rilke to Lotte Hepner, Munich, 8 November 1915   168

18 The Epic Side of Truth 173
Daniela Helbig
Walter Benjamin to Gershom Scholem, Paris, 12 June 1938   178

19 'A Shit on a Pedestal' 187
Antoine de Baecque
François Truffaut to Jean-Luc Godard, May–June 1973   194

20 A Philosophy of Dance   201
Ada Bronowski

Maurice Béjart to Nahuelt, Christmas 2000   207

List of Contributors   211
Acknowledgements   213
Notes   215
Index   239

INTRODUCTION
Ada Bronowski

Here are twenty letters written by twenty intellectuals and artists as disparate in time, age and circumstance as a Roman Emperor and an English seventeenth-century Viscountess, a retiring third-century BC philosopher and a twentieth-century film director. Twenty unique voices converging around central questions about how to live our lives. From: how to face death? To: how to make life bearable? From: how to get pleasure? – and for that matter, what is real pleasure? To: what is happiness? And how not to waste time? How to be good? What does it mean to be bad? Can we change? Twenty private letters tackle these eternal and universal questions.

None of these letters were written for a wide audience and none of the writers – or almost none – ever thought we would be reading them. In this respect, the letters collected here are not part of a public exchange of views – a practice which reached its apogee in the post-Renaissance and pre-Modern Republic of Letters, in which the great discoveries of the Scientific Revolution and the ideas of the Enlightenment were made public.[1] The opposite traits run through the letters collected here, in that they are deeply personal and, genuinely or performatively, private. No competitiveness, no rush for first place; nor is there any brilliantly mean lampooning for the entertainment of others. The privacy elicits discourses which lay bare sincere and urgent responses to the hard questions of life, which no human can escape. Yet, where privacy itself plays an argumentative role in support of the truth of what the letters intimate, the questions they address naturally open the scope of these letters. As such, their writers, knowingly or not, make room for us all as 'brothers and sisters in humanity' to quote Flora Tristan.

The reflections developed in the letters are addressed to a friend: it is first, the friend in the flesh, anchored in the historical context of the correspondence: the man called Menoeceus, Epicurus's good friend, André Jacopssen, Giacomo Leopardi's Swiss friend whom he met in Rome in the winter of 1822, Madame de Tessé, Germaine de Staël's Parisian friend, Mahatma Gandhi's distant cousin Maganlal, Maurice Bejart's last star dancer affectionately nicknamed Nahuelt. But this friendship, strengthened through the impact of the confidences imparted in the letters, bursts forth out of the historical context. Through each of these addressees, it is each and every one of us who is shaken up to change our lives in the light of the urgent wake-up calls that resound in these letters.

The letters are philosophical in the sense that the Greek philosopher Plato first gave to the word, that is, that they follow paths to truth or a truth and indicate to the correspondent directions for how to follow that path. The paths proposed are not framed by any particular coded literary genre; nor do most of the twenty authors belong to the distinguished academic field called philosophy. Indeed, half of the authors presented here have no official or unofficial affiliation with the academic discipline; a handful of them have a nodding acquaintance with it, which means that they have a complicated relationship of belonging and not belonging to a mainstream canonical representation of the academic discipline; and as to those who firmly belong to that mainstream canon, they appear in their letters to a friend as surprisingly non-conforming, and at times, even as challenging some core tenets and doctrine to which their names in history have been attached. This is perhaps most evident in a letter from René Descartes who, in reply to his epistolary friend, Elisabeth, destitute princess of Bohemia, realises, perhaps, that to be a dualist in theory works very well, but it does not square with reality and lived experience. Did Descartes recant (in private) and was he not really committed to a separation of the mind from the body? Did a woman, not enlisted in any philosophy course at any university, open his eyes to his errors? The answer can be found in Chapters 5 and 6 of this volume.

The twenty authors presented here make up a parallel philosophical tradition in the margins of the canon, in the shadow of the Republic of Letters, developed under the protection of the private letter. For some, this is because they are women who, historically, were forced into the margins of philosophy and were only able to find a welcoming place to think and create under the protective shield of private correspondence. Others created new disciplines in themselves and had no establishment to rebel against or fawn upon. Others have a 'sensibility' as Leopardi calls it, which makes them hybrid thinkers who belong to no one discipline and whom the academy has never been able to pin down to one specialism: half philosopher, half poet, half dancer, half political activist, half film-maker, half playwright.

A famous sonnet from 1908, 'The Archaic Torso of Apollo',[2] by Rainer Maria Rilke ends abruptly and out of nowhere with the injunction, imploration or resolution: 'you must change your life'. Rilke captures a moment of realisation and determination that, in different forms, the letters in this volume explore and develop. Where, in the microcosm of the poem, it is the fascination and wonder felt at the sight of a headless ancient sculpture that moves the poet to call everything into question, in each of the letters presented here, it is the macrocosm of everyday life which prompts analyses and discoveries of a deep truth hidden within the shapes that are perceived through experience.

It is that rallying cry to which Rilke gave poetic force and to which, explicitly or implicitly, the writers answer in these letters. Rilke famously wrote a series of *Letters to a Young Poet*, in which is displayed the capacity of the epistolary form to serve as a magnifying glass onto the analysis of the processes of creation. In this collection, another letter of his is presented, which applies that capacity to the examination of the lived experience of disillusion and fear. The letter expresses discursively what in the poem is effected through rigidity of form and sublime imagery, but the underlying message is ever the same: that not even experience is immediately given and that we must learn also to perceive it (see Chapter 17).

Pain and paradoxes give way to poignant admissions of the impossibility to reconcile ideals with reality: thus Leopardi reverts, desperately, to the capacity of the imagination to console us from such irreconcilable differences (Chapter 12), where the ancient god Kronos, given new life and power of speech through the satirical second-century essayist Lucian of Samosata, persuades his addressee that dreams are not so desirable after all (Chapter 4), whilst Henry David Thoreau exhorts his friend to embrace reality as it is, divested of the artifice and idealisations projected onto it (Chapter 14). The same impetus, though to very different ends, breathes enthusiasm into Johann Joachim Winckelmann who urges his friend to go and see for himself the works of art of antiquity to properly comprehend what is beauty: no books, no reproductions could ever substitute that first-hand experience (Chapter 10).

The letter charges its writer to acknowledge the concreteness of experience, not to hide behind theory or behind finely chiselled works of art, finished products of a complete philosophical treatise – no rhetorical subterfuge, just truth or, at least, a truth: that is what Elisabeth of Bohemia urges Descartes to do when her own experiences clash with his theory (Chapter 6), or Friedrich Schiller when he writes to Johann Wolfgang Goethe to tell him, urgently, that there is something wrong with pure rationalism, however compelling the theoretical order is shown to be (Chapter 11). This is also what the choreographer Maurice Béjart explains to his young friend: it is only the lived experience of motion that brings out of oneself, one's own true self (Chapter 20).

In the heart-to-heart, soul-to-soul conversation which these letters lay bare, it is no surprise that the reconciliation of the mind with the body is re-enacted from one letter to another as an unavoidable piece of evidence to contend with. We cannot pretend that the union of soul and body is not of central importance to our lives: thus Oscar Wilde, in the heart-wrenching introspective letter he writes from prison, articulates a new philosophy of the senses that must at every step satisfy both the desires of the mind and the desires of the body (Chapter 15); thus Epicurus warns that the body must be taken care of for the mind to be free to make the right choices and ensure that we live a good life (Chapter 1). New rules for new appetites are given by Marcus Aurelius who explains to his teacher of rhetorics that he can no longer indulge in defending indifferently both sides of an argument; he is now committed to only ever defending what he is convinced is true (Chapter 3); such new rules, to help counter fears and unknowns, are discovered by Rilke in his letter that sounds the causes for unhappiness (Chapter 17), or by Flora Tristan in a remarkable letter about the dawn of a new system of love where women decide and men comply (Chapter 13).

The letter form is a form of liberation: liberation from requirements to prove through logical demonstration, views that are too urgent not to share as soon as possible; liberation from the fear of saying something which is incongruous or contrary to mainstream ideologies; liberation from pomposity and peremptoriness. Great men appear humble and the humble appear great: this is the case, literally, in Lucian's invented correspondence between the lapsed god Kronos and a self-nominated representative of the poor, who starts by telling us that 'he is most esteemed by that god' (Chapter 4).

The question of money: what to think of it, how to handle it, whether to desire it, a bit, a lot or not at all, is also a recurring theme. Precisely because of that constant acknowledgement that the mind without the body is not much use, the answers to the question of money are never the expected sanctimonious expressions of moderation or disdain for wealth; rather, much more searching and ethical explorations of its place and use in life are developed. Kronos tells the poor that money makes the rich wretched, at the same time as it makes the poor poor only because they foolishly admire it. Seneca turns the expression 'time is money' on its head, by explaining that this is literally true, since the only real currency is time itself; we are all squanderers and getting poorer by the day (Chapter 2). François Truffaut mocks the rich for thinking of redeeming themselves by investing in left-wing socialist films and mocks those who make such films, in this precise case, Jean-Luc Godard, for thinking that giving out a wad of cash can compensate for an utter lack of sympathy and personal involvement (Chapter 19).

There is a morality which evolves and deepens from one letter to the next, but it is not an old-wive's tale of good versus bad. The singularity of each author renews, with each letter, the value of right and wrong, magnifying the importance of moral integrity and a personal relation to the good, happiness and duties owed to oneself and others. Walter Benjamin thus crushes the sentimental simplicity of right overcoming wrong in a vividly lucid analysis of the greatness of Kafka, concluding that there is 'hope but not for us'. The best that we can aim for is failure: for in realising our failure we move closer to self-realisation (Chapter 18).

In a personal letter, there is space to think in more depth, without bravado, about failure, a much more common experience than its opposite: Epicurus explains it is better to fail for the right reasons than gain fluke success. His brothers-in-arms from across the centuries and the continents understand him as considering failure as the opportunity to finally pause and examine oneself in what becomes, in the words of Oscar Wilde, 'an intensification of personality'.

There is nothing like a letter to spell out the dynamics of a relationship: who holds the upper hand and who desires to seduce whom. Catherine the Great, eighteenth-century empress of Russia, appears in a letter to a courtier as both impressing him with her mastery of Enlightenment principles and at the same time superseding these principles with a refined sense of realpolitik which sees the practical limitations of such well-intentioned philosophy (Chapter 8). In her letter, the question of what freedom truly is cannot be quashed even as she betrays its universalist aspirations; the letter becomes thus a home to her better side. The same question runs through a letter from Mahatma Gandhi who enjoins his friend to yet another plea for self-realisation rather than a mindless submission to orders from above, be it for the liberation of their country, India. In self-realisation lies freedom: 'emancipate yourself ... you are yourself India' he writes (Chapter 16). Until then, a man lives in exile from himself: Germaine de Staël thus laments her exile from Paris, not only because of the physical distance from her friends, but also because she feels separated from her better self, from all those people who spoke the same language of the heart and mind. The letter comes, then, to assuage the division one feels from one's own self (Chapter 9).

The privacy of the letter also allows for earnest criticism. Harsh words are not gratuitous piques but serve to unfold a sober and clear-headed analysis, which societal rules governing the borderline between politeness and scandal, usually block or turn to spite. But in a letter, Walter Benjamin can deliver to his friend's ears alone a scathing rebuke of Max Brod in whom he identifies yet another great mystery about Kafka, that they should have ever been friends! He hypothesises that Kafka entrusted the destruction of his works to Brod because he knew he would not obey his request (Chapter 18). Winckelmann, in his letter, is free to ruthlessly dismiss the mannerisms of the French style of art criticism, challenging thereby Enlightenment aesthetics (Chapter 10); and, in a defining letter, Truffaut calls Godard 'a shit on a pedestal', not to insult him so much as to draw out, in a breathtaking letter, a description of the moral contradictions of the artist caught between moral absolutes and the demands of the here and now of the real people living and suffering around him – a contradiction which is further complicated by the question of what counts more, film or life (Chapter 19).

The letters are arranged chronologically; each is introduced by a specialist in the field, giving an in-depth analysis of the major themes and placing these in relation to relevant biographical and bibliographical works. Each letter is thus a doorway through which to enter the worlds of some of humanity's great thinkers.

1 BE PRESENT!

Epicurus to Menoeceus

Ada Bronowski

From amongst the ancient Greek philosophers, Epicurus (341–270 BC) stands out for having been a profuse letter writer, writing letters to friends, students and family in which he never failed to impart some pearls of wisdom, extracted from a very personal philosophical engagement. His letters circulated widely, even the most evidently personal. A letter from Epicurus to his mother, for instance, ended up being engraved in stone, some 500 years after it was first sent, on a portico in Oenoanda, a small outlier Greek city, at the south-western tip of present-day Turkey. In the letter, Epicurus reassures his mother who has been having bad dreams about him. He urges her to stay focused on the present, on what she can see and touch here and now and not worry about thoughts and impressions of things which are not directly present to her. He refers to his trademark concept of 'disturbance' ('*tarachē*') which is what one must stay away from at all costs, so as to reach the opposite state, that of 'absence from all disturbance', ('*ataraxia*') another trademark concept. His solution: 'take courage mother!', be wary of thoughts which bring to mind what is not present now.[1]

Epicurus was probably not the first son, nor will he have been the last, to tell his mother not to worry about him. But there is something about the *Letter to Mother*, as this stone-engraved fragment has come to be known, which makes both the letter and the kind of son Epicurus was, exceptional. It is a combination of two things: on the one hand, the immediate and sincere concern for his correspondent's moral and psychological improvement (namely that it is in his correspondent's power to achieve the ultimate goal of life, absence from worry), on the other hand, providing simultaneously a philosophical argument for why it is both necessary and possible to do so. The argument is simple in appearance: only what is here and now is true. It summarises a complex and elaborate theory of sensorial representation, by which our sense-organs are receptive to projections produced by other objects; when our sense-organs are switched off, as during sleep, that exchange of data cannot occur; therefore, there is no truth in dreams. In a few short lines to his mother, Epicurus has condensed the heart of his philosophical doctrine, skipping over the theory in a way that can only be achieved within an intimate letter, relying on respect for his interlocutor as a means of persuasion and an urgent and sincere desire to solve the problems of everyday life, beginning, as here, with nightmares.

Epicurus wrote over forty-five treatises and books of philosophy, themselves containing multitudinous volumes, for instance, a monumental work entitled *On Nature* composed of 37 books. They have all disappeared. Save for bits of sentences salvaged from carbonised papyri, Epicurus's prodigious output did not benefit from the zealous copying of texts which was the only means for the perpetuation and dissemination of texts in antiquity. The reasons for this editorial tragedy are not purely accidental. Epicurean philosophy has always irked. It poses a threat to institutions, whether they be social, civic or religious, by promoting subversive ideas, which can easily be framed as anti-social. The doctrine thus famously favours pleasure over duty; it denies, not so much the existence of god or gods, but rather any form of intercession from us to them or them to us; perhaps most subversive of all, it gathers physical, cosmological, and astrological evidence that there is nothing special about human beings, since we are, as everything else, but the momentary products of a haphazard meeting of atoms, which assemble and will disassemble to infinity, regardless of anything we do, think or say.

And so, the letter acquires, in the hands of Epicurus, a double significance. Formally, it is well adapted to the thoughts of Epicurus. For, just as the dialogue is the form which specifically expresses the kind of radical questioning of everything which characterises Plato, the letter imparts Epicurus's utter conviction that he holds the key to a happy life. No need for endless demonstrations, the recipient of a letter can trust that Epicurus would never lie to him or her, but simply that there is an urgency to put into practice Epicurus's discoveries, because it is imperative to change our lives for the better. Alongside this doctrinal framework, the letter form is also a strategy for the survival and diffusion of doctrine. For, under the cover of a humble, inconspicuous letter to friends and family, the eminently mobile, relatively short format of the letter is, for Epicurus, the guarantor of the survival and perpetuation of his thought.[2]

We can see as much from his letter to his mother, which we can easily imagine she was proud and happy to share, perhaps first and foremost with her other sons whom we know spent time in Epicurus's school in Athens and were also engaged in a philosophical practice in the wake of their brother, whom they greatly admired. They are perhaps at the origin of the dissemination of the letter to their mother, she who 'carried within her such atoms which would combine to produce a sage', as one of her sons reportedly said.[3] The school Epicurus founded in Athens and in which he taught for thirty-five years, was not so much a school as a meeting place, in a garden, in which anyone interested, from slaves, to prostitutes to politicians could assemble and, following Epicurus's example, practice and discuss the means and the benefits of a life devoted to his philosophical discoveries. One important discovery is that philosophical advice needs to be recalled to the mind, often and regularly, by re-reading and repeating its pithy formulations. Thus, if a friend is far away, it is essential that, although he cannot partake in the discussions in Athens, he can be reminded of the main and crucial elements of doctrine. What can a good friend do for his friend, other than send a letter, which, by the very act of reading it, will recall in the recipient, all those life-changing ideas? Everything in Epicurus's letters resonates with the febrility of a wake-up call: no bland and conventional 'Best wishes' at the end of his letters, notes a perceptive biographer, but personal, exhortative enjoinders: 'May you do well', 'Live your life to the utmost'.[4] A letter from Epicurus is an intellectual vibraphone, in which each word strikes a chord. But, precisely because the letters are such intimate gestures towards a change of life, they also are permeated with a universal aspiration. We are, all of us, that friend.

In a letter addressed to his friend Herodotus, Epicurus writes that he sends him a summary of 'the main points of his doctrine' because, actually, that is 'enough' (*Her.* 35 and 83[5]). It takes a very generous character, a special kind of philosopher, to say of his original, painstaking, school-founding doctrine, that there is no need to go into its details (though Epicurus in those very same lines, reminds his friend that he has provided them elsewhere). The main lines are enough. What is more, Epicurus generously writes up for his friend a summary of all he needs to know. Beyond a question of character, Epicurus's 'enough' is also a philosophical agenda.

Three letters have arrived to us in full, copied out by the biographer Diogenes Laertius in the tenth and final chapter of his collection, *The Lives of the Eminent Philosophers*, devoted to the life and thought of Epicurus and published almost 600 years after his death. Diogenes Laertius took the Epicurean 'enough' to the letter. He selected these three letters as encapsulating the Epicurian philosophy in its entirety. The letter just mentioned, addressed to Herodotus, is principally devoted to the theory of atoms and how they aggregate into perceptible bodies; the second letter addresses questions of the behaviour of the earth, sun and stars set against the proof of the infinity of possible worlds; the third letter, which is the letter presented here, addressed to Menoeceus, discusses the conclusions to draw from those scientific observations, namely how to live one's life once we realise that the world is made up of atoms and is configured the way it is now by pure chance and that, even though it might be destroyed any day, it is hardly the end of the infinite universe.

The main theme which runs through the letter to Menoeceus is the relation between the present time and the presence of things. It is a relation which, from the very first sentence, Epicurus frames as one which only the practice and study of philosophy can properly bring to light. The play on 'present-presence' is pervasive throughout the letter.[6] It forges the unifying goal of the life project Epicurus enjoins us to embrace. All the big questions of life: god, death, a healthy diet, being self-sufficient, can be resolved once we get our heads round what it takes to be present to what is present.

The contrast between young and old is transformed, from the beginning, into a contrast between youth that feeds on the delusion of having time and is thus stigmatised as the age of procrastination and old age which is already saturated and has grown too tired to act. It is always either too early or too late. But, from the start, Epicurus makes us a promise: if we practice philosophy, a reverse temporality will take place. The young can at the same time be old, and the old can continue to be young. A change in perspective is required: paying attention to what is present now. What counts is the 'health of the soul', which is described a few lines later, brought about by identifying 'the things that make us thrive'. The crucial element here, is the appeal to 'the things', also qualified as 'the things which are present' and whose absence requires that they be restored to us. For these things to be productive of happiness and thus guarantee the health of our soul, we must come to be aware of them. It is not so much their influence, as our paying attention to them, which puts them in our possession: we have them by paying attention to them. That is how they begin to fill our here and now.

Epicurus is no dualist. He does not think that our bodies are separate from our souls and that our souls have a life beyond our bodies. He confirms as much in the letter: when death is present, we are not; when we are present, death is not. This formula is both famous and famously frustrating in its attempt to be consolatory – a consolation thwarted by a nagging question as to how this is supposed to effectively help.[7] But it establishes one thing: that our life is the life of our body. Its death is our death, there is no surviving soul or a soul whose life is separate from the body. And yet, from the start of his letter, Epicurus entreats his friend to focus on his soul, implicitly suggesting that it is the body – in its youth or old age – that misleads us, by diverting our attention from what makes us happy, to a misguided apprehension about what will happen or what has already happened to our bodies. The body, Epicurus seems to suggest, is trapped by time's arrow, whereas the possibility to find happiness, tranquillity and satisfaction rests with a certain activity of our soul.

The letter is structured around forceful injunctions that speak directly to the soul: 'you must study philosophy', 'you must pay attention', 'you must reflect', 'you must remember'. These injunctions convey both the urgency of the task at hand and the double-direction in space and time with which that task is concerned: here and now. Such exhortations echo a philosophical tradition crystallised by Socrates' appropriation of the Delphic maxim: 'Know thyself'. Epicurus's letter culminates with a final exhortation which cannot but resonate with the Socratic motto, as Epicurus urges Menoeceus to 'train yourself to pay attention'. Epicurus has subtly transformed the Socratic command. 'Know thyself', as Socrates notes, is an injunction whose apparent simplicity hides the greatest, if not an insurmountable, challenge.[8] But Epicurus's 'train yourself' opens up the possibility of actually realising the injunction.

The Epicurean formula opens a horizontalisation of our expectations: we have at arm's length what it takes to live fulfilled and happy. The search is not within ourselves, but around us in recognising what is present to us. At the heart of the difference between Socrates and Epicurus is the way each thinks of the self: a soul which is at odds with its body (Socrates), or a soul which is its body at its best (Epicurus). However, the distinction is not a straightforward clash between Socrates who thinks the two are separable and Epicurus who thinks they are not. For Epicurus too is concerned with the 'health of the soul'. A more subtle dialogue is, in fact, engaged between Epicurus and the dualism of his philosophical rivals.

As the letter progresses, we are told to embrace the transience of life, which Epicurus calls 'the mortality of life' (*Men.* 124). Rather than being apprehensive about the end of our lives, we should see its ending as a source of pleasure throughout our actual life. For the enjoyment of our lives lies with its ending: we make the most, not of the length or quantity of our time, but of its intensity – an intensity borne out of the fact that it has a beginning and an ending. In that way, 'our concern with living well and our concern with dying well, is one and the same' (*Men.* 126). To master this elasticity of time is to master the nature of our desires. Some desires are natural, some are 'vacuous', that is to say, they are not motivated by any reason (and are more of a whim than a desire). But not all natural desires have the same claim to our regard for them: some are necessary, some are not. Amongst the necessary desires, further divisions deepen Epicurus's analysis of the self: some desires are necessary for our happiness, others are necessary for the absence of discomfort to our body (which the twentieth-century philosophy of pathology will call the need for 'the silence of the organs'[9]), whereas others still are necessary to live. Integrity of the body and life are not the same thing. Rather, there are three levels of life: mere survival, clinical bodily integrity and living one's life properly.

This is Epicurus's answer to Plato and Aristotle who also set out three levels of life: the acquisitive life of multiple desires, the ambitious life of public engagement and the contemplative life.[10] Epicurus has exploded the hierarchy implicit in his rivals' division. Both for Plato and Aristotle, attaining the contemplative life, the superior and only truly happy life, is reserved for the happy few; those whose intellectual capacity – to resist all or most pleasures of the body – will eventually enable them to contemplate truth and possess wisdom.

For Epicurus, the life of fulfilment is not over and above the body, but with and through the body. He puts it in terms of the weather, providing us with a psychological weather forecast: there is a 'storm in our soul' (*Men.*128), a *winter of our discontent* which befuddles our soul. To assuage it, we must align soul and body. Maintaining our bodily integrity is one thing but enjoying that integrity is another. From 'the silence of our organs', we must find the silence after the storm, which is a silence in our minds. This Epicurus analyses as a calibration between pleasure and pain. He goes to some length in the letter to pinpoint our errors of judgment about present fears at future pains and future fears at present pains. It inevitably comes down to our blindness to the present and to what is within our reach here and now.

Under the mild and gentle appearance of a friend giving advice to a friend, Epicurus rips apart every aspect, custom and usage that constitutes life in a community. The iconoclastic force which sweeps through his letter burns, to this present day, with the same radical fervour. Everything that we are used to, we should get unused to: we think of god, or the gods, as sharing values and feelings with us? We are wrong; the whole point of being a god is to be completely indifferent to humans. We have accustomed ourselves to think of death as an evil. But death is utterly different from what we know, so we cannot think of it on any common terms with our lives. It is, in every way, nothing to us. We have been accustomed to think of pleasure in terms of quantity and accumulation? Wrong again, pleasure is anywhere where there is no pain, or any future pain. Hunger is a pain, so the simplest food which eliminates hunger is the greatest pleasure. We are used to thinking of luxury and opulence as a good, but luxury is a dependence on outward things, and surely to be independent is best.

A final warning goes to the defenders of necessity and of causal determinism whom Epicurus refers to as the 'physicists' (*Men.* 134). There can be no necessity. All there is, are indestructible moving atoms, which, every once in a while, swerve randomly. Things happen by chance, which means that we are free. Being free, it is we who decide our actions. This is the reason, as the final bombshell lands at the end of the letter, that not all success is good. Sometimes failure is better than success, that is, when it derives from well-reasoned plans; success is the fruit of mere chance. With this final nuance, Epicurus also distinguishes himself from his closest rivals, the Stoics. The Stoics divide actions into what is up to us and what is not up to us. For the Stoics, as long as we do all that is in our power to do and thus plan correctly, whatever the outcome, we have done well; neither success nor failure is in our power. For Epicurus, the outcome counts, but only when taken together with the rational planning for it. Failing well is the result of a well-governed soul and body, whereas success by mere fluke is a recipe for disaster, foul weather in the mind and outside.

Epicurus to Menoeceus[11]

3rd century BC

Epicurus to Menoeceus, all good wishes!

(122) No one, however young, should delay studying philosophy. Nor, even as we become old, should anyone tire from the study of philosophy. For there is no too soon or too late for anyone when it comes to maintaining the healthy state of the soul. To say that the time for philosophy has not yet come, or that it is long gone is like saying that the time to thrive and be happy is not yet come or that it is over. And so, young and old, everyone must study philosophy! When you are old, you do it so as to rejuvenate by feeling grateful for the good things from days gone by. And when you are young, you do it so that, though you are young, you are old at the same time because you do not fear the future.

So, it is crucial to concentrate all our attention on those things which make us thrive and happy. If happiness is present with us, then we have everything. But when it is absent, we must do everything to obtain it.

(123) All those things which I have unceasingly recommended to you, please do them! Concentrate all your attention on them. Consider them to be the ABC of the good life.

And the first thing to think about concerns God, you must think of him as an immortal living being who is blessedly happy, as indeed he is described under the common notion of God. Do not, then, attach to him anything besides his immortality. Do not attribute to him anything which clashes with his blessed state. But conceive of everything and only those things which can protect his blessedness along with his immortality – that is how to think about him!

For gods exist. And knowledge of them is evident. But they are not like the multitudes believe them to be. For these people do not protect the notion they have of what makes gods, gods. And so, sacrilege is not when someone denies the gods worshipped by the multitudes, but when someone ascribes to the gods the opinions of these multitudes. (124) For these are not pure and primal preconceptions, but false representations, formed by later additions from claims people make about the gods. On the basis of such representations, the greatest calamities are thought to be brought about by the gods onto bad people, whereas benefits follow for those who are good. But what this comes down to is that people get habituated to feel an affinity to particular virtues no matter what, approving other people who are like them, whilst considering as alien anyone who is not like them.

Next you must get used to this: to thinking that death is nothing to us.

All good things, as all bad things, come from sensation. But lack of sensation is death. Therefore, a correct understanding that death is nothing to us makes the very mortality of our life enjoyable not because it adds infinite time to it, but because (125) it takes away the desire to live forever. For nothing is terrifying in being alive once you understand that nothing is terrifying in *not* being alive.

So someone who says he fears death not because it will cause pain when it comes, but because it is painful now since it will come in the future, is a babbling fool. For what is present now and is giving no trouble is causing an imaginary pain in one's expectation of it. It turns out therefore, that the freakishly scariest of all evils, death, is nothing to us. Precisely because, whenever we are present, death is not present; and when death is present, then it is us who are not present. Therefore, death is nothing: neither for the living, nor for the dead, since for the living, death is not present, and for the dead, it is they who are no longer present.

But at times people flee death as the greatest of evils, and at other times, they choose it to put an end to the evils in their lives.

(126) The wise man, however, does not think lightly of his being alive, nor does he fear not being alive anymore. For life is not distressing to him, nor does he consider not being alive to be an evil. But just as, with food, it is not the greatest quantity of whatever there is but the tastiest that we would choose, in the same way a fruitful life is not the longest but the most pleasant.

So if you recommend to the young on the one hand, to live well and to the old on the other hand, to end their lives well, you're making no sense, not only because life is to be embraced in any case, but also because to be concerned with living well, and to be concerned with dying well, is one and the same concern.

Much worse still is to say that not to be born is a good thing,

> And once born, to pass through the gates of Hades as swiftly as possible.[12]

(127) For the person who says this, if he is persuaded by what he says, how come he does not get up and walk away from life? For this is what he should be ready to do forthwith, if indeed he is so sure of his decision. But if he is joking, then he is a fool to speak so about things which are no joking matter.

You must remember that the future does not belong to us, nor does it wholly *not* belong to us, so that we should not trust blindly that it will happen, nor should we deny ourselves all hope, as if it were most certain that it will not come about.

And you must consider this: that when it comes to our desires, some are natural, but others are vacuous. There are also differences amongst our natural desires: some of them are necessary desires whereas others are merely natural. And even amongst the necessary desires, some are necessary for our happiness and thriving, whilst others are necessary for the body to be free of discomforts, whereas others still are necessary just to stay alive.

(128) An uncompromising theory of desires refers every choice we make and every aversion we endorse back to the health of the body and the state of tranquillity of the soul, for this is the aim of a blessedly content life. It is for the sake of this end that we do everything we do, so as not to endure physical pain, or have our souls burdened with troubles. And when once we arrive at this state, all the stormy weather in our soul dissolves. The living being need no longer roam around, trailing after some thing or other it is missing, and in search of something new to enhance the well-being of the soul and the body.

For we are in need of pleasure only when we are in pain because of the absence of pleasure. But when we are not in pain, we are no longer in need of pleasure. And this is the reason why we say that pleasure is the beginning and the end of the blessedly happy life.

(129) For we recognise pleasure as our primordial good, congenial to our nature. Indeed pleasure is the first thing we take into account for all our choices and aversions. And it is pleasure which has the final say, since sensation is the criterion by which we judge each and every good thing as good. And since pleasure is our primordial good and we are born to seek it, precisely because of that, we do not choose each and every kind of pleasure, but rather, we often forgo many pleasures when greater distress follows from them. And there are many afflictions that we think are worth enduring over pleasures, because a far greater pleasure awaits us after having patiently borne these afflictions over a long period of time. So, every pleasure, because of its own intrinsic nature, is good, but not every

pleasure is to be chosen. Just as also every kind of pain is bad but not all pain must automatically be avoided.

(130) It is indeed by gauging pleasures against pains and looking at the benefits of the one compared to the inconveniences of the other, that each and every pleasure or pain can be judged properly. For we treat something as good which after some time turns out to be bad, and vice-versa, we treat something as bad, which, it turns out, is good.

Now we think that to be self-sufficient is a great good. But not so as, in any event, to support ourselves with as little as possible, but rather so that, if we have not got a lot, we can be content with the little we have. For we are genuinely persuaded that the people who enjoy opulence to the utmost are those who have the least need of it. For all that is natural is easy to procure, and only the object of vacuous desires is hard to come by. Simple food affords just as much pleasure as the expensive foods of an opulent lifestyle, when once the pain of need has been removed. (131) Bread and water give a person in need the highest of pleasures.

So getting used to the simple lifestyle, and not to opulence, enhances one's health. It renders a man unflinching in the face of the necessary requirements of life. And when at intervals, we come into periods of opulence, it places us in a better position to deal with it and prepares us to be fearless in the face of good or bad fortune.

So you see when we say that pleasure is the goal of life, we are not speaking of the pleasures of the profligate or the pleasures found in sensual indulgence. That is what ignorant people think, and those who disagree with us or who misunderstand us. But what we mean by pleasure is, for the body, not feeling any pain, and for the soul, being unburdened from any trouble.

(132) It is not wallowing in drinking parties and revelling, it is not the enjoyment of young boys and women, nor yet the taste of fish and the other dainty foods which make up an opulent dinner table – no, it is none of these which give rise to a life of pleasure. What does is sober reasoning, the kind which meticulously examines the reasons for each one of our choices and aversions and rids us of the opinions from which great confusion takes hold of our souls.

And the foundation for all this, and which is also the greatest good, is prudence. That is why prudence is even more precious than philosophy, for from it are born all the other virtues. It teaches us that it is impossible to live pleasurably without also living prudently, and honourably, and justly, nor can we live prudently, honourably and justly without also living pleasurably. For the virtues stem naturally from the life of pleasure, and indeed the life of pleasure is inseparable from them.

(133) And now, tell me, do you think there is someone who is in a better place than such a man? A man who conceives of the gods as holy; who is fearless, whatever happens, when it comes to death; who has figured out what is the goal of nature; who understands that the limit to all good things is whatever is easily fulfilled and available, and that either the duration or the intensity of bad things is short-lived. And as for fate, which some people present as master of all things, he laughs at that, and rather says that some things happen by necessity, some by chance, and some due to our own actions. For we cannot be made accountable for what happens by necessity, and he sees that what happens by chance is uncertain, but what is due to our own actions is unregimented. It is those latter actions which are naturally accompanied by blame or its contrary.

(134) For it would be better to believe the myths about the gods rather than become the slave to the fate the physicists speak of. In the myths, there is some hope for intercession promised us through honouring the gods, but fate is intractable.

As for chance, our man does not consider it to be divine, as most people think of it (for a god would never do anything without order), nor does he think it is an unreliable cause. For he does not consider that it is by chance that good or bad are allotted to human beings in view of living the blessedly happy life – or not. All chance does is to furnish us with starting points leading either to great goods or great evils. (135) He thinks that it is better to fail through bad luck having reasoned well, than to succeed by chance not having reasoned at all. It is far better that in our actions, our sound judgement does not lead us to success by mere chance.

Pay attention to these things, and all those related to them, train yourself day and night, and train your fellow human beings. And then, never, neither in your waking hours nor in sleep, will you be troubled. You will live as a god amongst men. For a man who lives surrounded by immortal goods is nothing like a mortal being.

2 THE PRICE OF TIME
Seneca's First Letter to Lucilius
Christelle Veillard

Reading the *Letters to Lucilius*, we are drawn into a conversation between the philosopher Seneca (4 BC *circa*–AD 65) and his friend Lucilius. It is a conversation which evolves from one day to the next, touching on various topics, as the events of the times roll by. When Lucilius carelessly uses the word 'friend' to designate an acquaintance he himself says he does not fully trust with his own affairs, Seneca rebukes him and reminds him of what it takes to be a true friend (*Luc.* 3[1]). A true friend must prove himself, for instance by taking the time to write out and share the principles of philosophy in a letter. Thus, when Lucilius says he is working relentlessly at philosophy, Seneca congratulates him on his efforts to become a better person, but not without putting Lucilius on his guard: by getting too wrapped up in his studies, Lucilius runs the risk of 'playing up the part of the philosopher', by which Seneca means that he might end up merely looking the part, and attracting attention though he himself will not be paying attention to what really matters. For a philosopher is not the man who parades a dishevelled beard, and sleeps on the floor (*Luc.*5). The warning is given in passing, light-heartedly as befits the friendly tone of an intimate letter.

Seneca, in his letters, as a friend and teacher, lavishes encouragement and advice, but is also, at times, effusive about his own struggles to become wise. He is now reaching the end of his life and has retired from public life: 'I have retired from the world and from worldly affairs, starting with my own' (*Luc.* 8.2). The letters were written between AD 63 and 64, shortly before Seneca's death in 65. Lucilius, though roughly the same age as Seneca, still holds public office and is an official of the highest rank, for he is, in this period, the procurator of Sicily. We may suppose, therefore, that the correspondence makes up for the physical distance, which weighs upon the two friends. In his *Natural Questions*, which Seneca wrote during the same years, he offers an explanation for these letters:

> We must flee from the world and retire within ourselves. [...] Though we might be separated by the sea, I will strive to guide you, leading you by the hand to a more worthy goal. And, so that you should not suffer from loneliness, I will from here, engage in conversation with you. We will be united by the best part of ourselves.[2]

The 'best part of ourselves' is our soul, which we must spend our entire lives improving.

Throughout their correspondence, Seneca adopts a peculiar stance. He is a friend writing to a friend, keeping this friendship alive, consoling and advising Lucilius, whilst sharing with him his own problems. But, beyond this meeting of two minds, Seneca broaches a discussion with the whole of humanity. Through Lucilius, Seneca speaks to all of us who will ever read him: he is speaking to posterity. We have here the indication that this correspondence, however private, was from the start thought out by its author as a composition piece, with a specific philosophical content and ultimately destined for publication. If the only letters we have are Seneca's, it is because only the words of the teacher are edifying and meant to be remembered. Seneca declares with conviction: 'I can make the names I take with me endure through time' (*Luc.* 21.5). He promises Lucilius an everlasting fame, following in the footsteps of Epicurus who, when he made Idomeneus the addressee of his letters, had declared – so claims Seneca – that: 'if fame is an inducement to you, my letters will make you more renowned than all the things which you honour and for which you are honoured' (*Luc.* 21.3). Lucilius and Idomeneus occupy parallel positions: both are powerful and famous politicians of their day, but both owe their posthumous fame to their friendship and correspondence with a philosopher. Only philosophy brings true fame, the lasting memory of their names through the centuries, because only philosophy can master time.

This is precisely what the very first letter to Lucilius is about, in which Seneca gives his first piece of advice:

> Here is what you should do my dear Lucilius: reclaim yourself from yourself! And time, which until now – either because you were forced

or without you realising it – has been stolen from you or has just slipped away, time, I say, you must catch hold of and preserve.

Luc. 1.1

Having reached a period of his life in which he will rapidly begin to lack time, Seneca reminds Lucilius that time is his most precious possession. It is, in fact, the only good of which we are the sole masters and commanders. It is of this good that we make the most liberal use; for we waste it without thinking, as if we had an endless supply. We spend it in an absurd way, in useless or frivolous activities; worse, we let others dispose of it, depriving ourselves of the only thing which is absolutely ours, abdicating our own rights on ourselves. Who has not lost a whole hour, listening, without paying much attention, to the boring discourses of a sycophant? Who has not wasted time daydreaming, when they should have attended to a myriad of important tasks? Seneca warns Lucilius and, through him, he warns each and every one of us:

> think about it, a great part of our life slips through our fingers when we do wrong, an even greater part is lost by our doing nothing at all, and the whole of our life passes by as we are always doing something other than what we should.
>
> Luc. 1.1

Seneca, the Stoic philosopher, upbraids us about the fact that we are absent from our own existence, we have forgotten to pay attention to our own lives. It is, therefore, a matter of urgency that we reclaim possession of ourselves, by finding a way to get rid of this state of non-presence to ourselves. The role of the friend consists of pointing out these errors of ours, by sharing with us his own experience.

What is the cause of this strange absence from oneself? It is to be found in our attitude towards death – as simple as that: we believe that death is yet to come, whereas, in fact, death has already happened. Seneca here makes use of a classic Stoic element of methodology: that of revisiting the precise definitions of things such as to discover their paradoxical core. From this rearticulated definition, we are then able to determine the correct behaviour to have towards things. How can death already be behind us? Does this mean we will not die? Or, perhaps even, that we are already dead? What is meant by this paradoxical claim, is that death is within time – the time which we no longer have at our disposal. This time, already lapsed, already spent, is, to all intents and purposes, behind us, in our past actions. Death is thus not something to look ahead to but something which accompanies us day after day, in all our actions, cannibalising every moment that passes. The remedy, then, is also quite simple: we must focus on the time we have left, the time we can make use of.

To reach out to the future, towards the time of our actual operative presence, is thus the first recommendation Seneca imparts to Lucilius: 'Hold on to each and every hour' (*Luc.* 1.2). Seneca creates striking aphorisms in his *Letters*, which still resonate to this day. Their role is to galvanise the soul, to drive Lucilius to change his behaviour, and pull him out from this drowsiness, which might feel comfortable but is, in fact, harmful:

> Precepts have great weight in themselves, especially when they are woven into poetry, or condensed into prose aphorisms.
>
> *Luc.* 94.27

Aphorisms have the advantage of piercing straight into the soul, without the need of further explanation; they stir the soul to action by awakening its more noble instincts, which otherwise lie dormant. Seneca repeatedly insists that we are inclined by nature towards virtue, for the seeds of virtue are within us and it is enough to arouse them for them to develop (*Luc.* 108.8). This awakening occurs through a momentum communicated to the soul by way of an imprinting on it – the result of a well-formed aphorism, a condensed formula for truth, which is striking by its self-evident nature and thereby hits its target. It sets us in motion, in that our heart is touched, our mind is enticed and our desire for virtue is aroused. Seneca evokes the example of how, in the theatre, an audience bursts into applause at a well-turned phrase, which thus meets with instantaneous approval from everyone. The souls of the members of the audience adhere, as if instinctively, to the content which has been enunciated, without needing any proof, because they feel in agreement with what has been said (*Luc.* 94.28). The truth is immediately recognised by the soul and stirs it into action. For this reason, poetry has an advantage over prose because it pierces our souls more swiftly:

> For, as Cleanthes used to say, 'just as our breath makes a more resounding sound after passing through the narrow tube of the trumpet, from which it then erupts through its large bell, in the same

way, the restrictions of verse endows thought with greater resonance'. We hear the same things distractedly, and they are less striking when they are expressed in prose; but when rhythm is added and a noble thought is restrained within the norms of metre, the very same thought hurls out towards us like an extended arm.

Luc. 108.10

The comparison with the trumpet leads us back to the Stoics's physical conception of the soul. The soul is a warm breath, which loosens and tightens, depending on which objects it meets. It is also possible to bring about in it a certain kind of disposition thanks to well-turned sentences: the breath of the soul clashes with that of the spoken phrase; the force of the clash is determined by the degree of compression of the phrase, in form as in content. The more compressed the phrase, the greater the concentration of truth contained within it. The compactness of poetic discourse produces a tightening of the tension in the soul, which is the physical condition necessary for the kind of strength which anticipates the state of the virtuous soul. The soul of the wise has such a high tension that it is comparable to a fortification against which all external attacks come up short. This metaphor has met with a remarkable posterity in the writings of Marcus Aurelius, emperor of Rome and Stoic philosopher who lived a century after Seneca and who forged the image of the soul as an impregnable fortress and the inner citadel.[3] Seneca applies this method of poetic compression to his prose by formulating striking aphorisms, which are easy to remember. The letter form is thus an experimental middle ground. Though not poetic, it is porous to aphoristic expression and free from the prerequisites of the philosophical treatise, in which lengthy discussions and arguments are required to prove the validity of truths, but fail to capture our imagination by the expressive force of those truths.

It is with just such an expressive aphorism that Seneca ends his first letter:

It is too late to start saving once you've reached the end. For what is left at the very end is the worst, and there is only very little of it.

Luc. 1.5

Seneca warns us that it would be an error to hoard our time, when we have already spent most of it, which is Seneca's case, and also that of

Lucilius. There is also a touch of humorous irony in depicting the end as vile and yet, however repellent, there still is too little of it. Seneca points at a hapless greediness which wants no matter what, even if whatever is left to take is no good. The point is not to become a time miser to the extent that we become paralysed and immobile, thereby letting what time is left to us go stale. Seneca tells us how he himself tries to apply his method:

> like someone who leads the high life, but who is also scrupulous in his accounts.
>
> Luc. 1.4

Not to become stingy with one's time, but to make use of it wisely, with joy and splendour, fully acknowledging the life that is left to us. No sadness, no dismay: 'no one is poor if whatever miserable share is left him is enough for him' (*Luc.* 1.4). Seneca draws up a new economy in which it is not so much that time is money, but that money is time. This shift raises the stakes considerably by devaluating the worth of any kind of thing money can buy. The relentless obduracy of the philosopher-turned-accountant draws the line at what is and what is not replaceable. Seneca thus identifies the one thing which can never be replaced and which, therefore, is the only thing of worth, which is time. By insisting and expanding on what seems at first to be only a metaphor, Seneca goes beyond the reassuring safety of figurative speech to shake Lucilius up into truly fearing destitution. Poverty and wealth are now to be measured according to the currency of time, which can easily make paupers of us all.

Time is thus a new gold standard, which, as Seneca says, should be the starting price we ask for before undertaking any course of action. Just as keeping our accounts in good order is meant to help us stay on top of our budget, so now, with the new economy of time, being precise about rates and allowances should make us better equipped to use our time well.

Though the truths imparted are harsh, the letters of Seneca to Lucilius are also ultimately a work full of optimism: they are meant to bring support to all the souls who will read them, now and for all centuries to come, in what is both a homage paid to time and a victory over it.

Seneca to Lucilius

AD 63–64

Greetings from Seneca to his friend Lucilius[4]

(1) Here is what you should do my dear Lucilius: reclaim yourself from yourself! And time, which until now – either because you were forced or without you realising it – has been stolen from you or has just slipped away, time, I say, you must catch hold of and preserve. Be convinced that things are as I write: that some of our time is forced from us, some of it is surreptitiously removed, and some of it vanishes like evaporated water. The most shameful loss, however, is the kind due to our carelessness. And if you think about it, a great part of our life slips through our fingers when we do wrong, an even greater part is lost by our doing nothing at all, and the whole of our life passes by as we are always doing something other than what we should.

(2) Give me a man who puts a starting price to his time, who appreciates the value of each day, who understands that he is dying every day! For this indeed is where we are mistaken, that we see death far away in the distance ahead, but a great part of it has already been and gone. Whatever part of our lifetime lies behind us, it is in the clutches of death.

Therefore, my dear Lucilius, do what I write you to do: hold on to each and every hour. And then this will happen: that you will depend less on tomorrow, if you take the upper hand on today.

(3) For as we put things off till later, our life runs past us. Lucilius, nothing belongs to us, only time is ours. Nature put us in possession of this one single thing, as fleeting as it is slippery, from which anyone who wants can expropriate us. How foolish can mortals be that we let ourselves get credit for having obtained the most insignificant and worthless things which can easily be replaced; but no one deems himself in any kind of debt, who is in receipt of time, though that is the one thing that not even a grateful recipient can ever repay.

(4) You might be wondering what I myself do, who am meting out these precepts to you. I will confess to you in all frankness: just like someone who leads the high life, but who is also scrupulous in his

accounts, I keep an accurate balance sheet of my expenses. I cannot say that I do not waste anything, but I can tell you what I waste, why I waste it and how I waste it. I am accountable for the reasons of my poverty. But my situation is that of many who are rendered penniless for no fault of their own: everyone excuses them, but no one comes to their aid.

(5) What then? I do not think a man is poor if whatever miserable share is left him is enough for him. But that does not mean I do not prefer that you keep what is yours, and this is as good a time as any to start doing so. For, as our elders had understood, 'It is too late to start saving once you've reached the end'. For what is left at the very end is the worst, and there is only very little of it. Be well.

3 THE SELF-PUNISHING STUDENT OF A DOTING TEACHER
Marcus Aurelius to Fronto

Ada Bronowski and
Gweltaz Guyomarc'h

The epistolary exchange between Marcus Aurelius (121–180), emperor of Rome from 161, and his teacher of rhetoric, Fronto (100–166/7) extends over 30 years. It begins around the year 139 when Marcus is 19 and has already been elevated to the rank of Caesar: he knows that he is destined to become emperor. Fronto is about 40 years old. He comes from the Roman province of Numidia in Africa (now part of Algeria). A lawyer by profession, he is a well-known and well-respected teacher whose students hail from amongst the highest dignitaries of the Empire. At the time the correspondence begins, Fronto had already been Marcus's tutor for some time.

Unlike other famous correspondences in antiquity, for instance Seneca's *Letters to Lucilius*,[1] Fronto and Marcus Aurelius, it would seem, never thought of making their letters public. The most plausible hypothesis for the survival of the letters through the ages is that their publication was due to one of Fronto's descendants. Although this exchange is between two well-known figures in their own times as in later times, many of the letters display what may seem as a surprising degree of intimacy and sincerity between two friends. Most of the letters are private, as is evident from the unhampered freewheeling style of writing and the way both correspondents linger on details from everyday life, from physical ailments to the year's grape harvest.

The first reason for the correspondence is pedagogical: Fronto's aim is to complete Marcus's education. He sends his pupil reading lists with writing exercises. He corrects Marcus's letters and speeches, giving specific advice on the order or choice of words and images. Everyday events become excuses for exercises in rhetoric, for example when the two dispute the merits of sleep.[2] In some letters, Fronto launches into more theoretical accounts, discussing the different rhetorical genres[3] or making more small-scale observations such as how changing one letter in a word can alter its meaning completely.

But at every occasion, advice, theory, directives for improvement and even soft reproofs are given by the master with the utmost solicitude and care not to hurt the feelings of his student, so as only ever to encourage and boost Marcus's self-esteem. The whole correspondence is sustained throughout by an emphatically affectionate vocabulary. At times, it reads like an exchange between lovers rather than between a teacher and his student. For example, Fronto says that he never sees an image of Marcus without kissing it. And, despite or because of the reproaches he receives, Marcus never ceases to declare that he loves his master as much as he loves himself, writing to him even when he knows he will see him the following day and always with tender gratitude. In truth, such reciprocal declarations of affection are more a staging of the pedagogical relationship than an erotic exchange. It is in part an educational tactic, and in part, an affectation, which Fronto does not reserve for Marcus's benefit alone. Fronto uses the same mannerisms when he writes, for example, to Lucius Verus, Marcus's adopted brother.[4] And so, though it has been suggested in some recent scholarship,[5] there are no constricting reasons to suggest a physical relationship between Fronto and Marcus. Such a relationship, under the reign of Antoninus, would have been highly problematical in a context of growing rigidity in social mores – all the more so in imperial circles – in the aftermath of the famous and infamous loves of the emperor Hadrien.

The strategy from Fronto's perspective is to instil a practice of goodwill: goodwill as a form of pedagogy. This takes the shape of praise, as when Fronto tells Marcus one of his texts could find its place in 'a work by Sallust' whom Fronto greatly admires.[6] Generally, it is a method which derives from a certain understanding of human nature. Fronto thus writes to Marcus: 'humankind is by nature obstinate when criticised but is easy to endear through compliments.'[7]

In the face of such goodwill, the student is compelled to feel shame when falling short of his teacher's expectations. The high standards that affection and benevolence uphold are thus more powerful in keeping the student in check than stern words of rebuke. And yet, Marcus expresses a fear that his teacher is not critical enough of him as a result of his blinding affection for him.[8] As a result, he displays an almost compulsive pursuit of shaming and reproof of which the letter presented here is but one striking example. Reproof fills Marcus with gratitude towards his master, for he is then reassured that he is on the path of progress. He clings to the content of the admonition as the key to truth and knowledge.

In one of the earliest, if not first letter we have from the correspondence (dated from 139), Marcus expresses the joy he feels from the reproaches his teacher makes, because that is how he learns from his teacher 'to say the truth' – an arresting formula from a philosopher in the making.[9] In this letter, he explains that in his reproofs, Fronto does not correct superficial errors of style, but directs Marcus in the art of saying what is true, by showing him how to distinguish it from deceptive and ambiguous language. This is a first adumbration of what will constitute the heart of the letter presented here: namely Marcus's philosophical interpretation of the role and nature of rhetoric. For Marcus wilfully steers the practice of rhetoric Fronto teaches him, towards the philosophical pursuit of truth, reading into Fronto's admonishments about form, a deeper incitement towards the discovery of truth. Such an approach to rhetoric and its usage is redolent of Stoic doctrine.[10] It is far from clear, however, that Fronto endorsed this view of rhetoric, or that he intended his affectionate reproof to open up such deep tunnels of thought.

In the letter presented here, dated around the year 146, Marcus's conflicted approach to rhetoric is entangled with increasingly deeper levels of shame and guilt. On the one hand, he is ashamed and feels guilty that he has not done the homework Fronto had set him, though he had time enough to do it; on the other hand, he is consumed with the shame of not being a good enough and virtuous person, having been woken up to his moral shortcomings by the study of the works of the philosopher Aristo.

This letter is hotly debated amongst interpreters and has often been taken as the premise for Marcus Aurelius's conversion to philosophy. First and foremost, it lays bare the effects of a cossetted education on an extraordinary and self-demanding individual.

Racked with guilt for being a bad student and a bad human being, Marcus writes to his teacher, not in fear of admitting his shame but, on the contrary, to transform his shame into a self-imposed injunction to overcome his admitted failings, and thus to improve. The letter form enables Marcus to enter a candid analysis of the levels of shame he feels, precisely because they play into Fronto's pedagogical intentions, in which coaxing into improvement through soft shaming has ever been the mode of communication. In this letter we therefore get an insight into the development of the future philosopher–emperor, whose reputation to this day would be sealed thanks to the writing of his *Meditations*, a modern title given to a text which is a cross between a diary and a private notebook, in which self-analysis and self-criticism constitute the core of a philosophy of endurance and strength of the will.[11] The appeal and reliance on his friend and master is the projection onto a figure of authority of the trigger for internal resolve. Trust, friendship and the pedagogical imperative to make progress turn Marcus's letter to his teacher into the student's reckoning, in which he comes to terms with his own responsibilities both as a student and a human being.

The letter is rooted in everyday preoccupations and events, yet it is all the while shrouded under a constant appraisal and internalised scrutiny. It begins with Marcus complaining about the vanity of one of his friends, Gaius Aufidius, who displays contempt towards Marcus for being all privilege and no competence. What is interesting is how Marcus transforms this event into a first level of self-shaming in the eyes of his master: for, whilst he mocks the conceit of his friend, he also realises that in writing about it, and revealing that he is upset by his friend's taunting of him, he gives undue value to it, showing himself to be vulnerable to something which should not affect him. He himself anticipates his master's reaction: 'So what, might you ask?', he writes, conjuring in this way, the figure of the benignly reproachful teacher, putting him to shame for being disturbed by such trifling matters.

Marcus thus puts in motion the shaming mechanism that will constitute the rest of the letter. For he is confessing to the shame of being hurt by the teasing of a boastful friend, who himself was trying to shame Marcus as a privileged idler compared to the hard-earned self-professed success of Aufidius, the outsider (from Umbria), who gained his standing through toil and intelligence. Marcus reassures Fronto that he has made peace with Aufidius, but he is also intimating that the taunt hit a nerve because of Marcus's nagging fear that Aufidius might be right.

The main part of the letter is then devoted to the mixed feelings raised by Fronto's impending arrival: pleasure but also shame. Marcus admits to not having completed the work assigned to him by his teacher. He gives the reason for this: it is because he has been absorbed by the reading of the works of Aristo. The identification of this Aristo is controversial, but it is very likely that he is the Stoic philosopher Aristo of Chios (third century BC), known in particular for having, within the Stoic system, forgone physics and logic for the sake of ethics alone – and this, with a radical emphasis. For Aristo was opposed to the common Stoic claim according to which some things, though not good in the absolute sense, are nevertheless preferable if one can have them, such as health or staying alive. For Aristo, there is only one good, and that is virtue. It is possible that such radicality was attractive to the young Marcus – perhaps more than merely attractive. For Marcus goes on to describe a profound mental and physical upheaval as a result of his study of Aristo – a crisis characterised by contradictory states:

> Aristo's books are doing me good right now, but at the same time, they make me feel bad (...) That is why I punish myself, I get angry, I am gloomy, I have a '*crise*' and become jealous of everyone and everything, I go without eating.

This '*crise*' (rendered in our translation by borrowing from the French to mirror the effect in the original text), Marcus uses a Greek word to designate it (*zēlotupō*) in his otherwise fluid Latin, as if to underline the state of estrangement and alienation he is in.

The reason for this paradoxical and strenuous state of crisis is of a deeply moral order: Aristo shows him how to be a better man, whilst at the same time exposing to him his own moral inferiority and the distance between his capacities and what it takes to be a properly good man – precisely those inferior capacities which his friend Aufidius had already scorned. In other words, Marcus is experiencing the shock of apprehending the gap between how things should be and how things actually are, between what one should do and what one, in fact, is doing. The power of Aristo's writings consists in their addressing the real questions about life, appealing to the raw concerns of the life of the future emperor. This experience is so powerful that, for now, the only solution Marcus finds is to give Aristo's book 'a rest', to devote himself, at least for the moment, to his studies in rhetoric and catch up on his homework.

But, as he promises to devote himself to the task his teacher has set him, he also anticipates that he will not be able to fully accomplish the assignment. For he is, by now, too much under the influence of Aristo's philosophy to work on merely oratorical skills. That is to say, he can no longer defend both sides of an argument, which is the supreme art of the orator. He warns his teacher that from now on, he will only be able to defend one side of an argument: that where his convictions lie. He implies that his mastery of rhetoric is, from now on, the expression of his moral integrity.

It is, once more, a sense of shame which has impelled Marcus almost to rebel against his teacher of rhetoric. This is the shame he feels from Aristo himself: long dead the Greek philosopher may be, but that does not stop his new disciple from living up to the expectations set out by Aristo's philosophical precepts. And so, the salutary and gentle shaming theorised by Fronto the pedagogue has magnified in Marcus the philosopher and transformed into an inexorable motor for life-changing resolutions. For Marcus, progress is vital and necessary, but also hard to enact since it is always the fruit of overcoming bad tendencies. It is the feeling of shame generated not only from an awareness of one's inadequacies, but crucially from admitting to them, which ultimately drives him to action. This, in itself, is a philosophical stance. And so, the relationship between Marcus and his living teacher, Fronto, is tested against an apparent clash between the practice of rhetoric and the injunctions of philosophy.

Fronto keeps philosophy at a distance. Philosophy is not useless, he readily allows, as it can provide meat for eloquence: the great philosophers, Socrates at the forefront, did not forego the use of rhetoric.[12] But throughout his letters, Fronto can be seen to praise rhetoric *against* philosophy, because it does not help to assuage the sufferings of life. So, it was certainly not Fronto who suggested that Marcus read Aristo; his recommendation was rather that Marcus read some plays – Marcus reassures him at the end of his letter that he will get to that recommendation after reading some Cicero. Eloquence, for Fronto, unlike philosophy, is accessible to everyone and is as natural as laughter. It is the application in words of one's culture; indeed culture, as Fronto writes to a different addressee, 'belongs to the orator' and, rooted within human practices, it is the opposite of 'divine matters' which, in this context, have a pejorative connotation and which Fronto says 'are best left to philosophy'.[13]

As we can see in Marcus' letter, he is by no means abandoning rhetoric for the sake of philosophy. Moreover, in contrast to Aristotelian and especially Platonic philosophy, Stoicism considers rhetoric as an integral part of philosophy. As we mentioned earlier, Marcus sees Fronto's teaching of rhetoric as inculcating in him the science of 'saying the truth'.[14] This indicates that Marcus considers Fronto's lessons to be a crucial part of his own personal philosophical awakening. Marcus, what is more, did not wait to read Aristo before becoming interested in philosophy: he was introduced to Stoicism from a very early age, as he recounts at the beginning of his *Meditations* (1.7). If reading Aristo was undoubtedly an enduring influence on Marcus, it fits into a long evolution which does not crystallize into a disinterest for oratory and even less so in a disinterest for his beloved teacher.

It is Marcus himself who tells us that, from his exchanges with Fronto, he got something much more fundamental than lessons in rhetoric. In book I of his *Meditations*, Marcus offers a gallery of portraits of all the people he thanks for making him the man he has become. In this strange compendium, unique in all antiquity, not all Marcus's friends are mentioned, only those who are worthy of being role models. Fronto is mentioned early on (1.11), but not for his lessons in rhetoric, rather for having taught Marcus about

> the malice, caprice and hypocrisy that accompany absolute rule, and that generally those whom we regard as being of noble birth are quite devoid of humanity (*astorgoteroi*).

This last term, *astorgoteroi* in Greek, echoes its opposite and extolled quality, *philostorgia*, which indicates warmness of heart and a spontaneous sense of humanity which Marcus gives Fronto credit for in their correspondence. In one letter to Fronto, for instance, Marcus signs off, reverting to the Greek, with a friendly apostrophe: 'farewell best of masters, you most humane of human beings!'.[15] It is Fronto who explains why the word is only ever cited in Greek: it has no Latin equivalent, 'given that no one in Rome possesses this virtue'.[16]

For Fronto, *philostorgia* is a form of intimacy between two people, requiring absolute honesty and loyalty without failure. For Marcus the Stoic, the term is charged with philosophical connotations. It is not a term reserved for human feelings but one used for all animals feeling love and affection for their family and friends. To be wise is to know how to extend and transfer that love to the whole of humankind. *Philostorgia* is thus, properly speaking, philanthropy, as Chryisppus, one of the founding fathers of Greek Stoicism, had already theorised – a virtue which Marcus exalts in his *Meditations*. It is the love and humanity contained within *philostorgia* which Marcus says guarantees a love free from passion (*Med.* 1.9) and which he must preserve so as not 'to become too Caesar-like' (*Med.* 6.30). This is where Fronto's lessons most clearly bear their fruit. Against the moral undoing which power may lead to, love and humanity are bulwarks. *Philostorgia* is also associated with the goodwill one should display towards others and which Marcus considers to be the very mark of virtue (*Med.* 3.12; 6.47). It is, in fact, this feeling which characterises the disposition of the good man (*Med.* 4.25).

The correspondence between Fronto and Marcus Aurelius is the backdrop to the development and practice of this *philostorgia*. The exchanges produce the occasions for it, in which the humane and loving teacher is a model of whole-hearted affection, who enjoins his student to express himself with sincerity. However natural, friendship needs to be learned and to be worked at. More than its content, therefore, it is the very fact of the exchange which is, in itself, of importance. Fronto teaches Marcus much more than rhetoric. Call it the truth, call it love, friendship or humanity, only a correspondence, and what is more, a correspondence which is long and constant, could give the future philosopher–emperor the space to learn this *philostorgia*.

Marcus Aurelius to Fronto

AD *146–147*[17]

My dear master,

It's Gaius Aufidius, he is over-excited. He is praising his own soundness of judgement to the skies! He says, there never was a more sensible man (and I am not even exaggerating!) to come from Umbria to Rome. So what, might you ask? He wants to be extolled as much as a judge as an orator. And when I laugh, he taunts me: it is easy to sit next to the judge staring with your mouth open, he says, it is another matter entirely to do the actual judging, that is glorious work. This is aimed at me. But in any case, the matter has now been settled. That is a good thing, I'm happy to say.

As for your arrival, it brings me joy and makes me anxious all in one. That it fills me with joy is needless to say. But why anxious too? I will confess it all to you, so help me god! It's the work you set me to write, I haven't even written down the first word of it! And it's not as though I did not have time to spare. But it's Aristo, his works are doing me good right now, but at the same time, they make me feel bad. For when they teach me about how to be better, they are undoubtedly doing good, but when they also show me how much my own abilities lag behind compared to these elevated ideas, then your student often blushes so deeply, and gets so enraged with himself! For in all the twenty-five years since I was born, I was not able to assimilate to my soul not one scrap of these good opinions and pure principles. That is why I punish myself, I get angry, I am gloomy, I have a '*crise*' and become jealous of everyone and everything, I go without eating.

I am in the thrall of these worries at the moment, and postpone daily to the following day, my commitment to write. But now I will come up with something. And, just as a certain Athenian orator once warned an assembly of his countrymen, 'sometimes the laws must be allowed to sleep', I will put Aristo's books to rest, begging them leave of absence for a short while. Instead, I will devote myself entirely to that poet of the stage you recommend – though first, I'll be reading a few of Cicero's shorter speeches. But, when I do come to writing, I will only defend one of two positions, for as to defending both sides on one and the same question, Aristo, though momentarily at rest, will never allow me to go that far.

Be well, my best and most admirable teacher.

My wife sends greetings.

4 A PHILOSOPHY FOR THE POOR FROM A CYNICAL GOD

Kronos to the Poor, from Lucian of Samosata's *Saturnalia*

Alberto Camerotto

Kronos's letter to the poor appears to be a letter about happiness. For its aim is to find a route to happiness, though that route might seem paradoxical and contrary to expectations. In his letter, nothing is as it first seems to be, however: sardonic advice and caustic warnings are the tools and raw material from which this route to happiness is constructed. Its discussion evolves against the backdrop of a utopian quest, formulated at the start of the letter, that of a desire for a world in which everyone is equal and in which there is no more injustice.

The letter presented here is the second letter from a sustained correspondence in which the nodal figure is the god Kronos. Lucian of Samosata (125–180 *circa*), essayist, erudite, satirist and philosopher recreates the real-false conditions for the plausibility of this letter collection: it is as if we were to find some old letters in the attic, only that the letters are from an old forgotten god. In the first letter, someone – someone who speaks for the poor – writes to Kronos. As the person indicates in his letter, this is not the first time he has done so, but this time, finally, Kronos writes back and so the exchange begins. After the letter presented here, which is Kronos's first reply, comes a letter which takes the opposite tack in which the god writes to 'the rich' discussing the impending festivities around the

Saturnalia. In the last letter of the collection, the rich write back to the god.[1] The letters belong to a larger set of texts devoted to Kronos, written with reference to a period of the year called *Kronia*, otherwise known as the Saturnalia celebrations, when the god Kronos returns to rule for seven days.[2] Kronos is a god from a different age, a Golden Age, before the world became dominated by Zeus and the other gods of Olympus.

Kronos is a special god. He is a god of otherness, a very important and polyvalent quality,[3] for he is an obsolete god, surpassed by the times and the generations; he has left his own privileges and power behind. In so doing, he has freed himself from convention and the usual shackles of custom and society to take on a different kind of role – perhaps also, to reserve for himself the right to be free from the relentless duties tied to managing the world and its mortal inhabitants. It is a distance which signifies happiness, just as Epicurus describes how the gods live, far away and detached from the affairs of mortals.[4] But precisely because of this distance, Kronos also has the capacity to see things from a different angle. From his mannerisms and choice of words in his letters, he is also a cynical god, an odd kind of philosophical god. He is paradoxical even in his commitment to non-commitment, harbouring within him a secret ideology driven to search for an impossible utopia. He is a god who does not keep silent, but, untethered, makes full use of his freedom of speech, that Greek idea(l) of '*parrhēsia*', serenely provocative free speech, which characterises the ancient Cynics.

He is, in short, all set to play the part of the satiric hero.[5] There are also echoes in him of Dionysius with his own ambiguities, and at times also of Prometheus, with his brazen free speech, whom Lucian had already reinterpreted elsewhere as a sophist.[6] But, as far as satirical strategy is concerned, Kronos could also be considered as an *alias* of Lucian himself, with all his ambiguities and his contradictions. On the one hand, the intimation is that it is useless to think that we will hear truths coming from this god: he can play the philosopher, but one thing is for sure, he has abandoned any form of dogma. On the other hand, as a god, he gives up on all pretences and equivocations as well, so it is likely that he will make some revelations. In any case, nothing guarantees that it is good to believe him. He is the mouthpiece for the simple – and for that reason, the most powerful – truths of satire, which are destined to become principles for life for anyone capable of truly understanding them.

The themes running through the correspondence are typical of satire: rich *vs* poor, excess, luxury, vanity. The inequalities of a social system are laid bare, in which the rich are forever richer, with ostentatious displays of their wealth, which turn out to be all the more shaming as they are revealed to be utterly vacuous. The squandering of goods becomes the symbol of absolute egoism. And yet, though the poor are ever more crushed by their poverty, there is no ethical legitimation which can save them. For in this world, the selfishness of the rich is mirrored by the envy and awe of the poor. There is no escape; but, in becoming aware of the state of things, there is a possibility to start over. Sure enough, the celebratory injunctions of the Saturnalia festivities would seem to allow for a temporary 'revolution', but the Saturnalia celebrations are also a time for satire.

Details from the everyday prevail in the letter between Kronos and his correspondent, 'me', as he appears in the initial greeting. Between Kronos, the god and his addressee, there is a sense of familiarity and a relationship which, from some angles, may remind us of the relationship between Seneca and Lucilius, which Lucian is evidently imitating and mocking.[7] For even the themes of the discussions are similar to those Seneca discusses: poverty, slavery, wealth, the misuse of goods, the corruption of life, the right attitudes to take, what choices to make. Stoic Seneca has, however, morphed into cynical Kronos.

To understand Kronos's advice to the poor, it is useful to bear in mind the complaints addressed to him in the first letter of the exchange (*Sat.* 19–24). There, an unknown mortal writes to the god, instead of praying. He complains about what is happening on earth, as any one of us could do. It is a banal everyday sort of letter, complaining also about the postal service, since letters get lost or are not read, or never answered. The writer mentions in that respect, a previous letter which went astray. The manner of address is that which is expected in a letter, with all its simplicity and concreteness. The problem posed is the inequality which makes life unbearable and human society shameful. The chasm between the rich and the poor is likened to the difference between an ant and a camel, or gold and something worse than lead. Human society in this state is simply a ridiculous monstrosity, with one foot in tragedy, the other in farce. Only laughter can come from such a sight, laughter which makes all the masks fall, revealing the absurdity and the embarrassing dissonance on which society is founded. No one can justify with a witty turn of phrase such profound inequalities, for they are not the fruit of merit. This is inequality, pure and simple.

Kronos, by name and deed, conjures utopias. And making utopias come true is what we have been led to expect from a god who was sung by the poets as a Golden Age ruler.[8] We expect to hear the wisdom gleaned from that original paradise lost in which reigned every sort of abundance, the absence of all worry, toil and pain for everyone with no exception.

But here and now, all sense of justice seems to have disappeared. The rich seem exaggeratedly happy: they have everything, they can do anything. But surely the poor could also be happy, if only they learned how to be content with the little they have? We shall see what Kronos has to say about that, but first we must recall the rule of the utopian city from a well-known fragment of a poem by Crates the Cynic philosopher (365–285 BC *circa*): on his imaginary island of *Pera*, the expensive delicatessen of the rich are of no avail, all you need there, is 'thyme, garlic, figs and bread'.[9] Kronos's poor complain of having only some cress, thyme and onion at their disposal. The echo to *Pera* is difficult to mishear but what was praised over there is here bemoaned. By the end of his letter to them, however, Kronos will show the poor that those are, in fact, secret objects of desire for the rich.

It would be wonderful if Kronos could make a reverse revolution happen and turn things back to how they were at the dawn of time. He has the power to change everything: his words say as much, as he speaks of freedom, change, transforming things though they seem frozen for ever as they are. In the plea from the poor in that first letter to Kronos, the poor consider him capable of changing the very laws of nature. There would finally come about that in which no one dares to believe any longer: equality, equality between all humans, starting with an egalitarian redistribution of all goods. Small things to begin with: the invitations to Saturnalia lunches should really be 'much more democratic' and everyone should have the same amount of food and wine.

The first letter ends with a remarkable curse upon the rich: gold-digging giant ants, from Herodotus's *Histories*, are called upon to transport the wealth of private citizens to the public reserves.[10] This curse on the rich is, despite appearances, based on the very same utopian vision in which private fortunes end up in the public treasury of an ideal city. Against selfishness, there is but one remedy: everyone must put their riches in common. We could say this is a communist idea, that of a political project for a rational and egalitarian division of all goods to fight against inequality which Hesiod and Aristophanes had already decried back in their day. It is an idea which is found in all utopian visions and which we find, of course, in Thomas More's *Utopia*.

But then comes Kronos's reply, with the letter presented here. The overpolite salutation at the start is clearly written in by the mortal who wrote to Kronos to begin with, since he refers to himself as 'me, whom Kronos greatly esteems', thereby implicitly commenting – and self-congratulating himself – on the fact that Kronos has deigned to reply to him. But the intrusion of 'me' in these greetings also indicates that our man is purposefully sharing with us a letter he personally received from the god. The self-congratulatory tone of the greetings is, in any case, immediately dispelled by the brusque tone with which the letter begins. All the complaints, wishes, hopes, all the wishful thinking about utopia are reduced to idle talk. Requesting that goods be redistributed is put down to pure folly. Kronos disengages immediately from any form of responsibility with regard to the affairs of the world. He truly seems to have become an Epicurean god. This is all due to his personal history and, if we believe him, his own choice. Kronos's only fields of expertise are games, revelling, singing and getting drunk. These are the main pastimes that are approved during the seven days of the Saturnalia.

There are traces in Kronos of the '*spoudogeloion*', the hybrid tone which is half serious and half in jest inherited from Aristophanes and Plato's *Symposium*. The responsibility of eliminating all inequalities belongs to Zeus who, nowadays, holds sway over the world. All the serious business is in his hands. But as Kronos writes this, he infuses his words with an implicit tone of understatement, in which he fully acknowledges the utopian vision he has been called upon to realise. And so, though it seems that initial expectations are being disappointed, the disillusion is itself set out in ambiguous terms which are deceptive in appearance.[11] For Kronos recognises a rallying cry in the protestations and aspirations addressed to him. He knows exactly what his addressee is talking about, because these thoughts about equality are precisely his ex-domain of expertise.

Utopia begins with equality: either everyone is rich or, just as well, everyone is poor. Kronos is well aware of the radicality of the Cynics's idea which could resolve all the problems of society.[12] But under Zeus's regime, the oldest of gods has a very reduced margin of action: lasting only the time of his celebratory holiday, he can only tend to the inequalities pertaining to his specific jurisdiction. Thus, at most, he can make some recommendations to the rich: that, during the time of the Saturnalia, they should be generous to the poor with the leftovers, the hand-me-downs and their invitations to their charity banquets – more or less as we do today at Christmas time. Kronos appears to be benevolent and somewhat paternalistic towards the poor. At first blush – and more than we would have expected – he is concerned with legitimising the hypocrisy and anticipating the eventual remonstrances of the rich and their petty charity.[13]

This would be almost embarrassing, were it not for Kronos's eccentric reversal of perspectives even as he promises to scold the rich. For where he, at first, seemed patronising, he now appears as a full-blown cynic, joining, in this way, a long Greek tradition which is largely perpetuated in the works of Lucian. For his message is the following: the happiness derived from wealth and power is a trap. It looks golden from the outside, but inside it is a ragged misshapen patchwork. For to be rich is to be filled with worries, fears and troubles. It is better to avoid wealth: a philosophical principle which becomes a classical encomium of poverty. Kronos has had first-hand experience. Thus, to find happiness, the oldest of all the gods recounts how he gave up his wealth and power to others. If we think lucidly of the way of life of the rich, torn between banquets and all manners of excess, extravagant luxury and depravation, then inequality becomes paradoxically lucky for the poor. For excess of any goods is not good for human beings. We must learn this time and time again. One can have too much of a good thing: eating till you burst is where luxury and vice become synonymous with illness and pain. A lesson as relevant today as it was in the second century, with our own contemporary problems of obesity and generally with too comfortable a life in the midst of a world overflowing with consumerist obsessions. Having everything is not what is best for mortals. Idleness and indolence soon transform us into corpses.

It is by acknowledging the truth of this state of affairs, that we can hope to bring about the only possibility we have of changing the world and turning things around. If wealth makes us unhappy, then poverty means salvation and happiness, just as is claimed by the paradoxical ideology of the Cynics. Moreover, wealth has even worse surprises in store. If you are rich, all human ties and all your most cherished relationships are necessarily warped: for you can trust neither your friends, nor your children, nor your wife. Even love becomes a matter of profit, prostitution and lies.

The problem no doubt comes down to the perception and interpretation of reality. The triumphant outward spectacle of wealth arouses the admiration of the poor, who stare in awe at the gold and the glitter, the white horses and shiny carriages, all to the greatest satisfaction of the rich. Here lies the aberration. And this is where satire can have an effect: for what we need is to modify our cognitive system. We need to operate a shift of perspective following the classic rules of philosophical refutation given to us by Socrates' *elenchos*, the method which helps unmask convention and shake up common opinions. If there is the slightest chance for a revolution close at hand, it can only come from this sort of conscious realisation. For in fact, it is the rich who need the poor as witnesses and admirers of their wealth. Without witnesses, wealth would come to nothing.

What needs to be done is to dismantle the hypocrisy of society: it is the habits and conventions of society which eat away at any possibility for justice. But it is the poor who are responsible for it. A different way of thinking about reality must be put into practice. From that perspective, Kronos becomes a satirical hero, capable of exposing the lies of our world. Wealth and the pursuit of the superfluous are only made for show, for social ostentation.[14] Luxury is utterly useless, it is meant only to create astonishment and envy, and that is all there is to the social prestige of wealth and the possession of goods, which but few people can afford in any case. So, it will suffice to deactivate the mechanism by which wealth is sought, by dismantling the logical and social trap: if the poor no longer pay tribute to wealth by their admiration of it and their shameful obsequiousness, gold will immediately lose its value. It will in fact, become, from one moment to the next, the most vile and abhorred thing, just as it happened in the ideal Athens of another utopian philosopher created by Lucian, Nigrinus from his eponymous dialogue, *Nigrinus*, and just as we find it in Thomas More's *Utopia*.[15]

The cynics take the prize at the end, as the letter concludes on a prevailing note of paradox and cynical detachment. Kronos can mete out his advice thanks to his position as an observer of reality: because of his detachment but also because he has inside knowledge of both ways of life, having once been rich and now, being wilfully poor. It is good to think of living as best we can in the moment, with the ability to laugh at everything. And since it is the time of the Saturnalia festivities, one should focus on enjoying the party. For the moment we start seeing reality for what it really is, all that we admire – wealth power, and beauty – appear as fleeting and subject to the implacable principle of '*oligochronia*', the principle of evanescence. One certain outlet for equality remains, one implacable law which is the same for everyone: that we are destined to leave on earth all our wealth and all our poverty, no distinctions made. But who knows if that is not itself the utopia, or rather the dystopia, of the afterlife? . . .[16]

Kronus to Me

From Lucian of Samosata's Saturnalia, 25–29, a December between AD 160 and 175[17]

Kronus to me, whom he greatly esteems, greetings!

(25) What is this madness of yours, my good man, writing to me about the present state of the world and urging me to make a redistribution of goods? Don't you know that's someone else's job? The current lord and master of the world should take care of that sort of thing. I'm surprised at you, you must be the only man left who doesn't know that I am king no more. Sure, I used to be king once upon a time, but that's all over. I divided my dominion amongst my children. The concerns you raise, that is what Zeus mainly takes care of. My own responsibilities such as they are, extend to boardgames, merrymaking, singing, drinking and the like and for all of seven days a year and not a day more. So, when it comes to those more important things that you speak of: wiping out inequality, making everyone either equally poor or equally rich, that is what Zeus should sort out for you. But if someone has been wronged in his holiday rights, or has been cheated out of his share of fun, that is where I can be a judge in the matter. So I will be writing to the rich about those dinners, and that measure of gold and the clothes, telling them they should get these things delivered to you people for the holiday celebrations. You are right to mention these things. They are just and fitting requests that the rich should honour, unless they come up with a good reason against doing so.

(26) Generally speaking though, you should know that you, the poor, you are very much deceived and mistaken about the rich. As if they were really blissfully happy, as you imagine them to be! That only they should be living some kind of life of pleasure because they eat lavishly opulent dinners, drink good wine, get to sleep with handsome boys and beautiful

women, and have the softest clothes to wear! You have absolutely no idea what it's like. The worries these pursuits bring with them are no trifling matter. The rich man must keep an eye out for every single thing: lest the butler gets lazy or steals when no one is looking; lest the wine goes bad and the grain infested by weevils; lest the thief should steal his precious drinking cups; lest the people be persuaded by sweet-talking populists, scaremongering the crowds about his presumed aspirations to rule tyrannically over them. And all this is but a fraction of his troubles. If you people knew what fears, what anxieties the rich man has, you would think that being rich is to be fled at all costs.

(27) And then, what about me?! Do you really think that, if being rich and ruling were good things, I would ever have been so delirious as to let those things go and give them up to others? Do you think I'd do that and accept to sit down in my place like a private citizen and let myself be ordered about by someone else? But, because I knew all about these concerns which necessarily assail the rich and powerful, I fled from power; and I did well.

(28) And now here you are, coming to me crying about these people gorging themselves on wild boar and cake whilst you, for your feast, make do with some cress, thyme or an onion. Well, let us look into this matter in more detail. In this very moment, both diets are surely equally pleasant to taste and equally painless. But afterwards? That's when things take a different turn completely. It is not you who, the following day, wakes up with a hangover like they do because of all that wine they guzzled, nor do you, as they do, because they are too full, let out stinking and foul belches. But those are the benefits they reap! And, having rolled about most of the night with boys, women, or whatever their lechery impels them towards, they readily catch consumption, pneumonia, or an oedema from all that debauchery. And just look at them, can you spot anyone amongst them who is not as pale as a ghost and who does not actually look like a corpse? And who amongst them reaches old age on his own two feet, rather than on the eight feet of his litter-bearers? They are covered in gold from the outside, but inside, they are nothing but a patchwork of random bits and bobs like the clothes used for actors on a stage, patched up from all sorts of worthless rags.

You, the poor, you never have fish for dinner, you hardly know what fish tastes like, but then, no gout, no pneumonia. Don't you see that you are off the hook for those sorts of things as well? And indeed, for any other consequence which follows from such causes. And, I'll tell you this, it is not even possible for these people to keep eating these things every day, for there are limits to satiety. Mark my words, they'd sooner be hankering for a simple vegetable and some thyme any day, just as much as you desire rabbit ragout or pork chops.

(29) It does not bear telling you about all the other woes these people endure, from the wayward son, to the wife in bed with a house slave, or the lover who yields out of necessity rather than pleasure. Quite generally, there is so much you people have no idea about. You see only their gold and their glitter. If you ever see them driving out on their white carriages, you gape at them wide-mouthed and prostrate yourself at their feet. But if you would disdain these things, if you would not make such a fuss about them but deem them of little worth; if you would not turn around to stare at their sliver-coated carriage; if, while they were speaking, you did not look away from their faces to stare at the emerald ring on their fingers or touch the hem of their coats and marvel at their softness. But if only you would let them be rich all on their own, then know this for sure: it is they who would come running to you. They would need you to join them for dinner, so that they could show you the banquet couches, the tables and the drinking cups. For possessing all these things is of no benefit at all if there is no one to witness your enjoyment of them.

(30) You would discover then, that most of these things they possess, they possess for your sake, not because they are useful to them, but so that you can admire them.

These things I write to soothe you since I know both of these ways of life. And in any case, it is worth celebrating this holiday bearing in mind that soon enough everybody with no exception will have to leave this life. The rich will be abandoning their wealth, and you, your poverty.

But you may rest assured that I will write to them as I promised. I am sure that they will not wrinkle their noses at a letter coming from me.

5 REAL PHILOSOPHY FOR REAL PEOPLE

René Descartes to Elisabeth of Bohemia

Delphine Antoine-Mahut and Marie-Frédérique Pellegrin

The correspondence between René Descartes (1596–1650) and Princess Elisabeth of Bohemia (1618–1680) is exceptional on three counts. First and foremost it provides a major contribution to philosophy; secondly, it never ceases, for all that, to evolve as an intimate and private conversation; third and lastly, it stands apart from the philosophical correspondences of the time, since the exchange is decidedly disengaged from the restrictive codes of the Modern Era's Republic of Letters. The first two aspects must be placed in context: philosophical letters at the time were not written with the intention that they would stay private. But, on the death of Descartes, Elisabeth refused to let her letters be published alongside those that Descartes wrote to her. In this historical context such a refusal is unusual to say the least. It surprised and indeed annoyed Descartes' editor, Claude Clerselier (1614-1684) as the letters exchanged between Descartes and Elisabeth frame a whole part of Cartesian philosophy which would thus never be properly categorised or published – especially the part concerning moral and political philosophy. The letters also reveal the independent philosophical thought of Elisabeth herself.

The epistolary exchange between Descartes and Elisabeth is thus the laboratory of Cartesian moral philosophy and, at the same time, the diary of Elisabeth's moral and philosophical life, whose depth of insight is astonishing. The clash between the private and the public structures the very frame of thought which drives the whole exchange since Elisabeth is challenging in it, in private, the Cartesian philosophical positions. And so, it seems a natural ending to the exchange that Elisabeth should thus refuse to have it published.

The last remarkable aspect of the correspondence pertains to its breaking free from the epistolary codes at the time. For the correspondence brings together two very different people: a French philosopher, who is a middle-aged gentleman, and a young German princess. It is Elisabeth who initiated the correspondence. Incited to do so by the Dutch doctor Henricus Regius, from Utrecht University, she boldly writes directly to the most famous philosopher of the day and asks him very difficult philosophical questions. She pioneers in this way an original literary genre: the mixed-sex philosophical correspondence. For the letters exchanged between people of different sexes are, in theory, governed by strict literary and societal rules which prohibit serious conversations between men and women. By escaping accusations of pedantry, the private letter form itself becomes for Elisabeth a safe space allowing a woman to philosophise unhampered. Elisabeth often seems to be playing the role of the objector in the letters since it is Descartes' philosophy which is the topic of discussion, but the study she carries out of her own character and situation, as a creature of passion and reason constitutes in itself a work of philosophy, originating out of a philosophical introspection. It is therefore fitting to set side-by-side a letter from Descartes and a letter from Elisabeth (Chapter 6) to fully grasp the reciprocal to-and-fro of their way of thinking and making progress in their understanding of the self through an exchange with the other. Though the initial relationship had begun on an unequal footing, the epistolary exchange succeeds in creating a form of equality.

First: Descartes to Elisabeth, from Egmond, 1 September 1645

The correspondence between Descartes and Elisabeth is a testimony to the exceptional intellectual capacities of Elisabeth in a variety of domains, from metaphysics to mathematics. But her line of thought reveals that her main preoccupation is with the practical application of philosophy. In a previous letter, Elisabeth had asked what the point is of 'playing the role of philosopher' as Seneca does in his *On the Happy Life*,[1] if you do not give to each and every person the natural means to become happy? What margin of freedom does a real man or woman, of flesh and blood dispose of, when each is bound to a body and are part of the world? What is truly 'one's own'?

In the letter from 1 September 1645, Descartes moves on from a commentary on Seneca, to a reply to these questions in his own name. Each and every one of us can indeed have the experience of an illness which affects, either momentarily or on a long-term basis, our capacity to reason. Should we then conclude, against Seneca, that it does not entirely depend on us to be happy in this life and that we should therefore leave it to the contingencies of fortune? Or should we reject that which makes a human being a real human being, and not merely a pure spirit? And how should we preserve the requirements for rationality of virtue without all the while making virtue impossible to put into practice?

Descartes' answer consists of two main lines of reflection. Firstly, he assesses the various factors (what he terms 'indispositions') which are liable to hinder the free usage of our reason and thus our capacity to procure happiness for ourselves. Secondly, he refocuses the discussion on the true causes of our happiness so as to determine the swiftest means by which to exercise virtue. The end of his letter succinctly brings together all that we need to know for 'the true use of our reason in the conduct of life'.

To state that we can be happy in all circumstances and without any help from anything external to us seems to come down to withholding from the great majority of people, who are indeed seeking this natural state of bliss, the means to achieve it. In response, Descartes' first approach consists in acknowledging the actual impact of indispositions to the body in the everyday exercise of reason. This impact would seem soon enough to be identified as a principle of heteronomy, whereby reason would seem to be dependent on the body. However, most often, this indisposition is temporary, so that the dependence principle must be relativised in comparison with the more regular use of our mind when it is 'free'. For people acquire the habit of using their reason well and this usually suffices to counteract momentary dysfunctions. To be one's own is first and foremost to consider exercising virtue in the long-term.

This goes for the indispositions which can utterly disrupt the use of reason. All the more so, then, when it comes to those which merely alter our moods and even more so for those which result from changes of fortune. The less indispositions originate from within or the more they result from the encounter with something external to us, the less they will be able to alter our internal state. In addition, the more indispositions will have been harder to overcome at a later stage, the more having overcome them will corroborate and strengthen our internal state for the rest of our life. Habit, which is cemented through the trials of our lives, is thus the proof of how free will can overpower that which resists it the most. It is the habit of reasoning which reminds us of the urgency there is of 'thinking of oneself', i.e. remembering to reason, in those moments in which good fortune induces us to confuse true happiness with a mere contingent, however pleasant, heteronomy.

What kind of pleasure or satisfaction should we trust in then, when we seek true happiness?

If indeed virtue is the greatest good for man, the practice of virtue must surely bring with it the greatest satisfaction. But a real human being, in contrast to 'a mind on its own' is 'a mind insofar as it is united to a body'. He is, in this sense, a creature of passions. How can someone both declare that virtue makes man completely happy and at the same time reject all form of passion as Seneca does? Should we only allow ourselves pleasures of the mind?

Descartes argues first by appealing to the representative dimension of passions. He thus explains that often, though not always, the value we give to an object which we suppose is the cause of a passion is, in fact, detached from any relation of truth with this object. Passion exaggerates, amplifies, deforms the good (or the bad) which we imagine to be caused by this object. The imagination introduces in this way a hiatus between the representational force of the passion and a rational appraisal of the object – the latter usually operates only at a later stage, after the initial representation. The exercise of virtue then is, at best, second in line compared to the misfortune or the dissatisfaction which we actually feel and which are the results of our initial pursuit of merely apparent pleasures. There is thus a relation to time which is a fundamental dimension of true pleasure. The habit of reasoning, rooted within repeated trials, must also be associated with a constant requirement to be first in line – this must be down to the mind's own initiative. But it also must take stock of the long-term: that is to say, that the mind must maintain, and if needs be must recover, its prerogative over the course of time. For the mind understands by a simple calculation, that, when it comes to choosing between pleasures, immortal pleasures are of greater weight than those which do not last. This principle must be embodied before and after our individual existence: before, so as to serve us as a guide as far as theory is concerned; after, so as to shape our life experiences.

In conclusion to his letter, Descartes has given himself the means to distinguish between the act of 'mastering' the pleasures of the body from that of 'despising' them. The philosopher is indeed embodying his part and not merely pretending to 'play the role of philosopher': for he puts into practice his claims and instigates everyone else to 'tame' their passions instead of attempting to 'free ourselves' from having passions. Philosophy is put to the test and proves itself through this trial: for philosophy is not worth anything if it has no clear aims and practical results.

It is under the pressure of Elisabeth's concrete questions about real people and their real choices in life that Descartes has been forced, in his reply, to give – like nowhere else in his writing – an account of the 'true' use of reason within a grounded, concrete reflection on what makes a real human being.

René Descartes to Princess Elisabeth of Bohemia

*Egmond, 1 September 1645*²

Madame,

As I was uncertain whether your Highness was in The Hague or in Rhenen, I addressed my letter through Leiden, and that letter you have done the honour of writing me was delivered to me only after the postman who carried it to Alkmaar had left. This has kept me from expressing earlier how full of glory I am that my own judgment of the book that you have taken the trouble to read is no different from your own, and that my way of reasoning appears natural enough to you. I assure myself that if you had had the leisure to think about the things of which he treats as much as I have, I could not have written anything that you could not have noted better than I. But because the age, birth, and occupations of your Highness have not been able to permit this, perhaps then what I write will be able to serve to save you a little time, and my mistakes themselves can furnish you with occasions to note the truth.

When I spoke of a true happiness which depends entirely on our free will and which all men can acquire without any assistance from elsewhere, you note quite rightly that there are illnesses which, taking away the power of reasoning, also take away that of enjoying the satisfaction of a rational mind. This shows me that what I have said generally about all men should be extended only to those who have free use of their reason and with that know the path necessary to take to reach this true happiness. For there is no one who does not desire to make himself happy, but many do not know the means to do so, and often a bodily indisposition prevents the will from being free. Something similar also happens when we sleep, for the most philosophical person in the world does not know how to prevent himself from having bad dreams when his temperament disposes him to them. All the same, experience shows that if one has often had some thought while one has had a free mind, one returns to it often afterward, no matter what indisposition the body has. Thus, I can say that my dreams never represent to me anything upsetting. And without doubt, one has a great benefit from being accustomed for a long time to having no sad thoughts. But we are able to be absolutely responsible for ourselves only so long as we are in our own power, and it is less upsetting to lose one's life than to lose the use of reason. For even without the teachings of faith, natural philosophy alone makes us hope for our soul to have a happier state after death than that it has at present. No fear is more upsetting to it than that of being joined to a body that entirely takes away its freedom. For the other indispositions, which do not altogether trouble the senses but simply alter the humours and make one find oneself extraordinarily inclined to sadness, anger, or some other passions, they no doubt give trouble, but they can be overcome and even give the soul occasion for a satisfaction all the greater insofar as those passions are difficult to vanquish. I also believe something similar of all external obstacles, such as the brilliance of high birth, the flatteries of the court, the adversities of fortune, and also great prosperity, which ordinarily gets more in the way of our being able to play the role of philosopher than do misfortunes. For when one has everything one wishes, one forgets to think of oneself, and, afterwards, when fortune changes, one finds oneself the more surprised the more one put one's trust in it. Finally, one can say generally that nothing can entirely take away the means of making ourselves happy as long as it does not trouble our reason, and it is not always those things that appear the most upsetting that are the most harmful.

But in order to know exactly how much each thing can contribute to our contentment, it is necessary to consider what the causes that produce it are, and this is also one of the principal pieces of knowledge that can serve to facilitate virtue. For all the actions of our mind which bring us some perfection are virtuous, and all our contentment consists only in our inner testimony of having some perfection. Thus, we know of no exercise of virtue (that is to say, what our reason convinces us we ought to do) from which we do not receive satisfaction and pleasure. But there are two sorts of pleasures: those which pertain to the mind alone and others which pertain to the human being, that is, to the mind insofar as it is united to a body. These latter ones, presenting themselves confusedly to the imagination, often appear to be much greater than they are, especially before we possess them; and this is the source of all the evils and errors of life. For, according to the rule of reason, each pleasure ought to be measured by the greatness of the perfection it produces, and this is how we measure those whose causes are clearly known to us. But often passion makes us believe that certain things are much better and more desirable than they are. Then, when we have taken great pain to acquire them and lost, in the meantime, the occasion to possess other truer goods, the enjoyment makes us know their defects and from this arises disdain, regret, and repentance. That is why the true duty of reason is to examine the just value of all the goods whose acquisition seems to depend in some way on our conduct, in order that we will never fail to employ all our care in trying to procure those which are, in fact, the most desirable. In regard to which, if fortune is opposed to our plans and prevents them from succeeding, we will have at least the satisfaction of having lost nothing by our fault, and will not fail to enjoy the natural true happiness which will have been in our power to acquire.

Thus, for example, anger can sometimes excite in us desires for vengeance so violent that it makes us imagine more pleasure in punishing our enemy than in protecting our honour or our life, and we will expose ourselves imprudently to losing both the one and the other for this end. On the other hand, if reason examines what is the good or the perfection on which this pleasure drawn from vengeance is founded, it will find none other there (at least when this vengeance does not serve to prevent the recurrence of what we take offense at) but that it makes us imagine that we have some sort of superiority and some advantage over those on whom we seek vengeance. This is often only a vain imagination, which does not merit being valued in comparison with honour or life, or even in comparison with the satisfaction one would have in seeing oneself master of one's anger in abstaining from seeking vengeance.

And something similar occurs with all other passions. For there are none which do not represent to us the good to which they tend more vividly than is merited and which do not make us imagine pleasures much greater before we possess them than we find them afterward, once we have them. Because of this we commonly blame pleasure, since we use this word only to signify pleasures that often trick us by their appearance, and make us neglect other much more solid ones, which we do not so much look forward to and which are ordinarily those of the mind alone. I say 'ordinarily', for all of the pleasures of the mind are not praiseworthy, since they can be founded on a false opinion, as is the pleasure we take in slander, which is founded only on the fact that we think we will be valued more, the less others are valued. They can also trick us by their appearance, when some strong passion accompanies them, as we see in the pleasure of ambition.

But the principal difference between the pleasures of the body and those of the mind consists in this: the body is subject to perpetual change, and even its conservation and its well-being depend on this change; so all the pleasures proper to it hardly last. For these proceed only from the acquisition of something that is useful to the body at the moment it receives them, and as soon as this something ceases to be useful to it, the pleasures also cease. On the other hand, the pleasures of the soul can be as immortal as can it, so long as they have a foundation so solid that neither knowledge of the truth nor any false belief can destroy it.

For the rest, the true use of our reason in the conduct of life consists only in examining and considering without passion the value of all perfections, those of the body as much as those of the mind, that can be acquired by our conduct, in order that, being ordinarily obliged to deprive ourselves of some of them in order to have others, we will always choose the best. And since those of the body are the lesser, one can say generally that there is a way to make oneself happy without them. All the same, I am not of the opinion that we need to despise them entirely, nor even that we ought to free ourselves from having the passions. It suffices that we render them subject to reason, and when we have thus tamed them they are sometimes the more useful the more they tend to excess. I would have none more excessive than that which leads me to the respect and veneration I owe you and makes me be, Madame,

Your Highness's very humble and very obedient servant,

Descartes

6 GOOD INTENTIONS AND THE RESISTANCE OF REALITY

Elisabeth of Bohemia to René Descartes

Delphine Antoine-Mahut and Marie-Frédérique Pellegrin

In her letter of 13 September 1645, Elisabeth discusses the Stoic-infused ethics that Descartes has offered, by considering her own life as a case study. The best way to explore the impact of moral advice is to gauge its effects on one's own life. Elisabeth submits herself to an introspection. She frequently proceeds this way, in fact, throughout the correspondence. For she insists that one cannot put principles to the test other than in light of a personal experience, in which one attempts to put them into practice. In order to understand virtue, one needs to have the most complete understanding of the individual who is seeking to achieve it; only then will we be in the best possible position to recognise what, in his or her decisions and hence in his or her actions, belongs to the passions and what to reason.

In the first long sentence of her letter, Elisabeth offers a self-portrait of sorts. This single sentence is enough to settle a number of remarkable characteristics of a remarkable personality. She is the daughter of a deposed king and, as such, though of high birth, leads a 'life that is very trying', fraught with financial worries and a series of family tribulations and misfortunes (a broken engagement, an adulterous sister, a heretic brother and another brother living openly with a mistress). Elisabeth is also an especially sensitive person, as the rest of this letter shows from the moral question she chooses to reflect on, namely repentance. It is both the psychological and physiological characteristics of this sensitivity which are examined through the course of the letter.

All these aspects of her nature set Elisabeth at an even greater distance from the personality of Descartes. The introspection she offers of herself throughout the correspondence acquires in light of that distance, an emphatically didactic importance: it enables Descartes to become aware of moral sentiments which are not familiar to him and which he does not always think of. It is thus Elisabeth's intellectual capacity for introspection which makes her a unique and privileged interlocutor for Descartes. In their correspondence, Elisabeth's power of self-analysis is itself a challenge to Descartes' hypotheses in moral philosophy.

It is Elisabeth herself who underlines this capacity: she confirms having begun early on to rely on her rational capacities because of her many misfortunes. She agrees in this way with Descartes' theory that prosperity can make you stupid (!), but she adds her own personal explanation as to the precocious development of her intelligence: it is due to the absence of a guide (she is not shielded from the world by a governess to whom her mind would have been submitted). As with so many other portrayals of the great and wise (including the one Descartes makes of himself in his *Discourse on the Method*[1]), Elisabeth emphasises her early use of reason. This precocious wisdom is strengthened by the adversities she has suffered in her life which compel her to ask real questions, that is to say, philosophical questions.

External circumstances alone are not enough to account for such a fundamentally rational nature. It comes also from an innate quality of the mind, one which belongs precisely to 'wellborn minds'. Descartes had affirmed, at the very start of his *Discourse on the Method*, that 'good sense is the most evenly distributed thing in the world'. But we should not see in Elisabeth's idea of an aristocracy of the mind an anti-Cartesian stance. For in the dedication to Elisabeth of his *Principles of Philosophy* from 1644,[2] Descartes notes that there are but few minds capable of mathematical thought, even fewer who can grasp metaphysics and almost none that are capable of applying themselves to both. He adds that, as far as he is concerned, he has only encountered once in his life a person who was in possession of both kinds of intelligence and this was Elisabeth. Thus, for both Descartes and Elisabeth, though everyone is capable of reasoning, not everyone can reason with excellence, far from it.

But is excellent reason enough to be virtuous? This question leads on to the central focus of Elisabeth's letter, which has both a general and a more specific scope. Specifically, it consists in an examination of the complex feeling of repentance. But from repentance, Elisabeth draws out a more general moral dilemma: that of reason's incapacity to guide us absolutely when it comes to practical matters. This is her final critique of Stoic ethics. The examination of the position of the Stoic sage had commenced a few letters earlier in the exchange. In this letter, Elisabeth distances herself once and for all from the Stoic model, but this leads her to ask a yet more far-reaching question: namely whether moral action (and all the more so, political action) is not always disappointing, is not even always doomed to fail? For is it not the case that every moral or political action ends up in some form or other of repentance? By which criteria may we judge the value of our moral actions?

We must rethink the relation between the passions and reason. For the question is how to achieve a state of moral tranquillity if reason cannot, in fact, calculate all the parameters required for virtuous action. For there is a difficulty when it comes to making an efficient use of reason; this arises specifically in practical applications and does not surface at a purely theoretical level. Simply put, it is the fact that we have neither the time nor the intellectual capacity to anticipate all the necessary information before taking a decision and acting on it. We would need an 'infinite science' to perfectly determine the best way to act. Descartes thinks that he can find the correct definition of virtue by affirming that it consists in acting with resolve according to what we have judged to be the best thing to do. But repentance, a feeling which is at once acute and relatively common, confutes the Cartesian position. For Descartes, good intention (that is, the resolve by which good reasoning guides a firm will) is enough to establish the virtue of an action. The possible failure of this action does not tarnish its value, thus cannot give rise to repentance. And yet, Elisabeth observes, repentance is there. The presence of this feeling shows that we cannot be – and indeed are not – satisfied just as long as we have done everything we could to act well, even when we do not succeed. For we cannot be content if our action fails, even if we have enlisted all our resources of good judgement and firm will to bring it to fulfilment. Experiencing repentance shows also that the satisfaction we may eventually reap from an action is only ever fully brought out if all the consequences which follow the action can be fully measured and precisely valued. Repentance is, in fact, the result of two kinds of lack of control: the impossibility to calculate rationally before acting on the one hand (which is due to ignorance or simply the limitations of our understanding); the fact that not everything is rational in moral action on the other hand (for passions are causes for action too). In short, when it comes to action, we cannot calculate everything rationally and not everything in action is, in any case, a question of rationality.

This double-sided argument explains why satisfaction from one's action is more complicated to reach than Descartes thinks. For in practical matters (i.e. in questions of morality and politics) the value of an action cannot depend solely on the internal determinations of the action. For the action is gauged against its effective impact in concrete terms. To use an anachronistic vocabulary, we could say that Elisabeth is defending a consequentialist ethics whereas Descartes is a partisan of intentionalism in morality. Elisabeth's position is all the more interesting in that her brand of consequentialism is born out of a personal feeling, that of repentance, which is an expression of how reality resists our intentions and that this opposition cannot leave us indifferent to it.

The motivations for our actions are not purely rational, they include the passions. This is an important hypothesis that Elisabeth puts forward here. For she thereby suggests that reason and the passions are not necessarily opposed when it comes to morality and life. There is a whole aspect of action in which reason and the passions are entangled in a way which is so intricate that it seems almost primordial. Elisabeth thus proposes the idea of a 'tacit sentiment' which is approved by reason as a 'gift of nature', which shapes our inclinations without our being aware of it. But these inclinations, whether they lead us towards selfishness or altruism, are not without a rational foundation. They keep us alive and allow us to develop ties with others. They can therefore be positive when they succeed in finding a balance. We must therefore think philosophically about the nature of this possible balance. Its discovery broaches a further challenge for Descartes: if the passions are not in themselves bad, if a great number of them are even approved by reason and if living morally is to naturally combine reason with the passions, then it is necessary to redefine the notion of a passion. Furthermore, to understand virtue, we must explore the ways that reason and the passions can collaborate. Is there a way for reason to make use of the strength of the passions? These questions constitute the central concerns of Descartes' future *Passions of the Soul* from 1649.[3] We see them coming to life before our very eyes, triggered by Elisabeth's reflections, in this private conversation.

The letter also anticipates how the questions posed with regard to morality should extend to the political sphere. Elisabeth demonstrates that what is at stake when it comes to action is not only the internal satisfaction (of having done everything we could have) but also the external concrete results of the act. But she, a princess, is a person whose private actions can have consequences which go beyond herself and the merely private regrets they may generate. When Elisabeth refers to the 'persons governing the public', she includes herself; she thereby highlights an additional gap between herself and Descartes. We know that Descartes is largely uninterested in politics. In his *Discourse of the Method*, he even condemns the 'meddlesome and restless spirits'[4] of philosophers who interfere in such matters, when neither birth nor fortune legitimates their pretensions to govern. But Descartes' addressee is by birth and, at the whim of the wheel of fortune, a public figure and a political actor. For her (stimulated also by his later reading of Machiavelli's *The Prince*), Descartes will be led in later exchanges, to broaden his concerns to the political sphere, which here, are limited to questions of ethics.

This letter from Elisabeth shows how private and personal questions feed the philosophical realm. Her psychological introspection brings forth essential reflections. But for Elisabeth, the exchange is first and foremost personal. If philosophy is meant to heal, then this does not happen in broad, general terms. Rather, remedies must be for specific ailments: just as Elisabeth says in her very first letter from 16 May 1643, she considers Descartes to be the doctor of *her* soul and body. The letter constitutes both the diagnosis and the cure. Repentance is a passion which diminishes the satisfaction of the wise man or woman, a psychological pain which challenges the whole of our moral life and of its relation to virtue. Thus, diagnosing repentance as a passion which diminishes the satisfaction of the wise man or woman, the cure lies in the very analysis of this psychological pain. For the existence of repentance challenges the very foundations of our moral life and our relation to virtue and therefore requests a new theory to rise to the challenge.

Princess Elisabeth to René Descartes
The Hague, 13 September 1645[5]

Monsieur Descartes,

If my conscience were to rest satisfied with the pretexts you offer for my ignorance, as if they were remedies for it, I would be greatly indebted to it, and would be exempted from repenting having so poorly employed the time I have enjoyed the use of reason, which I have had longer than others of my age, since my birth and fortune have forced me to exercise my judgment earlier than most, in order to lead a life that is very trying and free of the prosperity that could prevent me from thinking of myself and also free of the subjection that would have obliged me to rely on the prudence of a governess.

All the same, neither this prosperity nor the flatteries which accompany it are, I believe, absolutely capable of removing the strength of mind of wellborn minds and of preventing them from receiving any change of fortune as a philosopher. But I am persuaded that the multitude of accidents which surprise persons governing the public, without giving them the time to examine the most useful expedient, often lead them (no matter how virtuous they are) to perform actions which afterward cause them to repent. And, as you say, repenting is one of the principal obstacles to true happiness. It is true that a habit of esteeming good things according to how they can contribute to contentment, measuring this contentment according to the perfections which give birth to the pleasures, and judging these perfections and these pleasures without passion will protect them from a number of faults. But in order to esteem these goods in this way, one must know them perfectly. And in order to know all those goods among which one must choose in an active life, one would need to possess an infinite science. You say that one cannot fail to be satisfied when one's conscience testifies that one has availed oneself of all the possible precautions. But this circumstance never arrives when one misses one's mark. For one always changes one's mind about the things that remained to be considered. In order to measure contentment in accordance with the perfection causing it, it would be necessary to see clearly the value of each thing, so as to determine whether those that are useful only to us or those that render us still more useful to others are preferable. The latter seem to be esteemed by those with an excess of a humour that torments itself for others, and the former by those who live only for themselves. Nevertheless each of these sorts of persons supports their inclinations with reasons strong enough to make them each continue all their lives in the same way. It is similar with other perfections of the body and of the mind, which a tacit sentiment makes reason endorse. This sentiment ought not to be called a passion because we are born with it. So tell me, if you please, just up to what point one must follow this sentiment (it being a gift of nature) and how to correct it.

I would also like to see you define the passions, in order to know them better. For those who call the passions perturbations of the mind would persuade me that the force of the passions consists only in overwhelming and subjecting reason to them, if experience did not show me that there are passions that do carry us to reasonable actions. But I assure myself that you will shed more light on this subject, when you explicate how the force of the passions renders them even more useful when they are subject to reason. I will receive this favour in Riswyck in the house of the prince of Orange, where we are moving, since this house is to be cleaned; but for this reason you have no need to change the address of your letters to

Your very affectionate friend at your service,

Elisabeth.

7 'No. Colours are real.'
Anne Conway to Henry More
Sarah Hutton

Anne Conway (1631–1679) was one of the few female philosophers of the seventeenth century and author of a short metaphysical treatise, *Principia philosophiae antiquissiame ac recentissimae*, published posthumously in 1690 and translated back into English as *The Principles of the Most Ancient and Modern Philosophy* in 1692. Letters were an important means for Anne Conway to pursue her interest in philosophy, even for her philosophical education. Since, as a woman, she could not attend university, letters made it possible for her to receive a high-level training in philosophy, which she did from the Cambridge philosopher, Henry More (1614–1687). She owed this good fortune to her half-brother, John Finch, who persuaded his former tutor to take her on as a pupil. He taught her by means of letters. Since More was a proponent of the new Cartesian philosophy, he may have been motivated to accept her as a pupil by the example of Descartes himself, whose high regard for another philosophical woman, Princess Elisabeth of Bohemia, is recorded in the preface to his *Passions of the Soul* and dedication to her of his *Principles of Philosophy*.[1] More's epistolary tutorials with Anne Conway were the beginning of a life-long friendship between them which was sustained by letter-writing. Sadly, most of Anne Conway's letters are no longer extant, so, much of the time her views must be accessed via More's replies: the letter reproduced here is one of 39 of her surviving letters now published in *Conway Letters*.[2]

Conway's letter of 3 December 1651 was written at a fairly early point in her study of philosophy, just a year after the start of her tutorials with

More, when Lady Anne was a newly married young woman. The juxtaposition of philosophical commentary with every-day matters and personal information is typical of her correspondence with More. These frequently refer, as here, to her state of health ('my being in physick'), witness to the fact that she suffered all her life from a chronic illness for which no cure or palliative could be found, though she consulted some of the most eminent physicians of the day, from William Harvey and Francis Glisson, to the Irish 'Stroker', Valentine Greatrakes. Though no cure was found, being in contact with such a wide range of practitioners and healers at the forefront of modern science opened new windows of reflection for Conway: on the one hand, on the relation between the metaphysical questions proposed to her by her philosophy professor and the more everyday questions about the health and pain of the body; on the other hand, more generally about the philosophical activity itself and new developments in science and medicine. The letter here exemplifies Conway's practice of interposing worldly news and deep philosophical questioning.

The first paragraph recounts the departure of her favourite brother and More's friend, John Finch, for Italy via France, to study medicine at Padua. Finch was a key intellectual mentor for his sister and kept in contact with her throughout his travels. He would become an anatomist of note in Italy, before embarking on a diplomatic career, first as English Resident in Florence and later as ambassador to the Ottoman court, exemplifying for Conway the figure of the well-rounded intellectual, versed in medicine, philosophy, and knowledge of the world.

The remainder of the letter is a continuation of Anne Conway's epistolary tutorials with More. Conway had previously sent More a letter arguing for the existence of a vacuum, a question on which hangs all of modern science. More had set out a series of objections to Conway's arguments (*Conway Letters* 22a). That is the 'controversy' to which our present letter refers. More's letter makes reference to an enclosure penned by her, which he returned with his comments. Unfortunately, the essay within the letter, which our present letter refers to as 'the enclosed copy' is now lost.

In the letter which we have, Conway expresses a mixture of self-deprecation and gratitude for More's 'favours' in commenting on her arguments. This is not untypical either of Conway, or other intellectual women of the period (Descartes' correspondent, Princess Elisabeth, exhibits the same tendency). It illustrates just how much Conway valued the opportunity to study with More. Despite expressing self-doubt about her intellectual capacities, she is unafraid to disagree with her teacher. This is evident from her reference to their previous discussion as a 'controversy', which implies the meeting of equal minds. Her frank appraisal of More's argument as more cogent than she thought possible ('defended with more reason than I thought the thing capable of') is a further marker of their relationship, as one between equals. It is also a token of More's own appreciation of Conway, who welcomed and encouraged this dialogue between equal minds, rather than a teacher explaining truths to a student.

More based his tutorials on the philosophy of Descartes, initially, as in this letter, using *Principles of Philosophy*, which More apparently translated for Conway.[3] The topics discussed here and in the lost enclosure (colour and light and the existence of a vacuum) all derive from Descartes. As far as we can tell from their correspondence, More's pedagogical approach appears to have been to set up a series of objections and replies to selected passages from Descartes, by inviting Conway to critique the selected passages, and then answering her critique, and getting her to respond.[4] The 'old controversy about whether there be a vacuum' which Conway mentions, refers not to More's previous letter but to an earlier one (*Conway Letters* 19b) in which More responded to a (lost) letter where she had defended Descartes' rejection of the void (Descartes *Principles* part 2, paragraph 18). In that letter, More proposed an argument to defend the claim that 'an empty space implies no contradiction'.[5] More was impressed by the 'strength and subtlety' of Conway's lost response, which elicited from him the letter to which she responds here.

Setting aside questions relating to space and the void, Conway picks up on More's Cartesian account of colour and sensation in the earlier letter, where he explains the difference between 'first and second notions'.[6] On this account, colours are not intrinsic to things, but result from the stimulus of the organ of sense by motion transmitted by the object perceived; as More put it, colours are 'modifications of the mind' which are 'formally in the soul causally in the object'.[7] In her summary of his view, Conway echoes More's wording and his example of a green carpet and white paper: 'that all colours are formally in the soul and but causally in the objects & organ, that green and white is not in your carpet and paper, but in your mind'.⁸ She notes the Cartesian source of his view, which she has checked out, and cites – specifically mentioning the relevant passages from Descartes *Principia philosophiae* [I] 67–71. She summarises them as follows:

> that colours are not really in the object apprehended by the eye, but that the motion of the optic nerves stirs up a sensation in us which we call colour and make it similitudinary so to that we think is without in the object when as nothing but a mere motion was transmitted from the object to our eye.⁹

Conway disagrees with both Descartes and More, to defend the view that colour 'is a real thing' by adducing observable phenomena which she thinks are not adequately accounted for in Descartes' theory. First, she invokes the evidence of an optical experiment by Kepler in which the image of 'lively landscape' was produced in a *camera obscura*. This image, Conway claims, could not be transmitted by the paper on which it appears, since, on Descartes' view, it is caused by another object. Her observations that the wall of the *camera obscura* or the glass window are not sensitive bodies capable of mediating images suggest that she was aware of the post-Keplerian idea that vision is mediated by a sensitive body (i.e. the retina). The source for this example is Sir Henry Wotton's *Reliquiae Wottonianae* (1651), which prints a letter to Francis Bacon describing the experiment. Whether Conway repeated the experiment herself is not clear. But she goes on to adduce another example which is based on her own observation, that an image reflected in a windowpane at night disappears in daylight. On Descartes' theory, that motion causes the image, Conway claims, it would be visible in daytime too. (Evidently, she hadn't read Descartes' account of this in *Dioptriques* at this point, and no doubt More would have pointed this out to her in their (now lost) ensuing correspondence). Nevertheless, these are intelligent comments which amply illustrate the 'candour, freeness and perspicacity of wit' which More noted that she shared with her brother, John.¹⁰ A candour, which is thus manifested through the irresistible tendency in Conway, to weigh in the perceptible here and now in a theoretical argument, as a warning that the body impinges on the purely mental. She thus, in all 'candour', undermines the whole of the Cartesian enterprise.

This letter indicates that the context for Conway's early interest in Descartes was scientific. The arguments proposed in this letter are many years' distant from the philosophy of Conway's maturity. Nevertheless, we can draw connections between her epistolary tutorials and her later views. Firstly, her early correspondence shows that, even as a young woman, Anne Conway was ready to challenge not just Descartes but also her teacher. This was, of course, part of her training as a philosopher, but arguably this critical training paved the way for her later critique of both Descartes and More in her *Principia philosophiae*, where she raises objections which lead her to reject the metaphysics of both Descartes and More, in favour of metaphysical monism. Precisely when she rejected the dualism of Descartes and of More is uncertain. But the ground was laid for such a move within the security and freedom of thought afforded by the private philosophical letters exchanged with More.

Secondly, even though in her *Principles* she repudiated Descartes' metaphysics, Conway, like Henry More, retained respect for Descartes' natural philosophy (science). She comments, 'that Descartes taught many remarkable and ingenious things concerning the mechanical aspects of natural processes' (*Principles*, p. 64). Another point of connection between this early correspondence and her mature philosophy is that in both she agreed with Descartes' denial of a vacuum – though in her case, in her *Principles*, this is a consequence of her substance monism: that 'the whole creation is always just one substance or entity, and there is no vacuum in it'.[11] Thirdly, although her philosophical system is constructed largely *à priori* as deduction from the nature of God, she frequently invokes 'daily experience' and observation in her arguments, as here in this letter. Conway's letters thus appear as an epistolary genre of their own, following no prescribed rules other than her curiosity and dialectical needs, those, that is, required to set out as broad as possible a frame of argumentation on a given philosophical problem. Peppered as they are with mundane news of everyday life, alongside reports regarding her chronic migraines, the Conway letters could be described as a philosophical laboratory in which experiments in mixing life and philosophy, body and mind, are carried out with the earnestness and seriousness of an original thinker writing in a seventeenth-century context.

Anne Conway to Henry More
3 December 1651[12]

Sir,

    Had I not been hindered from writing the last week by my being in physick[13] I should have told you then my brother had written to me from Paris; but the news of his health I know will not be unwelcome to you now; they staid in expectation of a wind till the second of November at Rye; and then had not sailed above 4 Leagues before it changed, by which means they were blown back again to Rye, but within 2 days after they had a wind more propitious so their designs which brought them safe in 12 hours to Dieppe; where they stayed only one day and allotted no longer time of continuance in Rouen, but hastened immediately to Paris; my brother took the first opportunity of sending to me,[14] and complained of the little time he had to write; which he desired I would make his excuse for not writing to you, when I presented his humble service to you; the next opportunity you will be sure to hear from him they have found out a messenger by which they can send once every month & I think oftener they will not write: Sir I humbly thank you for your last letter, for the pains you take in affording me a particular answer to every one of my objections. I profess it is an infinite pleasure I take in the reading your letters; filled with a great deal of reason they are always; but I pray Sir, What you term courtship in my former letter, let me entreat you to account as a real truth: for such in earnest are all the expressions that I can make of my esteem of your favours; the commendations you give the enclosed copy I sent you I must attribute to your great civility, and yet I shall rest confident that you will both pardon the weaknesses of what paper and also bear with any other I shall send you of the like kind; which belief your own expressions hath both caused & confirmed in me; but because my tediousness upon one subject may not weary you I shall lay aside our old controversy: whether there be a vacuum (which you have with much more reason defended then I thought the thing capable of), but you must give me leave to take notice of that part of your letter where you say that all colours are formally in the soul and but causally in the objects & organ, that green and white is not in your carpet & paper, but in your mind: in my reading over again the first part of Descartes I find him to say something not much unlike this: Paragr. 67, 68, 69, 70, 71 sayeth that colours are not really in the object as they are apprehended by the eye, but that the motion of the optic nerves stirs up a sensation in us which we call colour and make it similitudinary[15] so to that we think is without in the object when as nothing but a mere motion was transmitted from the object to our eye: now I would fain know, if nothing real which we call colour be without[16] the eye, what is the reason that if you stop all the light in a room and leave but one little hole, against which you place a sheet of white paper, why all the images should be represented on the paper so exactly that Kepler,[17] as he told Sir Henry Wotton,[18] drew by that means a most lively landscape; for all the colours, and images, he drew according to those lines he found transmitted from the object through the hole upon the paper. Now the paper certainly could not possibly be capable of perceiving motion nor could it transmit its motion from the object to the eye, for first the paper transmits the colour of white which is its own motion, and if it should transmit the motion caused by any other object, then why does not everything we look upon yield the *eidolum*[19] or representation of something else, for there's the same reason for it in regard that something is as well in a right line against any object that you see, as any object in a right line against the paper and then its very suspicious something streams from that object as its image,[20] because in the case I have mentioned and in the night time when the candle's light vibrates upon the glass, you will see in the window your own species or representation, which would incline me to believe that it would be so in the day time also but that the exuberant light which is in the air dissipates those little images, which if made by motion only there's no reason why it should not be in the day time as well as in the night for if the glorious beams of the sun would hinder the effects of motion from the object to the eye then upon Descartes' supposition there was nothing to be seen in the day time; and if the sun could not hinder there's no reason why in the day time the wall should not transmit the motion that object made upon the *globuli*[21] which was in a right line against the wall as if you make the room dark the paper should not only transmit its own motion to the optic nerve but also the motion it received from the object in a right line against the hole and itself: Sir this seems to incline me to the belief of colour to be a real thing; and that it is something more than Descartes allows it to be: I have not time at the present to add anything more to this: pray pardon the hast this is ended in by: Sir

Your most faithful friend & servant

Anne Conway

8 A PHILOSOPHER-EMPRESS IN A REVOLUTIONARY WORLD

Catherine the Great to the Prince de Ligne

Kelsey Rubin-Detlev

On the scale of European royalty, Catherine the Great came from relatively humble origins: she was born a minor German princess, named Sophie Auguste Friederike of Anhalt-Zerbst, in 1729. Renamed Catherine when she became engaged to the heir to the Russian throne, in 1762 she usurped the throne of her husband, the recently acceded Emperor Peter III and proceeded to rule Russia in her own right as Empress Catherine II. Reigning for 34 years until her death of a stroke in 1796, Catherine expanded Russia's territory and international influence, reformed its administrative structures and oversaw the blossoming of Russian secular art and literature. In addition to her role as an empress, she was a self-designated graphomaniac.

Largely self-educated and a great reader of Voltaire, Montesquieu, Plato and many others, she wrote in a wide range of genres, including two dozen plays, a history of Russia, some excellent memoirs and several thousand letters. These were addressed to a remarkable variety of individuals, from heads of state and diplomats, to her many lovers and to famous and not-so-famous intellectuals such as Voltaire and the German doctor Johann

Georg Zimmermann. These epistolary texts show her to be an astute politician, a charismatic conversationalist and a well-read consumer and producer of literature and ideas. She wrote in three languages: her mother tongue was German, but she was educated by a French governess and studied hard to learn Russian as soon as she arrived in her new homeland. She rarely wrote letters in German, largely to avoid being perceived as overly attached to her birthplace; her business letters within Russia and her love letters were primarily in Russian; but French was the language of sociability and of most intellectual exchange with Western Europeans. Catherine accordingly wrote the letter presented here in French.

Her addressee, Prince Charles Joseph de Ligne, was a Belgian nobleman in the service of the Habsburg emperors, a small-scale sovereign in his native estates, a military commander and diplomat and a great charmer and socialite. He first met Catherine on a visit to St Petersburg in 1780, when he participated in her private salon-style entertainments at the Hermitage; he was such a social success that, after his departure, Catherine granted him the honour of corresponding with her. She enjoyed continuing their witty repartees at a distance, but she also hoped that her new friend would speak favourably for her in the elite circles he frequented across Europe.

As Catherine's letter shows, the year 1791 was a tense time for her and for Europe generally. The French Revolution had not yet attained the violent excesses of the Terror, but blood had already been shed at the Bastille, the royal family forcibly detained in Paris and the social structure of *ancien régime* France dismantled. Catherine strongly opposed the Revolution as a threat not just to her crown, but also to the entire cultural and political world as she knew it. Nevertheless, she did not have the military resources to spend on intervening in France, since her armies were busy fighting a war against the Ottoman Empire and seeking to control unrest in Poland. Her statements against the French Revolution, made frequently by letter, were all the more important as an exercise of soft power against this menace.

What would it have meant for Catherine as an eighteenth-century monarch to write 'as a philosopher'? Alongside Frederick II of Prussia and Joseph II of Austria, Catherine is an exemplar of what has been called the 'enlightened monarch' or 'enlightened despot', a ruler who drew on the ideas of the Enlightenment. But these terms were rarely used in the eighteenth century; the more common notion at the time was 'philosopher king'.[1] Yet the term 'philosopher', especially in its French form, *philosophe*, was nothing if not polyvalent and contested. It had, of course, its etymological meaning: a 'lover of truth', which Plato had theorised in his *Republic* when he first suggested philosophers should rule the city and become properly speaking 'philosopher kings'. It could mean something like 'stoic', in the eighteenth-century sense of a person with outstanding force of character and the capacity to overcome the passions. But it could also refer to a sexual libertine or, worse, be used to denounce an atheist.

Voltaire, whom Catherine called her 'teacher', defined the philosopher in moral terms: 'All philosophers have had this dual character: in Antiquity, not one of them failed to give to men examples of virtue, as well as lessons in moral truths.'[2] Ultimately, though, the most famous usage of the term *philosophe* was as the label and watchword of those who, like Voltaire, believed in new progressive ideas and, at the same time, practiced refined sociability in conversation and in letters. We learn in the *Encyclopédie* entry 'Philosophe': 'The philosopher is thus an honourable man who acts in everything according to reason and who combines a spirit of reflection and precision with good manners and sociable qualities. Graft a sovereign onto a philosopher in this mould, and you will have a perfect sovereign.'[3] Sovereigns are not completely transformed by being philosophers: they remain sovereigns, in the sense that they continue to wield a great deal of power, often including the right to exert violence in war, but they also act according to reason and are polite and sociable. Catherine's letter to de Ligne arguably strives to embody this specifically eighteenth-century type of philosopher sovereign.

Most discussions of Catherine 'as a philosopher' focus on whether she heeded the instructions offered to her by the men who most vociferously laid claim to the title of *philosophe* in eighteenth-century France: famous writers like Voltaire, Diderot and D'Alembert who are generally considered to have been at the forefront of Enlightenment thought. If Catherine obeyed their recommendations, the argument goes, she was a philosopher; if not, she was not. However, such a definition of philosophy is obviously reductive and ignores Catherine's awareness that the *philosophes*' claim to possess exclusively the title of 'philosopher' was polemical and contingent. Although in the 1740s she wrote a (now lost) autobiographical 'Portrait of a Fifteen-year-old Philosopher', as empress, Catherine stopped applying the term to herself: she wished to remain aloof from partisan literary squabbles and she did not always share the views of the more radical writers who assumed the mantle of *philosophes* in the 1780s. Nonetheless, she continued to declare her allegiance to what she saw as the early-eighteenth-century definition of philosophy.[4]

This commitment manifests itself in her letter in (at least) three ways. First, she displays her philosophy by seeking to demonstrate moral rectitude and moral reasoning, as suggested by Voltaire's definition. Since her position of power required her to transcend gender categories, Catherine did not adhere to the primarily sexual definition of morality usually applied to women; she manifestly considered her sexual life irrelevant to the practice of virtue in civic life. De Ligne's nickname for Catherine was 'Catherine le Grand', intentionally using the masculine form of 'the Great' and thereby emphasising her success in incarnating the normally masculine ideal of the philosopher king. Second, the literary form and tone of Catherine's letter exhibit the eighteenth-century philosopher's ability to exercise reason while modelling 'good manners and sociable qualities'. Third, the claim to be a philosopher regularly implied a political statement. Catherine argues that the Revolutionaries cannot deserve to govern France because they promote their ideas through violence unsanctioned by traditional government structures. Instead, she insinuates, power should be held only by those who (like herself and de Ligne) can practice philosophy and deal with their problems through the Enlightenment values of civilised discussion and orderly social interaction.

Catherine rhetorically transfers her political message about the Revolution into the sphere of moral philosophy. A knowing reader like de Ligne would be able to decode her moral discourse as a sophisticated, indeed philosophical, approach to politics. Catherine casts her first direct criticism of the French Revolution as a miniature philosophical dialogue with de Ligne, responding to a comment in his previous letter: 'All nations degenerate, except for the one which Your Majesty electrifies.'[5] Following the eighteenth-century fashion for displaying one's knowledge in an elegantly offhand manner, de Ligne had converted into flattery the concept of anacyclosis, according to which every form of government eventually deteriorates into another, leading from monarchy through tyranny, democracy, and mob rule, ending up back at monarchy again. Most prominently expounded by Polybius in the second century BC, this idea was explored by several eighteenth-century thinkers, including one of Catherine's key intellectual influences, Montesquieu. The latter wrote in his analysis of the rise and fall of the Roman Empire: 'One of two things had to happen. Either Rome would change its form of government, or it would remain a small, poor monarchy. [...] [F]or, since people have always had the same passions, although the occasions that give rise to great changes vary, their causes are the same.'[6] Catherine curiously reworks this idea in answering de Ligne's compliment: 'I do not share your view that nations degenerate: my reason is that people are always people.' Whereas she strongly endorses Montesquieu's Enlightenment universalist affirmation that the same human passions exist in all times and places, she refuses to accept the notion that human societies must therefore proceed inevitably from one form of government to the next. She thus devises a pithy argument for the permanence of monarchy by dissociating the two elements in Montesquieu's formulation.

At the same time, Catherine wittily relates de Ligne's comment to contemporary political jargon. French Revolutionary propaganda asserted that the revolutionary process would 'regenerate' the French nation, creating morally renewed citizens for a new, republican form of government. In response, Catherine assumes a moralist's view. Beginning from the premise of a fixed human nature, she analyses the empirical evidence offered by the Revolution to produce a moral maxim: 'in order to behave well in this world, one must begin by having a good heart and a judicious mind'. She argues that the Revolution is doomed to failure precisely because its leaders fail to behave in a philosophical manner: 'inexperienced and rash', they do not use their reason to reflect on their actions and, as 'villains', they provide the antithesis of positive moral lessons.

The same gesture generates the imaginary academic prize competition that constitutes the rhetorical centrepiece of the letter. In approaching political questions from a moralist's perspective, Catherine follows the example of many eighteenth-century political theorists, including Montesquieu. Catherine called his *Spirit of the Laws* her 'breviary', but in her legislative and theoretical writings, as in her letter, she does not adopt Montesquieu's ideas wholesale. Rather, she adapts them to what she saw as Russia's needs. In the *Spirit of the Laws*, Montesquieu stipulates that while virtue is the guiding principle of democracies, honour governs monarchies; consequently, a monarchy's laws 'must work to sustain that nobility for whom honour is, so to speak, both child and father'.[7] Addressed, incidentally, to a father-son pair, de Ligne and his son Charles-Joseph-Antoine, Catherine's letter tacitly invokes Montesquieu's ideas to combat the French Revolution. She believed firmly in a close relationship between the nobility and the monarchy, not least because she was put and kept on the throne by powerful noble supporters whom she rewarded with money and great honours. In her letter, this practical experience helps Catherine to augment her previous observations and to affirm, through the conceit of the prize competition, that the French

Revolutionaries will be hamstrung by their incapacity to grasp the moral forces, such as honour, that underpin government. By her very ability to construct such an argument, Catherine exhibits by contrast her own status as a 'philosopher king'.

Similarly, her position on the origins of inequality between human beings intervenes in another key Enlightenment debate. Catherine disagrees with Jean-Jacques Rousseau, who contended that natural, physical inequalities between people could not account for moral inequalities in society. Instead, she moves closer to the position of Denis Diderot in affirming that natural differences between individuals contribute substantially to determining their moral qualities and success in society. She thus fights the Revolutionaries on their own turf: although they claimed to be the heirs of the Enlightenment *philosophes*, she seeks to demonstrate that they have forgotten the Enlightenment's lessons and that she is the better reader and moral philosopher.

Catherine displays her 'good manners and sociable qualities' by embedding her letter within the practices of elite sociability. The chattering tone of the letter and the mentions of social entertainments such as theatre, billiards and masquerades are essential to creating Catherine's persona as a civilised and reasonable individual. The aphorism ascribed to the courtier Lev Naryshkin – postulating that gaiety generates 'spirit' (i.e. the strength of soul required for true leadership) hovers between seriousness and mockery, in keeping with the intellectually informed but aristocratically nonchalant air of salon conversation. The dictum echoes the *Encyclopédie*'s definition by insisting that sociability goes hand-in-hand with boldness of thought and action. It allows Catherine to accentuate her epistolary persona as a sociable philosopher and thereby to reinforce her political point: in the first paragraph, she contrasts her own affable voice with that of 'those bizarre pens inked with venom, who contrive to invest all their ingenuity in each phrase, in order to foster troubles of which nobody has any need'. This accusation encompasses both the Revolutionaries and Catherine's other political enemies, such as the Prussians, who, rather than attack France, preferred a confrontation with Russia. The image once again converts political disagreement into moral qualities: Catherine's show of the Enlightenment philosopher's elegant cheerfulness is contrasted with the irrational villainy of her enemies.

Typical of its century in its intertwining of philosophy and politics, Catherine's letter also exemplifies the semi-private, semi-public nature of many eighteenth-century missives, which were often read and/or written collectively even when not intended for immediate publication. Just as the Enlightenment philosopher was no recluse, Catherine's letter is emphatically not an intimate confession of her innermost thoughts to a single addressee. Although she scolds de Ligne for publishing one of her letters, there are clear hints that Catherine expects this letter to reach a narrow circle of initiates beyond the prince. These secondary addressees include the Austrian diplomat Count Ludwig von Starhemberg (1762–1833), whose correspondence and conversations with de Ligne Catherine describes as complementary to her own and de Ligne's son, Charles-Joseph-Antoine. Her questions about honour and valour are in dialogue with the latter and not just because Catherine imagines Charles-Joseph-Antoine's response; this passage expands upon statements she had made in an earlier letter to the son and her laudatory tone suggests that she expected Charles-Joseph-Antoine would also get wind of this letter. Additionally, knowing de Ligne's status as an employee of the Austrian government, Catherine could expect him to convey her views to influential people beyond his family.

This might well apply, for instance, to the unambiguous political statements that conclude the letter, since one of Catherine's major foreign policy objectives at the time was to encourage Austria to support a monarchist counter-revolutionary offensive against France. To express the pressing need for such an intervention, she skilfully draws together the various motifs that appear throughout the letter, with her reflections on honour and nobility reaching a crescendo in the image of loyal French knights mounting their steeds to set France right. The very last lines of the letter epitomise how apparently personal, private reflections could bear significant political weight. She may present her grandchildren simply as having inherited her 'good-naturedness', but as her heirs they stand metonymically for the durability of the monarchical system that will overcome the Revolution.

In sum, Catherine here illustrates a specifically eighteenth-century mode of being a philosopher by letter. This was a matter of form and display as much as of content. By creating a contrast between her reasonable, moralising, yet stylish approach to political problems and what she characterises as the bad hearts and poor fashion sense of the Revolutionaries, Catherine trumpets her claim to be the philosopher king who deserves to rule, unlike those whom she portrays as creating only chaos and bloodshed in France.

Catherine the Great to Prince Charles-Joseph de Ligne

Peterhof, 30 June 1791 [8]

Prince de Ligne, Sir, if your last undated letter by its sheer size did not look much unlike a kite, then, at first glance, its contents in twenty separate paragraphs certainly gave it the appearance of a definitive treaty. You must forgive me for making such a mistake at a time when my mind is preoccupied with such things, having heard talk of nothing else these past ten to twelve months—not that the task has advanced by a single cubic inch.[9] But let us pass over to the contents of your enormous letter. The first point concerns gratitude. You aver that it is more than an impression: it is an engraving. You have found my weak spot there. I have always felt a distinct predilection for beautiful minds. Those with excellent memories who retain by heart that which has never been copied out but merely read aloud—why, I think you will punish them by not furnishing them any more material on which to exercise their talent![10] My prophecies resemble those of the Sibyls, whose own age I am now approaching; experience of the past afforded to those ladies some rights to divine the future. The beauty of the miniature portrait of Asia and Europe, which gave you such a great deal of pleasure, has not enjoyed universal acclaim.[11] This is just how things are. Everyone has their taste, and the proverb says that on matters of taste and colour, one must not argue. This is why I have no wish to take it up with any living soul; for, if I thought I was right, I would not change my opinion either. Those who read between the lines in that portrait have perhaps given the words more meaning than they contained. Anybody who sought a morsel of encouragement believed they had found it, etc. etc.[12] Oh, good Lord, what are you saying? How could one not adore a nation that says: 'Do not give anything up. We shall give you everything you need: take it.'[13] Ah, this is so lovely! If they add, 'We, too, do not want to give up anything', well, so be it. If we are not taking anything away, then what harm is there if these worthy men have spoken a few useless words in vain? I shall always love them better than your Belgians, forgive me! ... That superb light cavalry and a certain infantry that marches ahead joyously and grumbles impatiently about any move that does not abbreviate the path to victory – well, it is those people indeed who, working together, are able to lead matters to a positive outcome faster and with greater certainty than those bizarre pens inked with venom, who contrive to invest all their ingenuity in each phrase, in order to foster troubles of which nobody has any need.

I do not share your view that nations degenerate: my reason is that people are always people. What is absolutely clear, however, is this: if lawyers, judges, people who are inexperienced and rash, and people who are villains electrify a nation, in order to regenerate it, then they ruin it at the same time. Indeed, from all this and from other recent evidence I have seen, I would say that the result is that, in order to behave well in this world, one must begin by having a good heart and a judicious mind. Without these, one accomplishes nothing of value, and one dances, as the song goes, clumsily, getting off on the wrong foot. Of the magic lanterns in Warsaw, I shall say nothing.[14] They are clamouring for the Jesuits, of whom you seem to think highly. On that matter, I often said to my great and very dear friend, the Count of Falkenstein[15] (whom I shall forever miss), that I was preserving the species intact so that, when they were needed, I would have the satisfaction of offering them to Roman Catholic countries for free. Note that the King of Prussia had offered them, for his part, at a price of one ducat apiece. You must think that I take more pleasure in seeing people fight than Mr Freeport does, since you are advising everyone to attack, whereas he just thought it wrong to separate those who are hankering to come to blows.[16] Thank God your advice has not been followed, at least up to now. If everything of which you spoke were to happen to me, I believe that game of carom-billiards would deprive me of the time and wish to play billiards in the Hermitage.[17] We danced gaily in that spot this winter, as your cousin, Count Starhemberg, will have told you. In addition, there were theatricals before and after supper, and suppers after which we raced to a masked ball under the pretext of amusing the Alexanders and Constantines.[18] Everyone was enchanted to be there, myself most of all, and all were vying to have the best costume. Ah well, after all that, go on and try to tell me that the grand equerry is wrong when he argues in his way, and with his physic-comic nonsense, that gaiety is very good for imbuing what you call spirit, whereas seriousness, sadness, and especially monotony freeze one to the marrow of one's bones.[19] Do you not find it odd that it is I who tell you this about monotony! But I have something else entirely in my head: I think that the Academies should establish a prize, first of all for the question: *What becomes of honour and valour* – synonyms that are precious, I repeat, to heroic ears – *in the mind of an active citizen* under a government that is suspicious and jealous to the point of prohibiting every distinction? This is despite the fact that nature itself has granted to intelligent people superiority over the stupid, and that courage comes from a sense of physical or mental power. The second prize will be given for the question: *Is there a need for honour and valour?* If there is a need, then this is why emulation should not be prohibited or impeded by its intolerable enemy, equality. I seem already to hear the voice of your son,[20] crying out, 'No, no, there is no such thing, equality will not come about! It does not exist in nature. I have proven that and shall prove it again at every opportunity I can. The two crosses I wear on my chest, and the wound I sustained, attest to it. My father himself took pleasure in arranging those marks of distinction in the picturesque way that another prince wore them. Joseph II predicted that he would have yet more.[21] The same thing will happen to me, be certain of that.' Rats have devoured all the titles of Alexander and Caesar, but not their deeds. Every one of us knows those by heart. What the rapacity of the cats of our own day has produced I find it hard to say ... at least not even a mouse has been captured. I have not read more than seventeen pages of the *Works* of the late King of Prussia. Those done, I cannot say why exactly I closed the book and have never opened it again.[22]

We saw the Comte de Ségur arrive, conjuring up the spirit of the court of Louis XIV, in rejuvenated form.[23] You then found him to be truly enjoyable company during the trip to Tauris. At the moment, Louis Ségur is suffering from a bad case of the national consumption. I do not know whether the air of the Pontine marshes suits him.[24] The old French knights were well loved, but one really does not know what to make of an active, equal citizen with flat hair, a black tailcoat, a waistcoat, and a riding crop in his hand. Whether the declared enemies of all kings will spark the indignation of all the latter to go against them: that is another question that might generate more than one dissertation.

As for my fifty thousand lancers, they are too busy at the moment to go that far. For that reason, as you see, I have not stolen a march on anyone. There was a moment when I rejoiced to see the royal family out of Paris. Their safety, we were told, was owed to eight thousand French gentlemen. This joy proved short-lived, and, since their entourage put up no resistance against the Municipality of Sainte-Menehould, it is to be supposed that they existed only on paper.[25] If all the knights of France do not mount their steeds at this very moment, I despair of ever seeing them do so. I am very flattered by the trust you show me. You will always find in me the very same good nature that, it seems to me, you admire. I am confident that my grandsons, who at this very moment are jumping about me, will have their fair share of it, too. Alexander is four digits taller than myself, his brother comes up to his shoulder. If you saw them now, I think you would be pleased with them. Farewell, my Prince, rest assured of the continued sincerity of my feelings towards you.

9 FROM EXILE WITH LOVE

Germaine de Staël to Adrienne-Catherine de Tessé

Catriona Seth

Germaine de Staël (1766–1817) was a writer, philosopher and foremost intellectual of the post-enlightenment era in the aftermath of the French Revolution. On 30 June 1806, she wrote to Adrienne-Catherine de Noailles, Comtesse de Tessé (1741–1814), a strong-willed woman after her own heart whom she had known for a number of years. The letter does not deal with news or events. Staël does not comment on current affairs or her activities, but she does open a window onto her own soul. When she penned it, she was in Auxerre, at the Château de Vincelles. She had been there for some weeks with her children and a retinue of close friends and domestic servants. Why Auxerre? It lay 41 leagues away from Paris. In the next few months she moved to other provincial abodes, Rouen in Normandy and then a château near Meulan. She was circling round the capital: Napoleon had forbidden her from coming within 40 leagues of Paris.

Staël wanted to be allowed up to the French capital to plead for the reimbursement of a major debt the French State had contracted with her Father, the banker and minister Jacques Necker, before the Revolution. More importantly still, she wanted to return to the city she called home. A true cosmopolitan, born in Paris to Swiss parents with Franco-Prussian roots, she had become a Swedish baroness on marrying; she was a lifelong anglophile, would inspire partisans of Italian unity before the *Risorgimento* and introduced the French to German Romanticism. At Vincelles, in

1806, hoping for a permission to return to Paris, she felt herself to be in a no man's land both geographically and emotionally. She misses Paris because of what it stands for. She fears she may never be allowed back and that her banishment will only end with her death.

A lifelong defender of freedom in many guises, Staël could not bear to be deprived of her liberty to come and go as she pleased, to talk without reserve to anyone with whom she might come into contact, to have friends from across the political spectrum – even those with ideals far from her own. France and Paris, at various stages, become corollaries of her personal freedom: France needed to be free for her to be allowed to do as she pleased and the constrictions on her personal liberty were a form of metonymy of the state of the nation. For Staël, breathing French air was inspiration in itself. To the end of her days, as her posthumous *Considerations on the Principal Events of the French Revolution* show, she believed that having been young and in Paris in the heady early years of the French Revolution was a fortunate lot indeed: hopes were high and discussions spirited – at least in the circles she frequented as the daughter of a wealthy banker and finance minister and the wife of the Swedish ambassador and the lover of a French count who was briefly minister for war in 1791 (Louis de Narbonne). In 1806, Staël felt clearly that her happiest times were behind her and that, in moments of doubt, such as when she was writing this letter, her memories had come to haunt rather than sustain her.

Conversation for Staël, who hosted salons at different stages in her life, was an ideal way to foster creativity, to work through problems or to give rise to new thoughts. In 1800 she writes that she is impatient to see Mme de Tessé: 'The house in which she dwells seems to me the source of all the ideas which animate me and incite me to speak' (24 September 1800 to Adrien de Mun); in turn, Adrienne-Catherine de Tessé was reported to have said that were she to be queen, she would order Mme de Staël to talk all the time. Conversation was at the heart of Staël's fiefdom in exile, the Swiss château of Coppet, on the shores of the Lake Leman. There, during her absence from Paris, intellectuals from across Europe came together, drawn by her magnetism. The Schlegel brothers were fixtures – August was her son's tutor – Sismondi the economist, Wilhelm von Humboldt, Juliette Récamier, Staël's soulmate Benjamin Constant, for whom she served as a sounding-board and inspiration for much of his writing and many more of the greatest artists and intellectuals in Europe. Byron, for instance, dropped in several times. The guest-list across the years reads like a *Who's Who* of European intellectuals of the early nineteenth century and Coppet was the centre of a melting-pot for many aspects of modern liberal thought.

Writing and exile were closely linked in Staël's case: it was the publication of her novel *Delphine* which led to her being banished from Paris in 1803. In 1810, the destruction was ordered of the proofs of her work *On Germany*; the powers that be giving as their motive that 'This book is not French'. On a more positive note, her forced travels inspired some of her later works. Her trip to Italy, undertaken while she was forbidden to live in the French capital, gave her much of the background material for her second novel, *Corinne, or Italy* (1807), in which the ideas of Enlightenment philosophy merge with a modern Romanticism, recounting all the while the history of Italy against the background of a grandiose love affair between an Italian poetess, Corinne, and an English Lord.

Whilst Staël had no reason to fear for her life, enjoyed considerable financial means and could circulate freely as long as she did not come near Paris, she considers herself as belonging to a long line of great exiles – all men – as she quotes the names of Cicero, Bolingbroke and Ovid. She mentions the latter in a letter to a family friend, the writer Jean-Baptise Suard (1732–1817), saying that Burgundy is monotonous without music, education or books, comparing it to Ovid's Scythia. In stating that the Roman orator, the British politician and the Latin poet found exile harder to deal with than the thought of death, she is also implicitly suggesting the possibility of suicide. At a time when the Church condemned *felo de se*, she had written in support of those who took their own lives in her 1796 treatise *De l'influence des passions* and depicted several heroes and heroines who commit suicide in her fiction. The death of such characters generally acts as a way of showing they were superior to those who are left behind to witness their fate – during passionate love affairs, Staël was not averse to using the threat of suicide herself as a form of emotional blackmail. She also gave considerable thought over the years to the value of such an act.

Staël's 1812 essay on suicide develops typological and analytical approaches, showing that all suicides are not identical. She salutes the fortitude of many émigrés and stresses that 'The most severe trial imposed on the Frenchman is separation from his beloved country'[1]. The parallel between death and exile hints at the importance of happiness as giving a reason for living. Staël – who was a staunch Protestant – admits that she fears what lies beyond death and that this fear and her children act as a safeguard. This suggests that true strength is to be found within oneself. In her *Reflections on Suicide*, Staël comes to the conclusion that it is greater to be resigned to one's fate than to revolt and that whilst there can be some value in *political* suicide, one should always seek to gain solace from one's devotion to others rather than to end one's life. The consciousness of the tragic nature of human existence and a reasoned acceptance of one's fate can thus, paradoxically, encourage one to go on living, indeed, to find a true quality in life. The letter states how much Staël might gain simply by talking to Tessé and the way in which the meeting of minds makes one want to surpass oneself; it lights sparks in one's soul, gives one faith in others. There is no feeling of intellectual superiority on the writer's part. Quite the opposite: she needs others to thrive and demands much of their affection.

Staël missed her friends above all – even though many of them came to stay in Switzerland – and she missed the climate of Paris as it was in her early adult years, at once grave and scintillating, a heady time full of promise when everything seemed possible. Her ideal homeland was an intellectual one, a communion of minds able to be entirely open with each other, at once exacting and generous in their judgment. While her language might seem grandiloquent, especially when she is speaking of emotions, the idea that she suffered from a hyper-acute form of sensitivity is apparent elsewhere in Staël's personal writings. Here, she fears the extent of her pain is being underestimated by the very people who should be most sensitive to her feelings. It is by expressing them that she herself gains a better understanding of them, but she also hopes that, in Mme de Tessé, she will find an ideal listener, one who can really measure their depth. This theory of friendship, a common theme for letters through the centuries, is marked by the ideal of a transparent communication similar to the one defended by Rousseau who had been a major influence on Staël from the start of her literary career. It leads her here to the eloquent analogy about language according to which the exiled being lives in translation, in a state of otherness, striving to find means of expression for what could be understood almost implicitly by an intimate friend. This image goes beyond the hint that the writer felt she might have to settle in Sweden, her late husband's homeland, to raise her children. It engages with the notion of self-identification: Staël felt she could only be herself when expressing herself in French; the French language itself is analysed as an essential part of what made her who she was.

A year after sending this letter, Staël made a clandestine visit to Paris. She wrote to Mme de Tessé suggesting a meeting at the house of a mutual friend. A series of misunderstandings meant they did not see each other. Both women felt hurt by the fallout. A short time later, Staël, reacting to Tessé's compliments on her novel *Corinne*, said that, as a result of the incident, she had lost the hope of being loved by her friend as much as she loved her. She would subsequently express the wish not to be banished from the countess' mind which, she claimed, would be like losing a second homeland. Her terms, as often in her correspondence, are enthusiastic and generous, her warmth and need for affection are clear, with the raw experience of exile offering her a way of thinking through personal relationships.

After almost 12 years criss-crossing Europe, Staël finally returned to live in Paris in 1814. She had spent time in various parts of France, at her Swiss home in Coppet, in Germany and Italy, in Vienna, Saint Petersburg, Stockholm and London. Her exile was a very productive time and saw the publication of several major works and the preparation of others, some of which only came out after her death.

Germaine de Staël to Madame de Tessé

Auxerre, 30 June 1806[2]

Amongst the misfortunes of my existence, Madame, I count the fact that even the people dearest to me do not understand the sufferings caused by my exile. It is not Paris that I regret, but my friends and a career for my children: I must find a country in which to settle them if I cannot return here, and leave my friends, my language and my homeland forever.

To start one's life again in the midst of life, to break with the past without it ceasing to resonate, to create a new future entirely devoid of hope, never again to see that which one's heart holds dear or to demand cruel sacrifices, at the very least... I do not know if such a concatenation of suffering might not lead me to die of *a broken heart* in the next week. Now that I have told you this, Madame, you will understand me.

And in addition to this, to no longer be able to engage with a mind such as yours, to spend one's life lost in translation, constantly needing to explain one's very self, when mere hints were sufficient for us to understand one another; that one would improve from talking to you, from wanting to please you, from receiving from your soul a spark which made it possible to still believe in something noble and true, this is suffering indeed, which, I confess, is overwhelming. And I see that strong men – Cicero, Bolingbroke, Ovid – were better at defying death than exile; I am quite sure it is easier. But homesickness tugs at all the strings of the heart and I suffer not just for a moment, but night and day, every time I say or hear a word in French. I do not draw in a single breath without saying farewell to this land; and in truth, if I am still alive, it is because I have children and fear death's great unknown.

Farewell, Madame, can one speak to you otherwise than from the depths of the heart?

10 EROTIC AFFINITIES
Johann Joachim Winckelmann to Leonhard Usteri

Katherine Harloe

The posthumous letters of illustrious men always hold a great attraction for posterity. They constitute the individual entries in that great biographical account-book, whose principal is represented by actions and written works.[1]

This is how Johann Wolfgang von Goethe began the announcement of his then forthcoming edition of *Unpublished Winckelmannian Letters* published in the *Jena Allgemeine Literatur-Zeitung*, the literary magazine published in Jena, in May 1804. Goethe's words posit a general relationship between the personal correspondence of great men and their public words and acts. It is no accident that his reflections occur in the context of the publication of new letters from Winckelmann, since for Goethe and his contemporaries, as also for his nineteenth-century successors, it was he who, above all, would come to define a particular unity of aesthetic sense, philosophical or scholarly vocation and way of life.

Johann Joachim Winckelmann (1717–1768) was a noted historian and connoisseur of Greek and Roman art, whose rags-to-riches life story was given added piquancy and intrigue by his religious and sexual unorthodoxy and the shocking way his life ended: he was murdered in a hotel room in Trieste, at the boundary of the Austro-Hungarian Empire, in his fiftieth year. He left behind a series of much-admired antiquarian works, most famously the *Reflections on the Imitation of Greek Works in*

Sculpture and Architecture (1755) and the *History of the Art of Antiquity* (1764). He also left a corpus of letters to German, Italian, French and English correspondents, which began to appear in various editions within a decade of his death. The letter presented here was not included in Goethe's volume (which presented 27 previously unpublished letters in the possession of the influential patron of the arts, Anna Amalia, Dowager Duchess of Weimar). It first appeared – in heavily bowdlerised form – in a compendium of *Winckelmann's Letters to his Friends in Switzerland*, published in Zürich in 1778.[2] This collected some 80 letters, composed by Winckelmann between 1758 and 1768 to Swiss correspondents happy to characterise themselves in the volume's preface as his 'pupils'.

The volume's editor, Leonhard Usteri of Zürich (1741–1789), is also the addressee of the present letter. Known principally during his own, similarly short lifetime as a university professor and school reformer, he had, as a young man in 1760–1761, undertaken a cultural and educational voyage across Europe.[3] He had sat at the feet of illustrious men in Geneva, France and Italy and formed philosophical friendships, most notably with Winckelmann and Jean-Jacques Rousseau, which continued via letter upon his return to Zurich. The educational aspect of Winckelmann and Usteri's epistolary friendship is evident in this letter, which begins with the simple address, beloved of Winckelmann, 'My friend' – noteworthy for the unaffected simplicity of the salutation and subscription. Winckelmann goes on to instruct the younger man in understanding Greek culture, examples of true and insightful connoisseurship and the study of coins. This letter touches upon many characteristic positions of Winckelmann's published aesthetic writings: the necessity of an autoptic experience of works of art, seeing with one's own eyes and hence the necessity of travelling to Italy; the centrality of a proper appreciation of beauty to judgements of style, which was key to the capacity to judge the authenticity of putatively ancient works. Typical too is his privileging of Greek works over Roman ones and the trashing of contemporary French fashions in art and aesthetics. The trends which were represented, for instance, by Claude-Henri Watelet,[4] other authors of the *Encyclopédie*, or the circle of Frederick the Great. By criticising the latter, Winckelmann sets up an implicit opposition between Paris and the *Frenchified* tastes of Berlin and Potsdam on the one hand and Greece and Italy on the other.[5] The former are sites of false affect and artificiality, while the latter signify the true, natural and healthy appreciation of art and culture. This opposition is deepened throughout Winckelmann's published writings and in his correspondence with other young male Grand Tourists, such as in his first letter to Reinhold von Berg,[6] in which Paris is characterised as 'the seat of empty pleasures'.

Berg is, moreover, relevant to the opening and closing paragraphs of Winckelmann's letter to Usteri. These allude to Winckelmann's *Essay on the Capacity for the Sentiment of the Beautiful in Art, and on Education in It*:[7] an essay on aesthetic education that Winckelmann had just published, and which took the form of an open letter addressed to Berg. This 'treatise on beauty', as Winckelmann terms it, opens by borrowing a paederastic epigraph from the Greek poet Pindar to characterise its addressee as 'fair of form, and overflowing with grace'. It is notable for its homoeroticism in both tone and content, which is most apparent in the claim that 'those who attend only to the beauties of the female sex, and are touched little or not at all by the beauties in our sex, possess the sentiment for the beautiful in art but little in an innate, general, or lively fashion'.[8]

Usteri, notably, omitted from its first publication in 1778, any such allusion which was in fact present at the start and ending of our letter. In addition to obscuring the homoerotic material, his exclusion of the first and last paragraphs conveniently removes Winckelmann's *ad hominem* sniping at connoisseurial rivals, and his mockery of Frederick the Great. Left out from Usteri's edition too is the third paragraph, with its somewhat ungenerous characterisation of the famous neoclassical artist (and dedicatee of Winckelmann's 1764 *History of the Art of Antiquity*), Anton Raphael Mengs. What remains is the discussion of numismatic connoisseurship, the reference to Heinrich Füssli, and the discussion of the *Monumenti antichi inediti*, Winckelmann's major work-in-preparation. The selection suggests Usteri's desire not to offend anyone still living, and to foreground those aspects of Winckelmann's letters that may be considered of intellectual-historical or pedagogical value.

Yet Usteri's edition preserved other, similarly erotically risqué judgement, which occur fairly frequently in Winckelmann's correspondence with close male friends. Particularly notable is the passage in a June 1767 letter to Usteri's younger brother, Paul, in which Winckelmann justifies his aesthetic (or erotic?) preferences by reference to the higher beauty of males among many animal species, the fact that 'in every town one finds more beautiful young men than beautiful women', and the observation that the female breast, considered the height of womanly beauty, loses form as it ages.[9]

In the present letter to Leonhard Usteri, the topic is treated with less apparent didacticism and greater lightness of tone: Winckelmann teases Usteri for his initial response to Winckelmann's essay, which has not survived, but must have voiced surprise or displeasure at the text's homoerotic overtones. Winckelmann jokes that this response would cause him to doubt Usteri's natural good taste or Hellenic understanding, had he not already been convinced of the contrary. Winckelmann leaves the reasons for his conviction obscure and this only adds to the tease: what is the nature of the acquaintance that makes Winckelmann so sure that Usteri possesses the sentiment for the beautiful, despite the surface prudery of his response to Winckelmann's *Essay*?

The closing paragraph also finds an echo in the opening of the *Essay* to Berg, with its emphasis on the purity of an erotic affinity founded upon sight alone.[10] Winckelmann's appreciation of the object of his desire – whether Berg himself, the unnamed Florentine youth in this letter, or an ancient sculpture such as the Torso Belvedere – occurs *via* the eye. This privileging of the ocular, as the sense most proximate to the rational, is reflected in his aesthetic theory, which he develops as an interpretation of Platonism, in which the contemplation of ideal Beauty is carried out 'at a glance' through the mind's eye.[11]

In both form and content, then, this letter presents and enacts many of the key elements of Winckelmann's aesthetic theory and approach to the historical analysis: the privileging of an ocular aesthetic of beauty, the presentation of Italy as an indispensable locale of connoisseurial education and the privileging of Greek art and culture, presented as the epitome of the 'natural' and 'healthy' against the preciousness and artificiality of the modern French. It is no accident that these themes resound particularly in Winckelmann's letters to Swiss correspondents, for Swiss cities and citizens could (as in Rousseau's work) be seen as a bastion of ancient, republican liberty.

Johann Joachim Winckelmann to Leonhard Usteri

Rome, 14 September 1763[12]

My dearest Usteri,

On the basis of your letter from yesterday I would have drawn an unfounded conclusion about your good taste and your knowledge of the ancient Greeks. Indeed we think differently upon one point, or [rather] you are mistaken in your judgement. Had I thought otherwise, my treatise on beauty would not have been excluded from the *History*, as has in fact occurred, and I would have had to describe the Apollo after the manner of Watelet. So this error-prone scribbler, of such terrible reputation, is coming to Italy! His face must have no need of glasses. Doubtless he wishes to be short-sighted because it is fashionable. Hopefully the Germans will soon possess a translation of his poem, and perhaps, as with Schütz's edition of Keyssler, it will be prinked up with theological remarks. Poor Germans! And the most wretched of all are those in Berlin. I have not cultivated the art of deriving ten from five, but I can judge the article on beauty in the *Encyclopédie*: it is utterly worthless, and this is by the great D'Alembert! I should like to see this Patron, but not to make his acquaintance. The philosopher whose works you send me has superior thoughts. 'A pity he is a German', the hero of Potsdam will say, 'It is one of the best books I have read.'

My friend, you ask me for a lesson in the study of coins. What one can learn from books may be said; but the greater part consists in practical experience which cannot be set out on paper; so I do not know what I should write to you. For the writings of Baudelot d'Airval on the Utility of Travel, and those used by the lower classes of students, serve to create *impostori* rather than true connoisseurs. The scholarly part may be learned from books; as concerns the rest I myself am unashamed to confess that I am not always able to judge correctly. If I am in doubt over whether an imperial-period coin is ancient or copied, I summon an old beggar who, on account of his former trade as cheesemonger, is named Casciarino: he knows the answer. It's different with Greek coins, where beauty is at stake: in such cases I profess myself to be a capable judge once more. But the forgeries are only of imperial coins, not of Greek ones. And one can attain no thorough knowledge of coins away from Rome. If you would like to ask me questions I shall always answer them if I am able.

Of Mengs I have heard nothing in months, and have received no reply to my letters: perhaps I set down a word that must be weighed ponderously beforehand on a finely calibrated balance scale. In his household no one tells me anything except that he is in good health; I enquire no further, for good reasons.

I have not yet seen your Füssli. But your friend will not be able to await the publication of my work in Rome, even though a start shall be made upon the engravings next month. Some of the explanations are several pages long, even though I aimed at the strictest concision, and I doubt whether the whole work will fit in a single folio volume.

To conclude where I began, you are mistaken: this acquaintance did not begin in Florence but rather in Rome in the year just past. In Florence I only viewed the person who pleased me by sight; the time did not allow me to speak with him, and no inclination was as pure as this one. As for the rest, I care little for what anyone in Germany may think of me upon this point. In my *History* I have succeeded in giving strict moralists far more opportunity [for opprobrium]. More anon.

Your sincere friend,

Winckelmann.

11 RATIONAL EMPIRICISM?

Friedrich Schiller to Johann Wolfgang Goethe

Dalia Nassar

The friendship between Johann Wolfgang Goethe (1749–1832) and Friedrich Schiller (1759–1805) is possibly one of the most well-known literary and philosophical friendships and certainly one of the most celebrated. Statues portraying their friendship, with Schiller holding a manuscript in one hand, reaching out with the other to the laurel wreath Goethe holds in his, span the earth: from Weimar to Anting (China) via Milwaukee and San Francisco. Their friendship has been described as a collaboration 'like no other known to literature or art,' and although it spanned only 12 years (on account of Schiller's death), it was a friendship that fundamentally transformed both men. During those 12 years, Schiller and Goethe lived in close proximity to one another – Schiller moved back and forth between Jena and Weimar, while Goethe remained in Weimar –and yet, despite their physical proximity, despite the fact that Schiller was often in Weimar and Goethe regularly visited Schiller in Jena, they composed numerous letters to one another, sometimes daily. Their correspondence, which was first published by Goethe in two volumes in 1828–1829 and which contains over a thousand letters, was described by Goethe as possibly his greatest treasure.

Schiller, who was Goethe's junior by ten years, had moved to Jena in 1789 to lecture on history and had been hoping to meet the older, better known poet, for some time. But it was not until 1794 that the two men were able to have a proper conversation, a conversation that established their friendship and which Goethe documented in the essay 'Fortunate Encounter'. Goethe recounts that the two had been at a scientific lecture in Weimar and, upon exiting the lecture, discovered that both were equally dissatisfied by it. Schiller begins the conversation by criticising the lecturer's fragmentary approach to nature, to which Goethe responds that a different approach is clearly needed, one that does not regard nature as composed of isolated parts, but which seeks to portray nature as active and alive, as a whole that manifests itself in the various, fundamentally related parts. With some excitement, Goethe goes on to elaborate his theory of the metamorphosis of plants, his view that there is a fundamental unity that underpins plant form, that makes a plant *plant*. They are walking and talking, and suddenly Goethe realises that the two are standing outside Schiller's house, at which point, Schiller turns to Goethe and tells him that he disagrees. What Goethe is describing, the so-called 'form' of the plant, is nothing that can be found in experience. For it is an *idea*. Goethe, who was taken aback by Schiller's response, pauses for a moment, and then replies, with what one might imagine as a slight smirk on his face, that, well, he cannot but be thrilled by the fact that he can *see* ideas with his own eyes!

It is on this question of the relationship between experience and ideas – of what is actually involved in experience, of what can and cannot be seen and what it means to 'see', on which hinges much of their correspondence, friendship and also their disagreements. For in 1794 Schiller was a Kantian, convinced by the view that ideas are not in things themselves – in the objects – but in the human mind. It is the mind that generates ideas (such as totality) by which we are able to investigate the natural world. As such, however, these ideas are *only* assumptions, useful for research, and nothing more. We must, for instance, assume the totality of nature – that the objects in nature are connected to one another in some way – in order to investigate the relations between species. This does not mean, however, that nature *is in fact* a totality. For this is a claim that we cannot substantiate (we can never experience the *whole* of nature, only its various parts). The ideas, then, are mere guides, because they cannot be encountered or seen in experience.

In his 1795 *Naïve and Sentimental Poetry*, Schiller cast Goethe as upholding the naïve tradition of poetry and himself, by contrast, as a herald of the modern, or sentimental poetry, emphasising the disconnection between self and nature and a turn to subjectivity and interiority. Goethe agreed with this description. In the same essay 'Fortunate Encounter', where he speaks of their 1794 meeting, 'Goethe relates the reason why he had avoided Schiller until then: the two men, he writes, are 'antipodes' and 'nobody could deny that between two antipodal spirits the division is more than the diameter of the earth …'. Or, as he puts it in an 1828 essay that looks back at that early phase of their friendship: while Schiller 'preached the gospel of freedom, I wanted to preserve the rights of nature'.

Over their years of friendship, however, the two became less like antipodes, transforming through the instigation and inspiration of the other. Goethe read Kant with greater sympathy, while Schiller opened himself up to the possibility that ideas can be 'objective' (i.e. in the world). It is precisely this point on which the letter we have here hinges: Schiller seems to be getting it – and he is extremely excited about what he's getting.

Schiller composed the letter on 19 January 1798, five days after Goethe had published the essay 'Experience and Science'. Schiller's letter, written with some haste and under duress – he had been sick over the last few days, but cannot resist writing with what energy he can muster – is a response to Goethe's essay. This letter is the perfect embodiment of their productive friendship, and, as such, is also an exemplary philosophical letter: written *in medias res*, it is an expression of thought in action, of excitement and of a sense of urgency to communicate fresh insights – to test them out, to make sense of them – with someone to whom these still inchoate, but important, thoughts can be entrusted. It is, simply put, an expression of authentic and intimate communication, founded on a significant amount of trust.

As I noted, the two friends did not live far from one another, so the possibility of an upcoming personal interaction, a conversation, was very realistic. Nonetheless, Schiller felt the need to write down his thoughts and send them post-haste to Goethe, because he saw something in them that could not wait.

Schiller realises that this is 'a monologue' adding that he may be just interpreting everything according to his world view, his interests, but his ultimate goal is to hear what Goethe has to say about the matters at hand. The letter, then, is a mid-way point, a means of writing down, consolidating and communicating his fresh, uncensored thoughts to Goethe, to prepare Goethe for a conversation.

In the essay 'Experience and Science', Goethe distinguishes three kinds of phenomena or stages of knowledge: the empirical phenomena, the scientific phenomena, the pure phenomena. Each is a progressively more adequate way of grasping what one is seeing, when one is observing nature. The ultimate aim of the essay is to explain and justify the 'pure phenomenon' (i.e. the fundamental form that underpins a natural object – that makes it what it is – and demonstrate how such a phenomenon can be grasped). The aim, in other words, is to establish precisely what Schiller had denied: the 'idea' of the plant is *real*, it is that which makes the plant *plant* and not merely *ideal*, (i.e. in the observer's mind).

While the empirical phenomenon is available to every casual observer of nature the scientific phenomenon is achieved only through experimentation, 'by representing it under circumstances and conditions differing from those in which we first encountered it and in a more or less effective sequence'. The pure phenomenon, by contrast, requires discerning what is necessary or essential, excluding the accidental, or contingent – and thereby arriving at the essence or form of what is observed.

The key claim then is that the idea (the pure phenomenon) is not divorced from experience but achieved through it. The essay can thus be read as a continuation of that first conversation Goethe had with Schiller, an attempt to explain to Schiller what he means by an idea. But it is also Goethe's attempt to clarify for himself what he means by this experiential idea – something that he began to critically reflect upon following his conversation with Schiller.

Well before his encounter with Schiller, Goethe had had some important success in his scientific investigations. In the 1780s, Goethe joined a number of anatomists who had for some time been looking for the intermaxillary bone (i.e. incisive bone) in humans – a bone found in the upper jaw of amphibians, reptiles and mammals, whose discovery in the human would confirm a connection between humans and animals. In 1786, Goethe managed to find it – a fact that continues to surprise historians of science. How is it that Goethe found a bone that other (more experienced) anatomists had failed to locate?

The answer has to do with precisely his notion of an 'idea' or form. Goethe was convinced of the integrity of the mammalian structure, that the various parts developed in light of, and in relation to, the other parts. The heart, after all, cannot function properly without the veins, the arteries, indeed, the whole circulatory system. The fact that the parts are so dependent on one another belies a fundamental unity – *a unity that precedes and determines the various parts*. Furthermore, Goethe was convinced that this unity is not static, but transforming, flexible and dynamic. The shape of the heart is, after all, different in different beings – its shape, in other words, depends on the *whole of which it is part*.

The goal then, is to grasp the whole (the idea, the form) – and then one can easily discern the parts. This is precisely what Goethe did when he found the intermaxillary bone.

While some anatomists simply dismissed the idea of a bone connecting humans to other mammals (largely on religious grounds), others assumed that the bone in the human must be an exact replica of the bone in the ape. Goethe's insight was that the bone need not – indeed *cannot* – look like it does in the ape, because we must take the *whole* into account (the whole human body) and thus think of the bone as it would appear as *part of this whole*, not as an isolated part that is simply attached to the whole.

He was able to find the intermaxillary bone, then, not because he was guided by a static idea of what a mammal is or should look like, but by a dynamic idea: an idea that is, however, very difficult to articulate in abstract philosophical language, because it requires the constant practice of looking, comparing and observing.

Goethe attempts, nonetheless, to do this in 'Experience and Science' and Schiller is extremely excited by this attempt – he is starting to get what Goethe means. More importantly, Schiller does not only *get* Goethe's intention, he also *adds* to it – he elucidates the status of the 'pure phenomenon' and gives to Goethe the perfect term for his methodology: *rational empiricism.*

The letter begins with Schiller suggesting to Goethe that the best way by which to understand the distinction between the three kinds of phenomena – the empirical, the scientific and the pure – is by considering them in light of the table of categories (i.e. in light of the kinds of judgments that the various phenomena allow us to make). This means considering each of the phenomena according to the categories of quantity, quality, relation and modality (this division of judgments, which goes back to Aristotle, is the basis for Kant's own table of judgments).

The empirical phenomenon is the focus of common empiricism and concerns that which is immediately seen or sensed, what is here and now. In terms of quantity, the empirical phenomenon can only yield *singular* (rather than universal) judgments (*this* table here is green; *this* man is tall). In terms of quality, it can only assert the existence of things (x *is* y) rather than negate them (x is *not* y), oppose them to other things (x is *non* y), or compare them with other things (x *is like* y). When it comes to relations, common empiricism runs the risk of confusing what is accidental for what is essential (e.g. all swans that I've seen are white, therefore all swans are white) but does not actually commit the error, because it remains on the level of '*this* swan is white' – it never moves to the universal judgment 'all swans are white'. Finally, in terms of modality, the empirical phenomenon is only about what is actual (what is in front of me now) and thus cannot think in terms of the possible (what may be the case) or the necessary (what must be the case). There are significant limitations to common empiricism. However, it does have one important advantage. Because it remains bound to the phenomenon in its most immediate form, it does not ascend to the level of judgment – to making claims about the phenomenon that extend beyond what is right here. For there lies the source of error, which emerges when we move to the scientific phenomenon (i.e. rationalism).

Rationalism is the source of error, because it is less focused on what is before it and more concerned with the laws of thought itself – with what we can *think* rather than *perceive*. Thought and perception are, of course, not the same; the problem emerges when we mistake thought for reality.

But rationalism has numerous advantages. For one, it yields plurality rather than simple singularity (*many* men are tall) – but, Schiller warns, it should resist going further, to totality (*all* men are tall), which would clearly result in error. In turn, rationalism allows for negation – but it should be wary of isolating and separating those things which are, in nature, fundamentally connected. In terms of relations, rationalism aims to regard all things in causal terms (i.e. as causes and effects) but as Schiller once again warns, rationalism should be careful not to over-determine everything in causal terms, as that would yield a picture of nature that is purely linear: nature as an endless chain of causes and effects. Finally, rationalism abandons the actual (which is far too contingent for its purposes) but is unable to arrive at the necessary (because it can only concern plurality, rather than totality), which means that it is only concerned with the possible (i.e. the realm of logical possibility).

In contrast to both the empirical and the scientific phenomenon, the pure phenomenon, Schiller writes, is 'one with the objective laws of nature'. With the pure phenomenon emerges rational empiricism, the approach that Schiller ascribes to Goethe, which involves conjoining empiricism and rationalism. Only such an approach, Schiller argues, can grasp the objective laws of nature because it remains with what is given (via empiricism) but, through the capacities of reason, is able to note differences, draw comparisons and arrive at what is fundamentally essential. Or, as Schiller put it, 'in a word, it preserves fully the rights of the object . . .' How does it do this?

First, rational empiricism moves beyond both singularity and plurality, to unity, because it is concerned with what is essential and constant in the various manifestations before us. As Schiller explains, it aims to discern the unity *in* the multiplicity. In turn, rational empiricism is not concerned with mere affirmation (x is y) or mere negation (x is not y) but limitation, which involves seeing how things are both like and unlike other things, drawing connections rather than simply affirming or negating. When it comes to relations, rational empiricism pays attention to both the causal nexus of objects – determining their causal relation to other objects – *and* to their independence (i.e. to the fact that they are *not merely* effects or causes but *also* integral wholes, which are themselves *loci* of causal relations (e.g. an animal body is seen as an integral whole, rather than a mere outcome of various causes)). As such, Schiller explains, rational empiricism does not simply regard nature as an endless chain of cause and effect, but also discerns nature's 'breadth', the diversity and uniqueness of individual beings. It sees objects *for themselves* – and not merely as points in a chain. Finally, precisely because rational empiricism is concerned with what is constant, with what is essential, it arrives at necessity, at what *must be* rather than what (merely) is – which can be entirely accidental – or what may be – which is speculative.

One can arrive at the pure phenomenon, however, only through continuous and careful comparative study, study which remains with the phenomenon, but not with the *singular* phenomenon. Unlike rationalism, which can only arrive at plurality and thus mere possibility (if all the swans I have seen are white, then it is *likely* that *all* swans are white), rational empiricism discerns the fundamental character of its object and determines what makes it what it is.

In these few pages, Schiller elucidates Goethe's approach to nature in new and illuminating language and gives him a term for his methodology. Ultimately, for Schiller and certainly for Goethe, rational empiricism is the *only* approach to nature, because it alone yields necessity, which amounts to knowledge. After all, knowledge is what we know to be necessary, rather than accidental or probable. Such necessity is not – and this is the most important point – to be found in the mind, in our *way of thinking* (that would be Kantianism), but in the phenomenon itself.

Upon receiving the letter, Goethe was delighted by Schiller's exposition, writing in a letter from 21 February 1798 that the term 'rational empiricism' is so apt that he will adopt it to speak of his method in the future. Indeed, Schiller's term, which sounds like a contradiction, gets to the heart of Goethe's view that ideas can indeed be seen in experience. For the ideas we are talking about are not those of rationalism – which accord only with the logical laws of thought; and the experience we are talking about is not that of common empiricism – which is only of the singular and the immediate. Rather, Goethe's ideas emerge through experience, precisely because they are achieved through careful, repeated and comparative study, which conjoins the work of the physical eye with that of the mental eye, to arrive at a third form of vision: one which discerns what is essential (i.e. the idea or pure phenomenon).

Friedrich Schiller to Johann Wolfgang von Goethe

Jena, 19 January 1798[1]

It will be interesting and instructive to you, to examine the ideas, which you brought forward in that older essay and again in your last one, according to the *Categories*. Your judgment will be quite confirmed, and it will at the same time awaken in you a new faith in the regulative use of philosophy with regard to matters empirical. I will here confine myself only to a few modes of applying it, and moreover at once in connection with your last essay.

The idea of experience under the three different kinds of phenomena is entirely exhaustive if you test them according to the Categories.

a.

Common empiricism, which does not go beyond the empiric phenomenon has (according to quantity) always but one case, a single element of experience, and hence no experience; according to quality it always asserts but one definite existence without distinguishing it, without excluding it, without opposing it, in a word, without making comparisons; according to relation, it is in danger of conceiving what is accidental as substantial; according to modality it remains confined simply to a definite reality, without suspecting what is possible, or even leading its cognition up to necessity. According to my idea, common empiricism is never exposed to error, for error first arises when it is made the basis of a science. What it observes, it really observes, and as it feels no desire to make its perceptions laws for the object, so its perceptions may always, without any danger, be isolated and accidental.

b.

It is only with rationalism that there arises the *philosophical phenomenon* and error; for in this field the thinking faculties commence their play, and arbitrariness enters with the freedom that is granted to these powers which are so inclined to substitute themselves for the object.

According to quantity, rationalism always comprises several cases, and as long as it is modest enough not to represent plurality as totality – that is, to make objective laws – it is harmless, nay useful, for it is the way to truth, which can be found only when one understands how to free oneself from particular cases. When abused, however, it becomes hurtful to philosophy, because, as you yourself very clearly state in your essay, it will maintain the immense combining powers of the human mind at the cost of a certain republican freedom of facts; in short, because it regards mere plurality as unity and hence treats that which is no totality, as a totality.

According to quality, rationalism very properly contrasts the phenomena one with another, it distinguishes and compares, which (like rationalism generally) is also praiseworthy and good, and the only way to philosophy. But the despotism of the thinking powers spoken of above, manifests itself here also immediately by *one-sidedness*, by strictness of distinction, as before by arbitrariness of combining. It runs in danger of strictly separating that which is allied in nature, as in the above case it joins what nature separates. It makes divisions where none exist, etc.

According to relation it is the everlasting endeavour of rationalism to enquire into the causality of the phenomena, and to unite everything *qua* cause and effect: again very praiseworthy and necessary for philosophy, but likewise extremely hurtful owing to one-sidedness. I refer here to your essay itself which chiefly censures the abuse which occasions the causal relationship of the phenomena. Rationalism seems to be at fault here principally from the fact that, inadequately, it merely takes into account the length and not the breadth of nature.

According to modality, rationalism quits reality without arriving at necessity. Possibility is its immense field, hence its unlimited hypotheses. Even this function of the understanding is, as I think, necessary, and the *conditio sine qua non* of all philosophy, for, in my opinion, it is only through what is possible that a passage from the Real to the Necessary is to be found. Hence I uphold, as far as I can, the freedom and justification of theoretical powers in the domain of physics.

C.

The *pure phenomenon* which, as I think, is one with the objective law of nature, can be got at only by rational empiricism. But, to repeat it again, rational empiricism itself can never begin directly with empiricism; on the contrary, rationalism will in all cases first lie between them. The third category arises at all times from the union of the first with the second, and thus we also find that it is only the full activity of the freely thinking faculties together with the purest and the most extensive activity of the sensuous powers of perception, that leads to scientific knowledge. Rational empiricism, consequently, will effect both these things: it will exclude arbitrariness and call forth liberality: the arbitrariness which influences the mind of man towards the object, or blind chance in the object, and the limited individuality of the single phenomenon towards the power of thought. In a word, it will grant the object its full right by taking from it its blind power, and procure for the human mind its full (rational) freedom by cutting off from it all arbitrariness.

According to quantity, the pure phenomenon must comprehend the totality of instances, for it is the element of constancy in every one of them. Hence it again restores unity in the plurality, and that perfectly in accordance with the meaning of the Category.

According to quality, rational empiricism always sets a limit, as may be learnt from the example of all true enquirers into nature, who are equally removed from all absolute affirmations and denials.

According to relation, rational empiricism pays heed both to the causality and to the independence of phenomena; it sees all nature in a reciprocal state of activity, everything is determined alternately, and hence it takes good care not to allow causality to assert itself only according to a simple scanty length, but breadth too is in all cases taken into account.

According to modality, rational empiricism always penetrates to necessity.

Rational empiricism, in accordance with its idea, is indeed never exposed to abuse like the two preceding species of cognition; but one ought nevertheless to guard against a false and apparently rational empiricism. For in the same way as a *wise limitation* constitutes the real spirit of this species of rational empiricism, so a *cowardly* and *timid limitation* may produce the other. The fruit of the former is the pure phenomenon, the fruit of the latter the empty and hollow phenomenon. I have on several occasions observed that timid, weak minds – on account of too great a regard for objects and their variety, and from too great a fear of the powers of the mind – in the end, so limit and, as it were, hollow out their assertions and enunciations that the result is nil.

There is still so much to be discussed on this subject and on your theses, that I am looking forward to your coming in order thoroughly to enter into the matter, for it is only conversation that gives me actual help in quickly grasping and retaining hold of the ideas of others. In the monologue of a letter I am always in danger of only taking up my own side. I more particularly wish to hear you yourself discourse upon that which you call the direct application of cases to rules.

My poetical work has been at a standstill for the last three days, notwithstanding my having been quite in the humour for it. An affection of the throat, which has been going the rounds of our house, has at last attacked me also, and this trouble having come upon me just when I was in a state of great sensitiveness, produced by my work, I was very feverish all day yesterday. Today, however, my head is already much better, and I hope in a few days to have quite got rid of my troublesome visitor.

I congratulate you upon your new *xenion*.[2] We will, of course, put it *to action*.

The mad pranks which Herr Posselt is cutting before the public will not do his publisher any great injury.

People are asking here continually whether you are going to have Gotter's opera,[3] *The Enchanted Isle*, performed in Weimar.

As Herr Hirt has to some extent prepared people for your essay on *Laokoon*, do you not feel inclined to let it appear in the *Horen*[4]?

Farewell. My wife sends kind greetings.

12 'WHAT THEN IS HAPPINESS, MY DEAR FRIEND?'

Giacomo Leopardi to André Jacopssen

Luigi Capitano

Giacomo Leopardi (born in 1798 in Recanati and died in 1837 in Naples) was a peerless writer of prose and poetry, from his *Canti* to his *Moral Fables* to his posthumous *Zibaldone*.[1] His correspondence is made up of over 1,100 manuscript letters, sent to family, friends and scholars of his day.[2] Leopardi's exceptional genius was discovered early on by the literary critic and scholar Pietro Giordani (1774–1848) but his name began to circulate in Europe during the nineteenth century thanks to the Swiss philologist Louis De Sinner (1801–1860) and the French critic, Sainte-Beuve (1804–1869), such that the philosopher Arthur Schopenhauer (1788–1860) had boasted of being one of the 'three greatest pessimists' of Europe, along with Leopardi and Byron.[3] Nietzsche, too, was a deep admirer of Leopardi before ultimately rejecting him as a decadent. In the English-speaking world, amongst his most fervent enthusiasts were Thomas Hardy and Samuel Beckett.

Born into an aristocratic but impoverished family, the count Giacomo Leopardi had, at an early age, gained mastery in philology, poetry and philosophy. He was an auto-didact, studying in his father's library of over 12,000 books. He felt early on the imperious need to escape from the constricting settings of Recanati and began to travel, living in some of the most important cultural and artistic centres of Italy (Rome, Bologna, Milan, Florence, Pisa and Naples)[4] without, however, ever crossing the

Italian border. In Naples, at the feet of Mount Vesuvius, shortly before his death at age 39, Leopardi wrote a great symphony in verse entitled '*La Ginestra*' ('The Desert Flower') a spiritual testament of sorts, in which the infinitesimal size of our world and the destructive force of the volcano are counteracted against the 'noble nature' of the poet capable of calling out to the whole of humanity to join forces together against universal evil. His was a lunar and nocturnal nature, nourished by the works of the proto-romantic Edward Young as also, from amongst the English poets, Shakespeare, Milton, Pope and Byron. His philosophy, influenced amongst others by Locke, Pascal, Rousseau, Voltaire and the French materialists, is consonant with a radical scepticism and a negative philosophy which verges on nihilism.[5] Yet, he never renounces his 'illusions', which ground his vision of life and art.

The letter to André Jacopssen (1793–1864) written on the 23 June 1823 sketches in broad brushstrokes the negative philosophy of Leopardi and his poetics of the imagination. Leopardi had only met Jacopssen, the erudite tourist from Bruges, a few months earlier, in February and March 1823 during his first Roman trip,[6] when Leopardi was staying with his uncle, Carlo Antici, whom he mentions at the end of the letter. Leopardi sent Jacopssen a first letter, which is now lost,[7] to which Jacopssen would not reply until 2 June, which is the letter Leopardi in turn replies to on the 23 June, in impeccable French. Using the French language would open the doors – or so he thought – to a wealthy foreign patron, which was the only 'advantage' Leopardi thought he could get from his trip to Rome. It is more than likely that he had pinned his hopes of escape on Jacopssen.

This initial exchange of letters with Jacopssen, after his return to Recanati, inaugurated two years of epistolary exchanges (1823–1824). Their correspondence is infused with melancholy and pessimism, and also with intense reflections on the question of love.[8] In the letter presented here, the poet unburdens his heart, expressing intimate and deep thoughts which touch on the meaning of life, the search for happiness and the privileges of love and friendship. The written correspondence reveals a unique correspondence in thought and sentiments, sounding 'the depths of the heart', as Leopardi asks, in a hopeless, rhetorical question: 'where to find a heart capable of responding?'.

The worlds of these two young men – Leopardi is 25, Jacopssen, 30 – converge in an ideal of sensitivity, which is loaded onto the French term '*sensibilité*' and which both men cherish above all else. Leopardi writes: 'In love, all the gratifications reaped by vulgar souls do not even come close to the pleasure that one single moment of ravishment and deep emotion can bring.'[9] It is Jacopssen's own tone of confidence in his letter from 2 June, which incites Leopardi in turn to pour his heart and world out. He is transported, in his reply, by a wave of enthusiasm and gushing sensitivity. He begins with the portrayal of his ideal of 'the sensitive man, brimming with imagination', the Leopardian '*uomo imaginoso*', whom he had thought to discern in his friend and whom he conceptualised in his immense intellectual diary, the *Zibaldone*.[10] It is this ideal alter ego who would also inspire the character of the Familiar Spirit in his dialogue 'Torquato Tasso and his Familiar Spirit' from the *Moral Fables*.

Leopardi often professes a propensity for absence and solitude, but in his letters, it is not rare to find equally emphatic and effusive exclamations of affection; declarations such as 'I love you' pepper his correspondence, with family and close friends (in particular Pietro Giordani and Pietro Brighenti). But our letter here is nevertheless an exceptional document in this respect, especially considering that the two correspondents barely knew each other and that their friendship had been interrupted but a few short weeks into their acquaintance. Sure enough, they share a number of preoccupations, starting with a certain artistic and intellectual sensibility born out of a double veneration for the enlightenment and romanticism. They both love Canova and Rossini and both share interests in disparate readings ranging from Buffon's *Natural History*, Volney's *Ruines, or a Survey of the Revolutions of Empires*, to Madame de Staël's *Corinne*, Chateaubriand, Bernardin de Saint-Pierre and, most of all, Rousseau. Yet, their worldly ideals of travel could not be more different.

Jacopssen is a European tourist on his Grand Tour, erudite and ravenous in his desire to learn about places, landscapes, cities, museums, libraries, gardens and science laboratories, but also hospitals and charitable institutions for the poor. His is a philanthropic and polymorphous mind; all avenues of knowledge light up his curiosity in an indefatigable and self-teaching frenzy for learning. Jacopssen's life is 'a full life' as Leopardi would call it in the *Zibaldone* (4185–6): a life full of travelling which will take him across France, Switzerland, Italy and the North of Europe.[11] Though he shares the romantic ideal of 'sensitivity' and he, too, has suffered in his body and soul, Jacopssen remains a traveller of life in the outside world – not of the internal world of the mind. Leopardi is a traveller of the mind; he is the prototypical static traveller such as Fernando Pessoa would conjure a century later.[12] Pessoa's traveller is the man who wanders off in his imagination as if on the wings of 'the city brochures'.

Leopardi is used to travelling across libraries both real and imaginary. On his first trip to Rome, along with around 2,600 pages of his *Zibaldone*, he brings Cervantes' *Don Quixote*, a book on style by the seventeenth-century Jesuit Daniello Bartoli (himself a great traveller) and *Dialogues* of Lucian of Samosata, one of the sources of inspiration for Leopardi's future masterpiece of satirical prose, the *Moral Fables*. For Leopardi, his poetical imagination doubles up reality with phantasy. In the manner of the romantics, he is able to see, time after time, 'another tower, another country' (*Zib.* 4418). Such a traveller as he could only ever love 'through the lens of a telescope',[13] faithful to a Platonism of the imagination which again would be echoed in the works of Pessoa. This also explains Leopardi's lapses into the Rousseau-inspired 'land of chimeras', the only place, as Leopardi says himself, 'which is worth living'. It is Rousseau who writes in the *New Heloise*:

> The land of chimeras is, in this life, the only one worth living, and such is the nothingness of human affairs that, apart from the Being that exists in itself, there is nothing which is beautiful save from that which is not.[14]

An atheist, disenchanted with the world, Leopardi reveals in his letter that he fears the desiccation of his own capacity for imagination, which had always been so prodigious from his earliest age. Leopardi belongs to that species of restless beings, exiles in their own country, forced to roam from city to city, often the same cities which are on the map of the Grand Tour, without however, feeling any firm stable ground beneath his feet – no 'land' as he writes in his poem 'To Angelo Mai'[15] – and without ever finding his own reference point 'in any place at all' (*Zib.* 4287). Whereas Jacopssen is a man who is looking for something, Leopardi has a restless soul which is in exile, whilst his body is living in a contrived 'hermitage' in his 'native wild village', the small-minded papal stronghold of Recanati. Leopardi's escapes are, at best, long 'solitary walks' within the confines of a routine which is 'more unchanging than the motion of the stars' as he writes in our letter. Leopardi responds thus to his friend's words, who wrote in his letter from the 2nd June: 'for now the most monotonous and monochrome existence awaits me', adding a pessimistic gloss on the precarity of existence: 'from life to death, there is but one step'. They both enter a sort of competition, emulating one another as to who can immerse himself more deeply in the world of the other, with outpourings which verge on the intimacy of a Platonic love relationship. We should note that these are the months in which Leopardi is reading Plato intensely, intending to translate all the dialogues. It is thus not surprising that this letter should anticipate the themes of one of Leopardi's most enigmatic and metaphysical texts, which explores a similar platonic love trope, namely the poem 'To His Lady'.

Jacopssen's letter from 2 June was itself a response to the 'enchanting letter' from Leopardi which he had received, with great surprise, on his arrival in Geneva. As we can see, Jacopssen desired to propitiate himself to his new-found friend and he does so by appealing to his own sensitivity and their elective affinities. He writes to Leopardi: 'your letter discloses great depths of sensitivity in your character: that warms my heart, especially since I feel in myself a similar kind of moral susceptibility'. Jacopssen thinks that he is discovering in the Italian poet a disposition which is close to his own and that they are destined to agree on an 'infinity of topics', which will prove to be the basis for a true friendship. He tells Leopardi about a number of his romantic experiences, in which Jacopssen confesses to his friend, that 'his expectations were always disappointed', because they were too great. He takes a leaf out of his friend's own book and speaks about aspiring to an 'essentially negative happiness' which consists in 'not suffering'. Leopardi cannot not respond to this negative concept: 'the happiness of man cannot consist in what is real', is his reply.

Thus, 'it is all down to the imagination to provide a man with the only kind of positive happiness he is capable of'. Leopardi then confesses, in turn, that he has often come to desire from a distance, before facing disillusionment and reality: 'Many a time, I have refrained from meeting for a few days the object which had enchanted me in a delightful dream. I knew that the enchantment would have been broken by getting too close to reality.' It is a prelude to the attitude Leopardi would adopt soon enough, in addressing himself 'To His Lady':

> But there is nothing on earth
> that is like you; and even if there were a woman
> who had a face that resembled yours, by her movements and her
>   conversation,
> a copy of you though she be, she would be far less beautiful.[16]

What we have here is a poetical ideal of reality transfigured into an idea. Leopardi draws on the same idealised sensitivity when he describes the traits of his ideal friend, the '*uomo immaginoso*', the man who lives in his imagination, who is the Platonic lover, the representative fellow citizen of a no less utopian ideal society:

> I would agree, if you like, that virtue, like everything that is beautiful and everything that is great, is but an illusion. But had this illusion been a common one, had all men believed and wished to be virtuous, had they been compassionate, generous, magnanimous, full of enthusiasm – in a word, had everyone been sensitive (for I make no distinction between sensitivity and what we call virtue) – would we not all be the happier for it?

Leopardi's thoughts are as bitter as they are realistic, 'the world is ignorant of its own interests', he declares. Society, people, do not know what it is that would make them truly happy. They are in the thrall of a Machiavellianism and a utilitarianism which Leopardi contrasts with the ironic ideal of the useless. He evokes the figure of the *flâneur*, the urban wanderer, anticipating Baudelaire. He had even suggested 'The *Flâneur*' as the title for a Florentine journal devoted, jokingly, to the 'useless' and frivolous. The virtuous man (or 'The Gentleman', the title of an unfinished dialogue) is the sensitive man; the imaginative, magnanimous, enthusiastic, exceptional man – in sum, the man of genius. He is perhaps 'romantic' in the way he pursues, madly seduced by it, the dream created by his romantic and fantastical imagination; but he is not *only* romantic, as Leopardi suggests himself when he asks in his letter, almost coyly: 'Am I a romantic?' It is not by chance that the word 'genius', explained as having too much talent, is referred by Jacopssen to Leopardi. Jacopssen regrets that in life, such a condition is not the norm, but should be an exception. For only the exceptional man, (the creature 'from another species') has within him these superior traits of the genius. It would be a splendid utopia to find it everywhere. Jacopssen had spoken of 'the true human happiness, meant for the thinking classes', those who are capable of 'ineffable elation'. But man, as also animals, Jacopssen noted, is happiest when he is the less sensitive. This view, Jacopssen considered as congenial with Leopardi. But this tends to simplify Leopardi's negative theory. Jacopssen speaks of 'an essentially negative happiness', since the 'happiest' beings are ultimately those who have 'the least sensitivity'. Leopardi, however, turns around completely this negative vision of pleasure (though he does not renounce it). For he concludes his letter on happiness by maintaining that indeed, 'it is all down to the imagination to provide a man with the only kind of positive happiness he is capable of'. Thus the 'illusion' which imagination is capable of turns around that 'emptiness of existence' which had so preyed on him, he says, to make him consider its very nothingness as a real thing. Here lies the solution to the question about happiness with which the letter begins: if our options are either not to live so as not to suffer, or to unleash sensitivity so that it permeates everything, then we must make our sensitivity as powerful as possible. We must let it rule our lives.

What began as a logical puzzle: 'either we should not go on living or we should always feel', turns into a dilemma of Shakespearean proportions. It is resolved by considering it, not as an exclusive choice, but as the one crucial challenge of life. We must live to charge every moment of our lives with the power of our sensitivity. Thus, the most banal or outwardly humdrum routine, such as reading in the library and taking solitary walks, which are the sole outward occupations of Leopardi's self-described 'hermit's life' at the end of his letter, can be transformed into heightened internal states created by the imagination, full of taste, colours and wit, in contrast to the 'insipid and colourless and dull' outside.

Giacomo Leopardi to André Jacopssen

Recanati, 23 June 1823[17]

My dear friend,

I shall begin by thanking you for all the many expressions of kindness which you bestow on me in you charming letter, and most of all for the trust you display towards me when you tell me of the kind of life you are leading, of your thoughts, feelings and the state of your soul. All of this is infinitely interesting to me, and I can hardly tell you how much pleasure you gave me in communicating these details to me. For it is truly delightful to uncover the secrets of a heart such as yours. But it would seem to me to fall short of the affection you show me, were I to make an easy recourse to some ceremonial expression of circumstance. I therefore, do not thank you, but I merely assure you that my heart is all yours for ever.

My dear friend, it must surely be the case either that we should not go on living or that we should always feel, always love, always be hopeful. Sensitivity, that would be the most precious gift of all, if we could only know how to see it for its true value, or if there were something in this world to apply it to. I told you already that the art of not suffering is now the only art that I seek to learn. That is only because I have relinquished all hope of living. Had I not been convinced, from my very first attempts that all hope was utterly futile and frivolous to me, I would not wish for, nay, I would not even know of any other kind of life other than the life of enthusiasm. For a while, I felt the very emptiness of existence as if it were a real thing which was weighing down heavily on my soul. The nothingness of things was to me the only thing which existed. It was always present to me like a horrible ghost; I saw but a desert around me; I could not conceive of how one could submit to the everyday cares that life requires, knowing with certainty that all these cares will never come to anything. That thought so haunted me that it seemed I was almost losing my mind.

In truth, my friend, the world is ignorant of what is truly in its interest. I would agree, if you like, that virtue, like everything that is beautiful and everything that is great, is but an illusion. But had this illusion been a common one, had all men believed and wished to be virtuous, had they been compassionate, generous, magnanimous, full of enthusiasm – in a word, had everyone been sensitive (for I make no distinction between sensitivity and what we call virtue) – would we not all be the happier for it? Would not each single individual find a thousand riches in society? And should not society be dedicated to making illusions come true as much as it is possible to do so, since the happiness of man cannot consist in what is real?

In love, all the gratifications reaped by vulgar souls do not even come close to the pleasure that one single moment of ravishment and deep emotion can bring. But how to make this feeling last, or at least have it occur often in one's life? Where to find a heart capable of responding to it? Many a time, I have refrained from meeting for a few days the object which had enchanted me in a delightful dream. I knew that the enchantment would have been broken by getting too close to reality. And yet, I thought ceaselessly of that object, but I did not study it from what it was like in reality; rather, I contemplated it in my imagination, as it had appeared to me in my dream. Was it madness? Am I a romantic? You be the judge.

It is true that the tendency to always think things over and over, which is ever the way with sensitive minds, removes one's capacity to act, and even to feel pleasure. The overabundance of life within drives the person towards the outside world; yet at the same time, his nature is such that he does not know how to cope. He reaches out to the whole wide world, he wishes to be always full; however, every single object eludes him, precisely because they are all too small compared with his capacity. He demands of even his smallest actions, of every one of his words, of every gesture, of the movements of his body, more grace and perfection than it is possible for a human being to attain. And thus, he is never able to be pleased with himself, nor can he cease to examine himself. And, always distrusting of his own powers, he does not know how to do what everyone else does.

What then is happiness, my dear friend? And if there is no happiness, what then is life? I do not know. I love you dearly, I will always love you as tenderly, as obstinately as I used to love back then those lovely objects that my imagination would delight in creating. Those dreams, which you say make up a part of happiness. For indeed, it is all down to the imagination to provide a man with the only kind of positive happiness he is capable of. That is true wisdom, to seek happiness in the ideal, as you do. As for me, I miss those days when I could still look for it there. For I realise not without dread, that my imagination is becoming sterile and is denying me all the relief it used to procure me in days gone by.

This letter is already too long. The pleasure of talking about these matters with you, who explain yourself with such sharpness and depth of mind, has made me forget the other part of your letter in which you ask me who are our best philosophical writers. I will try to answer that question another time. But as to theologians, I am not even sure we have any at all, let alone if there are any excellent ones. I do not even think that there is any excellence to be reached in that domain. Your friend, the Baron de Hert (I think I do not know how to spell his name), has he come back home? How is he? Send him my regards and do please send me news of him. The good old abbot Cancellieri[18] is keeping himself as ever entertained writing books and publishing them. As for Antici, my uncle, he is leaving Rome to spend the summer at Recanati. I am in good health. I live here as if in a hermitage: my books and my solitary walks take up all my time. My life is more unchanging than the motion of the stars, more humdrum and insipid than the *lyrics* at the opera. Farewell my dear friend. Love me, if it is possible, as much as you deserve to be loved. Tell me about what you are doing, tell me about your plans, about your philosophical observations: the more you talk about these matters, the more pleasure you will give me.

I am, with the keenest affection and the most wholehearted devotion,

Your loving and sincere friend,

G. Leopardi.

13 A PHILOSOPHY OF LOVE
Flora Tristan to Charles Fillieu

Máire Fedelma Cross

What do we make of Flora Tristan's letter to a young man who had seemingly sent her a declaration of his feelings as an ardent admirer? Flora Tristan (1803–1844), the Franco-Peruvian pioneering socialist, feminist, essayist, pamphleteer and novelist, rejects her admirer on the grounds of moral superiority and independence as a woman. At the same time, she reaches out to him as a sister to a brother in humanity, urging him to rise to the occasion. The historical context is key to understanding how the personal and the professional mingle in this letter which is both a political manifesto and the foundation for a new philosophy of love.

The intriguing letter from Flora Tristan to Charles Fillieu, dated 30 July 1843, is quite unique, one of the rare instances in the published collection that would-be biographers could consider using subsequently as evidence of her personal circumstances.[1] The fact is that Flora Tristan left no account of where her affections lay in love after 1838 so there has been speculation as to why the beautiful woman preferred to remain aloof from the many men who wished to court her as she asserts in her letter to Charles F.

She had been married at the age of 17 to André Chazal, a Parisian engraver with whom she had three children, but hers was not a happy experience and she left the Parisian family home in 1825. Unable to obtain a divorce as it had been banned under the Restoration Monarchy, she was still married when she received this letter, but the manner of her firm rebuttal of Fillieu's advances implies that it was not for that reason that Flora Tristan dismissed Fillieu as a suitor. There is a more compelling reason. By 30 July 1843, Flora Tristan had thrown herself into her public life as a professional activist. In addition to being fully dedicated to the cause of emancipation for women by living the principles she preached, she was engaged full time in her political strategy for a workers' union, a tactic that required letter-writing to solicit support, though not the kind of support that Charles F. was proposing. Having distanced herself from the memory of her unhappy marriage she had seemingly little interest in pursuing any relationship, declaring that she belonged to no man.

She explains to Fillieu that without her gifts as a superior woman, her initial personal reaction would have been to treat the letter in a light-hearted manner, or even to embarrass him in front of others but, tempted as she is, she assures her suitor she would not ridicule him but respond according to her elevated principles to which she aspires in all circumstances.

In reading the embellished insistence on the role of a superior woman in her letter it is important to recall that Flora Tristan was part of the era of the emergence of an intelligentsia of thinkers and reformers wherein females had to struggle for recognition. In the same collection of letters, we read the response from one of her warmest supporters, the philosopher and socialist, Victor Considerant, to her request to attend the annual commemoration of Fourier's death: women were not welcome.[2] Flora Tristan persisted in her public engagement and used the identity of the superior woman to good effect as a shield against social prejudice.

A socialist activist, her published works written in hybrid forms of literature, travel writing and social critique were read and criticised. Her correspondence remained dispersed, unpublished and unseen until long after her death when Jules-L. Puech published her first major biography in 1925. As early as 1838 however, Flora Tristan had become established in Parisian circles as an outspoken female author having written two petitions to the French Parliament (*Chambre des Deputés*), asking for the restoration of divorce and the abolition of the death penalty. Her brochure *Necessité de faire bon accueil aux femmes étrangères* (1835) pleaded for the right of women to travel independently and in security and her book *Pérégrinations d'une paria* (1838) was an account of her epic journey to Peru to claim her inheritance from the family of her Spanish-Peruvian father who had died when she was a child.[3] Her parents had undergone a religious ceremony but failed to register their marriage with the civil authorities, hence her illegitimacy in the eyes of her powerful and wealthy uncle in Arequipa. The work was a severe condemnation of class and gender inequalities in Peru and, as such, its publication was denounced and destroyed there. It landed her in trouble in France too as Flora Tristan had prefaced it with an inclusion of her own life story linking her personal difficulties as an illegitimate daughter without resources and as an unhappily married woman to the lot of all women oppressed by laws of society. It enraged her estranged husband André Chazal to the point of planning to kill her. Chazal's defence lawyer used it to good effect against her in 1839 during Chazal's trial after he ambushed and shot her in the street outside her home. She escaped within an inch of her life.

That same year saw the publication of her novel *Méphis*, which Tristan mentions in her letter. There, she had extolled the Saint-Simonian ideals of a new social and moral order giving liberty and sexual freedom to both sexes and, in particular, ascribing a redemptive superiority to women. Her social activism began in earnest after the publication of her critique of capitalism in *Promenades dans Londres* (1840) and *Union Ouvrière*, first published in May 1843 and which ran to three editions in total by 1844.[4] These publications were funded by subscriptions raised from among her friends and acquaintances. Enter the first trace of her correspondent as one of her supporters: his name and occupation, 'Charles F., student', figures as No. 72 out of 102 in the list of subscribers to the second edition of *Union Ouvrière* published in January 1844.

The sentiments in the letter penned by Tristan to Charles are quite emphatic and make it one of the most personal and yet impersonal of the collection that covers her adult life from 1821 to September 1844, a few weeks prior to her death in November of that year. Her rejection was a tactic on her part to protect herself personally as an attractive woman. There is also the question of her rebuke to him for distracting her from the main reason for her existence, the cause of humanity. It falls into the category of an unsolicited letter, but rather than stooping to derision of his letter she makes an appeal to his loftier sentiments as a sister in humanity and directs him to channel his commitment to her by engaging in that cause. She demands devotion and dedication in her response. A close reading of this one letter gives us thus a deeper insight into the personality of Flora Tristan and the manner in which she treated individuals on initial stages of acquaintance. There is a contrast of emotions between her rejection of a love interest and her dedication to her cause as a full-time activist. Both were iterated as extreme emotions. There is indeed a performative dimension to Flora Tristan's letter: its author aspired to know many individuals on a professional basis, as a sister of the whole of humanity, aloof from emotional ties to individuals but also as a solitary woman removed from her experience of a disastrous marriage. Thus, as the critic and biographer Stéphane Michaud notes:

> It was without bitterness and almost in fun that she replied to the declaration of love from Charles Fillieu. Reducing her to one in his possession would not serve her ideas. She had a different idea of what love was, which she outlined in her books and especially in her life. She hoped for something else from men who said they loved her, to work for her [cause] rather than waste their energy in lovesick sighs.[5]

She contested the expectation of how an attractive woman should behave, responding to a love letter all the better to insist on her agency and escape from the constraints of society.[6] By July 1843 Flora Tristan had turned her back on a conventional lifestyle. Her 'own system' of relating to individuals in love and friendship was coloured by her decision to devote her energy to change, to improve the lot of the proletariat and women by proposing a scheme that would end poverty and ignorance, the two greatest causes of unhappiness according to her philosophy outlined in her book *The Workers' Union*. Her actions would mark her as a precursor to feminism. The language of the letter is an example of her dramatic interpretation of her own public role, and the *performative dimension* of the letter.[7]

At first it would seem that Tristan is writing to reject the advances of a lover but the letter also reveals Flora Tristan's self-conscious construction of her role as a professional activist through her relations with those both sympathetic to her cause and physically attracted to her through her conception of what a woman, a superior woman must be. A singular woman gives a singular response. If her correspondent has acted inappropriately, instead of blaming him she seeks to find the cause of the man's misbehaviour, an error in his reasoning which can be corrected to heal, to cure, just as she aspires to cure society's ills.

Tristan develops what is, to all intents and purposes, a proto-feminist philosophy of love in which she reverses the traditional order of love and seduction in two radical ways, not only in the order of courtship but also in the order of possession and domination. She explains to her romantic admirer that, faced with multiple choices, it is the woman who decides whom she loves; it is up to her to make the first move. The latter is not a subtle, coquettishly feminine nudge, but an unambiguous proposal to the man, of whether he accepts to belong to the woman. This topsy-turvy revolution in mores, which Tristan calls her 'own system', would have comical undertones were it not for the seriousness of Tristan's tone and her implacable commitment to live as she preaches – this very letter being an instance of the application of her principles to her own life.

The comical, naïve or simply idealistic becomes courage, elevation and dignity, embodied through the concept of the Saint-Simonian superior woman and incarnated body and soul in the real life of Flora Tristan. She is superior, that is, to the men and women of her time by living according to values that will only become norms in the future. Her superiority is not so much that of a mystical visionary but rather that of an uncompromising reasoner, whose lucid intelligence compels her to behave according to laws of reason regardless of her time and place. She is so convinced of her ideals she finds it self-evident that her uncompromising rationale will be accepted by her fellow activists, admirers and supporters. Flora Tristan makes it clear in her letter that she lives out this rationale ahead of her time.

Like many of her correspondents, Charles Fillieu, the student, outlived Tristan and went on to engage in the events of the 1848 revolution when the conservative regime of the July Monarchy was overthrown. In a search of digitised archives, we find traces of a Charles Fillien as a republican in the heady days after February 1848 when the Second Republic was proclaimed. He is cited as a cofounder of the *Club de la Fraternité* with Arthur Mangin and Antonio Watripon.[8] There is evidence, however, of a Charles Fillieu as a literary author of songs and a play.[9] These traces of Charles Fillieu as a literary artist would suggest he had the superior intelligence and emotional ability to understand the sense of Tristan's answer to him or, indeed, that the latter played a role in his intellectual and political awakening. His voice as Tristan's admirer is filtered through her answer to him, but, from the meagre evidence of his life after Tristan's death, we can speculate that he learnt from and was inspired by her example.

The Tristan–Fillieu correspondence is one part of a conversation; there is a danger of reading too much into the fragment, of taking the sentiments of the superior woman out of context. But to isolate one letter to an individual about whom we know so little can reveal much about the sender. Thus, whether it was Charles Fillien or Charles Fillieu, the focus is not so much on the intended recipient but on the content of the letter penned by Flora Tristan, the performer. The letter is not to a dear friend in the sense of a close personal lasting friendship: on the contrary. We have little historical indication about the circumstances. However, even though the letter is but a fragment of an acquaintance we can still gain an insight into the 'performative' personality of Flora Tristan setting herself up as a 'superior' solitary woman, as the ardent lover of humanity seeking to cure the cause of the ills of society.

Flora Tristan To Charles Fillieu
Paris, 30 July 1843[10]

Monsieur Fillieu,

A *superior* woman must be *superior* with everyone, and *in all circumstances* – this is how I have lived from the moment I came to be *aware of my superiority* and that is how I shall continue to behave.

I am at a loss as to the reason for the *more than inappropriate* . . . letter which you wrote to me yesterday after you left my home, why? – You were obviously under a *serious delusion*.

Were I a *prude*, I would send you back your letter, and forbid you from seeing me ever again, and I would utter your name only to disparage and sneer at it. Were I a *coquette*, I would show your extravagant letter to your friends, and, together, we could make jokes about you for a whole week. But since I am a *superior* woman, well aware of my *mission as a woman*, I will answer you in a very different manner –

Monsieur Fillieu, had you read my *Mephis*, I am sure you never would have sent me such a declaration – For you would have known that when it comes to love, *I have a system all of my own*, and I'll have you know, for your own improvement, that the systems which I enunciate in my works, I *realise in my life*. In preaching the independence of Woman, in desiring that she be perfectly free in all things, I want that, when it comes to love, it be she who takes the initiative – That she be the one to say to the one she loves: 'I love you. Do you want *to be mine*?' – This much shows you how I understand and consider what love would be between a woman and man.

But you see, my dear sir, as I write this to you, I feel *enough strength in me* to put into practice *now, in the present,* what humanity *will come to acknowledge in the future.* In all my life, I have belonged to no man – for always, *it has been me who has taken the initiative.*

Whenever I met a person whom I *liked,* or a man whom I loved, I said to the first: do you want to *give yourself to me*? And to the other: do you want to *belong to me*?

As for *declarations of love*, I have received hundreds of them and *never have I accepted a single man who addressed one to me.*

And now, sir, if you are truly *great,* truly *intelligent* and *good,* you will come to me as a *brother,* as a *friend,* but you must convince yourself that *never* will I be a *woman* for you. But if you do not have enough greatness in your soul to understand all that is elevated and sacred in my way of behaving, do not return and all will be over.

Your letter, however inappropriate, did not *offend me in any way.* It is since the age of 21 that I live alone and have had the huge misfortune of being a pretty woman; you must understand that I have received countless letters from *students,* from *second officers.* I am therefore used to this nuisance which comes with *wayward society* – I no longer get cross with those who *behave badly,* though it pains me. But I *study the cause* which makes them act thus, and I strive with all my power, to heal the *cause of the ill.*

Goodbye, my dear sir, I am your sister in humanity.

14 JUST THE MAGNIFICENCE OF REALITY

Henry David Thoreau to Harrison G.O. Blake

Rick Anthony Furtak

Writing to a slightly younger contemporary, his friend Harrison G.O. Blake (1818–1876), Henry David Thoreau (1817–1862) touches upon a number of themes that are developed in his justly famous book *Walden* (in which we find the heart of his philosophical ideas) and, to some degree, in other texts as well. He begins by asking: What is truly precious, and what is it to be impoverished? It is like asking: How do you define success? Thoreau challenges his reader to redefine poverty, wealth and freedom. 'Give me the poverty that enjoys true wealth' he writes in *Walden*.[1] 'If the day and the night are such that you greet them with joy, and life emits a fragrance like flowers and sweet-scented herbs, is more elastic, more starry, more immortal, – that is your success. All nature is your congratulation, and you have cause momentarily to bless yourself' (*Walden*, XI). We are rich, as he states later in the opening paragraph of this letter, if we can succeed in letting things alone[2] – or, more precisely, leaving *one thing* alone, even if it be only a winter apple that we allow to remain hanging on a tree. Against the technological impulse to assert our will and impose it on our environment, Thoreau speaks on behalf of what he sees as a rare virtue: *letting be*. It is when we cease to impose our purposes onto the world that we open ourselves to finding it wondrous and awesome. Shortly afterwards, in the same letter to Blake, he will recommend that this attitude be adopted towards God. Reverence is found not in supplication, he contends, but in minding one's own business, with an outlook of quiet receptivity. To pray is not to make requests but to listen.

Early in this letter, Thoreau also voices a concern with finding what is real, as opposed to false appearance. In doing so, he brings up a topic that persists throughout his writings: speaking broadly, we could say that Nature (almost always capitalised by Thoreau) provides a criterion of reality, as opposed to which the vagaries of culture and fashion are merely artificial. 'Shams and delusions are esteemed for soundest truths, while reality is fabulous' (*Walden*, II). Enjoining his correspondent to give things their proper weight, instead of making skewed evaluations, he urges Blake to acknowledge what is real and dismiss all that is merely superficial. Thoreau wishes to clear away prejudice and illusory opinion to find a rock-solid basis on which to establish 'a Realometer' (*Walden*, II), so that 'future ages might know how deep a freshet of shams and appearances had gathered' in human society. It is only *beautiful* laws that ought to prevail in an orderly *cosmos*, he suggestively adds: and we should find it liberating to abide by them, rather than wasting our efforts in futile resistance. What does Thoreau have in mind in this passage? As he writes elsewhere, 'the laws of the universe are not indifferent, but are forever on the side of the most sensitive' (*Walden*, XI). Furthermore, 'if one advances confidently in the direction of his dreams, and endeavors to live the life which he has imagined, he will meet with a success unexpected in common hours. He will put some things behind, will pass an invisible boundary; new, universal, and more liberal laws will begin to establish themselves around and within him ... and he will live with the license of a higher order of beings' (*Walden*, XVIII). Following the laws of the universe in this sense appears to mean gravitating toward what attracts us, what we find compelling, whatever draws us in with a sense of destiny. It also means being governed in our own lives by something akin to the regularity we find in Nature's laws and processes.

Borrowing a phrase from (among others) the Oneida Indians, which Thoreau learned about while he was preparing notes for a never-completed treatise on Native American thought,[3] he asks his friend Blake to align his own spirit with the Great Spirit, finding sustenance in it, suggesting that what inspires a person from within – what he sometimes describes as *wildness* – is an echo of a greater power to be found in Nature. The metaphysics that Thoreau is sketching out is kept rather indefinite in this six-paragraph guide for the perplexed, yet if we skip ahead further into the letter for a moment we get an intimation of what he means. The Muse, he says, 'should lead like a star that is very far off', like a polestar that provides us with orientation. As he counsels elsewhere, 'In the long run men hit only what they aim at. Therefore, though they should fail immediately, they had better aim at something high' (*Walden*, I). In other words, we ought to point ourselves toward the loftiest ideals, as toward a distant star. And how do we bring our guiding light into view? Thoreau seems to imply that the human spirit should be directed by Spirit in a more cosmic sense, our inner *daimon* directed by God. 'I say, God. I am not sure that that is the name. You will know whom I mean.' *Do* we know whom he is talking about? The term is admittedly vague. But Thoreau points out that 'the words which express our faith and piety are not definite; yet they are significant, and fragrant like frankincense to superior natures' (*Walden*, XVIII). Blake is hereby told not to compromise himself, but to believe in the aims he feels inwardly called to realise. 'It is by a mathematical point only that we are wise, as the sailor or the fugitive slave keeps the polestar in his eye; but that is sufficient guidance for all our life. We may not arrive at our port within a calculable period, but we would preserve the true course' (*Walden*, I). Such is the teleological appeal of Thoreau's philosophy: we are invited to have faith that our lives are blessed with a higher purpose.

Perhaps the most striking passage in Thoreau's letter occurs soon after he asks his friend whether he truly wishes to be alive – and it is uttered in response to some doubt that Blake has apparently confessed about whether life is meaningful. Placing the burden of proof on those who would argue that it is not or that such meaning as we may find in it is only delusive, Thoreau claims that there is no risk that we will overestimate its meaning or value. 'I am not afraid that I shall exaggerate the value and significance of life', he explains, 'but that I shall not be up to the occasion which it is'. He exhorts his interlocutor to rise to the grand occasion which life is, and to take his own existence seriously while he *is* alive. As Thoreau says in another context, 'Be it life or death, we crave only reality. If we are really dying, let us hear the rattle in our throats and feel cold in the extremities; if we are alive, let us go about our business' (*Walden*, II). We ought to put aside any concern that we will be duped if we lead our lives in accordance with what has moved us emotionally with the feeling that it is truly significant – whether that be a beloved, an enthusiasm or pursuit, or a sacred place. We should instead be concerned to avoid the dismal fate of letting such meaning as we might perceive be lost upon us because it is either overlooked or else not taken to heart. 'If men would steadily observe realities only, and not allow themselves to be deluded, life, to compare it with such things as we know, would be like a fairy tale and the Arabian Nights' Entertainments' (*Walden*, II). Note here that he describes the risk of delusion in terms of failing to see just how majestic reality can be – or, in the words of his letter to Blake – of having lived on Earth without noticing anything remarkable.

Opposed to this kind of obliviousness is the virtue of being attentive to the beauty of the world and regarding what we see in a charitable light: if we 'wish no ill to anything, apprehend no ill, cease to be but as the crystal which reflects a ray, – what shall we not reflect! What a universe will appear crystallized and radiant around us!' If we clarify our gaze in this way, we will find ourselves at the center of a dazzling universe. We should wish to avoid losing touch with the significance of phenomena due to a shortcoming in our own mode of observation. For Thoreau, the most reliable observer is one who can 'see things as they are, grand and beautiful' (*Journal*, 1/7/1857)[4] – that is to say, the beauty and grandeur of the world truly *are* there to be seen, even if we are not always able to discern them. We can all too easily fail to apprehend the value of being if we do not approach the world with the appropriate sort of affective orientation. It is all-important, then, to cultivate our perceptual capacities – and a good part of Thoreau's written work is dedicated to this endeavour. He articulates a vision of reality as significant and attempts to identify the subjective conditions that make us capable of becoming aware of this significance. When he says that 'the perception of beauty is a moral test' (*Journal*, 6/21/1852), he situates an ethical imperative within the context of aesthetic experience. Our conception of reality will be inadequate if we are blind to the world's beauty, he reminds his reader, and the content of experience depends upon the character of the individual's mind, defined by its mode of vision. 'It is something to be able to paint a particular picture, or to carve a statue, and so to make a few objects beautiful; but it is far more glorious to carve and paint the very atmosphere and medium through which we look, which morally we can do. To affect the quality of the day, that is the highest of arts' (*Walden*, II). By simplifying our life and developing a charitable and receptive outlook, we can open our eyes to the magnificence of reality.

As his letter draws to a close, Thoreau refers to something that Blake has said about his discussion of friendship – or 'Friendship', with a capital F – presumably in the 'Wednesday' chapter of *A Week on the Concord and Merrimack Rivers*, Thoreau's first book and the one he completed while living at Walden. It is in this chapter that we find his most sustained account of friendship, the goal of which is primarily to elevate one another toward realising our most lofty aspirations. Thoreau defines friendship in such exalted terms that it is difficult to imagine that any earthly relationship could quite live up to his ideal – as he himself admits, in the same journal entry that finds him arguing that a true friend should be approached 'with sacred love and awe' (*Journal*, 6/26/1840) and that we profane each other if we do not always meet on religious terms. Yet Thoreau has solid antecedent for the view that loving a friend means wishing good things for that person, wanting his or her life to be going well, as such a notion traces back as far as Aristotle.[5] His own view is distinguished by placing a strong emphasis on inspiring our friends and being inspired by them, not least through a willingness to criticize when they, or we, are falling short of being our best selves. The form of the personal letter allows Thoreau to address the most elevated demands of selfhood, while simultaneously speaking to the concrete, ordinary setting of his friend's life. It is entirely appropriate that he should tell Blake that any critical remarks he might have would be welcome: by offering them, Blake would be treating Thoreau as a friend ought to, by holding him to the highest standards and thereby providing him with 'a rare help'.

Henry David Thoreau to Harrison G.O. Blake

3 April 1850[6]

Mr. Blake,

I thank you for your letter, and I will endeavor to record some of the thoughts which it suggests, whether pertinent or not. You speak of poverty and dependence. Who are poor and dependent? Who are rich and independent? When was it that men agreed to respect the appearance and not the reality? Why should the appearance *appear*? Are we well acquainted, then, with the reality? There is none who does not lie hourly in the respect he pays to false appearance. How sweet it would be to treat men and things, for an hour, for just what they are! We wonder that the sinner does not confess his sin. When we are weary with travel, we lay down our load and rest by the wayside. So, when we are weary with the burden of life, why do we not lay down this load of falsehoods which we have volunteered to sustain, and be refreshed as never mortal was? Let the beautiful laws prevail. Let us not weary ourselves by resisting them. When we would rest our bodies we cease to support them; we recline on the lap of earth. So, when we would rest our spirits, we must recline on the Great Spirit. Let things alone; let them weigh what they will; let them soar or fall. To succeed in letting only one thing alone in a winter morning, if it be only one poor frozen-thawed apple that hangs on a tree, what a glorious achievement! Methinks it lightens through the dusky universe. What an infinite wealth we have discovered! God reigns, *i.e.*, when we take a liberal view, – when a liberal view is presented us.

Let God alone if need be. Methinks, if I loved him more, I should keep him, – I should keep myself rather, – at a more respectful distance. It is not when I am going to meet him, but when I am just turning away and leaving him alone, that I discover that God is. I say, God. I am not sure that that is the name. You will know whom I mean.

If for a moment we make way with our petty selves, wish no ill to anything, apprehend no ill, cease to be but as the crystal which reflects a ray, – what shall we not reflect! What a universe will appear crystallized and radiant around us!

I should say, let the Muse lead the Muse, – let the understanding lead the understanding, though in any case it is the farthest forward which leads them both. If the Muse accompany, she is no muse, but an amusement. The Muse should lead like a star which is very far off; but that does not imply that we are to follow foolishly, falling into sloughs and over precipices, for it is not foolishness, but understanding, which is to follow, which the Muse is appointed to lead, as a fit guide of a fit follower.

Will you live, or will you be embalmed? Will you live, though it be astride of a sunbeam; or will you repose safely in the catacombs for a thousand years? In the former case, the worst accident that can happen is that you may break your neck. Will you break your heart, your soul, to save your neck? Necks and pipe-stems are fated to be broken. Men make a great ado about the folly of demanding too much of life (or of eternity?), and of endeavoring to live according to that demand. It is much ado about nothing. No harm ever came from that quarter. I am not afraid that I shall exaggerate the value and significance of life, but that I shall not be up to the occasion which it is. I shall be sorry to remember that I was there, but noticed nothing remarkable, – not so much as a prince in disguise; lived in the golden age a hired man; visited Olympus even, but fell asleep after dinner, and did not hear the conversation of the gods. I lived in Judaea eighteen hundred years ago, but I never knew that there was such a one as Christ among my contemporaries! If there is anything more glorious than a congress of men a-framing or amending of a constitution going on, which I suspect there is, I desire to see the morning papers. I am greedy of the faintest rumor, though it were got by listening at the key-hole. I will dissipate myself in that direction.

I am glad to know that you find what I have said on Friendship worthy of attention. I wish I could have the benefit of your criticism; it would be a rare help to me. Will you not communicate it?

15 DE PROFUNDIS: A PHILOSOPHICAL LETTER

Oscar Wilde to Lord Alfred Douglas

Stefano Evangelista

In May 1895, Oscar Wilde was found guilty of 'gross indecency' and was sentenced to two years' imprisonment with hard labour. Only two months after the premiere of *The Importance of Being Earnest*, one of Britain's most public literary figures thus found himself suddenly disgraced. He was given the maximum penalty then contemplated by British law for homosexual offences under the so-called Labouchere Amendment of 1885. As a result of his sentence and of the bankruptcy that ensued, Wilde lost all his material possessions, including his house, books and art works, as well as the copyright on his writings. The most catastrophic losses, though, were intangible: his family (Wilde would never see his wife and children again), many of his friends and literary contacts and, above all, his literary inspiration.

Wilde's sentence came at the end of a series of three trials in which letters had played a fateful role. The first trial was actually instigated by Wilde, who sued for libel the Marquess of Queensberry – the father of his lover, Lord Alfred Douglas. Queensberry, a violent man and a bully, was worried that Wilde was compromising the reputation of his son. After several acts of intimidation, Queensberry personally delivered a famously misspelled card to Wilde's club in which he accused him of being a 'posing somdomite', or posing as a sodomite, as the phrase is generally glossed. This first letter of sorts was used by Wilde as his evidence for Queensberry's libellous behaviour. But things soon took a wrong turn, as Queensberry had more counterevidence than Wilde and his lawyer had anticipated, so he decided to withdraw, putting an end to the first trial. Emboldened by this victory, Queensberry then sued Wilde in return, which is how he found himself charged with 'indecency'. Queensberry now produced a love letter that Wilde had sent to his son, addressing Douglas as 'My Own Boy' and speaking about him in sexually suggestive language:

> Your sonnet is quite lovely, and it is a marvel that those rose-leaf lips of yours should have been made no less for music of song than for madness of kisses. Your slim gilt soul walks between passion and poetry. I know Hyacinthus, whom Apollo loved so madly, was you in Greek days. [. . .] Always, with undying love, yours, Oscar.[1]

On being questioned as to whether this letter entailed abnormal or immoral instincts, Wilde defended himself by claiming that it was to be viewed as literature rather than as a transparent record of his own sexual fantasies or practices. He truthfully added that that very letter had been set to poetry by the French author Pierre Louÿs for the Oxford student magazine *The Spirit Lamp*, edited by Douglas himself.

The Labouchere Amendment, under which Wilde was sentenced, criminalised male homosexual acts whether they took place in public or private. Letters such as this became crucial to its enforcement because they were one of the very few means that could prove that a sexual relationship had occurred in private between consenting adults. Douglas had been foolish enough to lose Wilde's love letter, which then found its way to his father who presumably purchased it from a blackmailer. Crossing the boundary from private to public in this most lurid way, the Hyacinthus letter made a grotesque spectacle of Wilde's intimacy with Douglas in the courtroom. To us, it highlights the ambiguous status of letters as texts that are precariously poised between the private and public – something that Wilde would come to exploit when he wrote his long prison letter to Douglas.

The extract here is the opening of the letter commonly known as *De Profundis*, which was written by Wilde in Reading Gaol towards the end of his sentence. For most of his stay in prison Wilde was not permitted to read or write but, during the second year, the regime started to relax and, as a consequence, Wilde was able to obtain some books and was eventually given access to paper. His letter to Douglas is the most substantial piece of writing that Wilde produced after the trials: in its entirety it comes up to roughly 55,000 words – the length of a short book – and it has frequently been published as an independent literary work.[2] In an ironic and perverse echo of the courtroom dispute over whether a private letter could be regarded as literature, the prison authorities did not allow Wilde to send it to Douglas on the grounds that it was too long and, therefore, in their view, did not count as a letter. When Wilde came out of prison, he entrusted the manuscripts to his friend Robbie Ross, instructing him to make two typescript copies and send the original to Douglas.

Wilde's foremost aim in writing to his former lover was to reproach him for having refused to share his suffering. Rightly or wrongly, Wilde felt that he had protected Douglas all the way through the humiliating ordeal of the trials, where his name had never been mentioned, even though he was Wilde's long-term partner. Wilde therefore expected in return tokens of loyalty and love, neither of which were forthcoming when he was in prison. Instead, Douglas had tried to publish some of Wilde's private letters to him in the French press – an episode to which he alludes in the extract – which Wilde feared might do further damage to his reputation. These are the circumstances behind the sense of betrayal that comes across so strongly in Wilde's words – a feeling of betrayal that is inextricably compounded with the memory of love. Love has given way to 'loathing, bitterness and contempt', negative feelings that Wilde wants to exorcise through letter-writing. In particular, he auspicates that 'bitterness', the first emotion that the letter conveys, might carry a redemptive quality – that it 'may be turned to joy'.

It is impossible not to hear in Wilde's words about 'sweet things changed to bitterness' an echo of Sappho's famous description of love as 'bittersweet' or 'sweetbitter' (*glukupichron*).[3] But Wilde adds to Sappho's fatalistic description of love as double-edged, the wish, almost the determination, that by writing and thus bringing back to life memories of time past, the very evocation of the past may sweeten the pain of the present, in an ultimate twist of the power of the writer. His determination that this should be so derives from a deeper, and more philosophical reason, namely that the evocation of the past, laying bare, that is, the sequence of events which have led to the present, is a way of unmasking wrongs in order to right them. It is a philosophical exercise of introspection whose conditions require the courage to admit the truth about past actions and face the shame and responsibility of acknowledging their faults. It is an introspection which Wilde valiantly takes on under the banner of the bittersweet eros, which makes the self-examination both worthwhile and necessary. Wilde knew classical literature and philosophy well; here he deliberately evokes Sappho's lyrical tradition to complicate and universalise his own experience. For all its valedictory rhetoric and intent, Wilde's letter to Douglas is, therefore, right from the start, a letter *about* the philosophical notion of love, its moral value and its revelatory power, capable of revealing to oneself the better part of man. It simultaneously gives his version of the story of the tragic relationship between himself and Douglas, and it writes that story into a history of homosexual desire sublimated as the purest form of a philosophically driven inquiry into truth and honesty that stretches from Greek antiquity to the present. The emotion of bitterness provides a thread through the social and cultural shifts that take place over the centuries, mitigated all along by its counterparts, reason and truthfulness which, by contrast, are unchanging moral ideals.

Wilde wants to show that love – even, crucially, a form of love that is stigmatised and criminalised by his society – can still have a redemptive power even from the depths of his loneliness. And love is also the emotion that, Wilde implicitly auspicates, will guide Douglas through the painful reading that will reveal to him his moral shortcomings, cutting through his skin like the 'knife of the surgeon'. Wilde knew from Plato's dialogues, especially the *Symposium*, that the Greeks viewed eros as a bond or emotion that facilitates philosophical exchange. He had adopted the Platonic dialogue form for his own philosophical dialogues, 'The Decay of Lying' and 'The Critic as Artist', in which elegant dandies discuss aesthetics and moral paradoxes in fashionable contemporary settings. He had celebrated the coming together of eros and philosophy in his short story 'The Portrait of Mr W.H.'.[4] Even from the dock in the court room he had made an impassioned speech in defence of a noble form of love between men 'such as Plato made the very basis of his philosophy, and such as you find in the sonnets of Michelangelo and Shakespeare'.[5] In the letter to Douglas this love – bitter, damaged and removed from its object – still functions as a medium for the attainment of an intimate knowledge of the self.

This merging of the literary and philosophical traditions that he saw in Plato, Michelangelo and Shakespeare was something that Wilde sought to recreate in the present. Glancing back on his career later in his letter to Douglas, he proudly declares to have made 'art a philosophy, and philosophy an art', which he goes on to gloss as follows: 'to truth itself I gave what is false no less than what is true as its rightful province, and showed that the false and the true are merely forms of intellectual existence. I treated Art as the supreme reality, and life as a mere mode of fiction'.[6] The letter to Douglas merges the philosophical quest for knowledge, self-knowledge and experience with the literary genre of autobiography. Wilde is conscious of distancing his written life from his life even as he writes it; or, to paraphrase his words, of substituting the reality of art for the fiction of experience, in a paradoxical twist whose ultimate effect is no less revelatory of bleak and painful truths about human nature. In this respect *De Profundis* follows in the tradition of Wilde's famous plays and fictions in being a self-consciously artful text, despite the claims to authenticity performed by the confessional tone. Wilde depicts himself as the tragic hero of a Greek drama, the gods presiding over his actions and his fate in a way that is beyond his control. He uses classical, often mythic, references to bestow a universal value to his personal story. In the extract presented here, he urges Douglas to remember that 'the fool to the eyes of the gods and the fool to the eyes of man are very different'; and, to describe Douglas's lack of self-knowledge, he writes that '[t]he head of Medusa that turns living men to stone, you have been allowed to look at in a mirror merely'. Wilde's words are the Medusa's head that will effect the traumatic transition from ignorance to wisdom. There is, in other words, a higher truth than the laws of society, a much more demanding truth which can only be reached by first facing the monster within – that monster which Wilde's Dorian Gray had magically exiled into a painted portrait.

It is the reference to the Oracle at Delphi that introduces the issue of self-knowledge that is at the heart of the letter. 'The real fool, such as the gods mock or mar, is he who does not know himself.' Later in the letter Wilde will qualify this claim as follows: 'People whose desire is solely for self-realisation never know where they are going. They can't know. In one sense of the word it is, of course, necessary, as the Greek oracle said, to know oneself. That is the first achievement of knowledge. But to recognise that the soul of a man is unknowable, is the ultimate achievement of Wisdom. The final mystery is oneself.'[7] The age-old Socratic quest for self-knowledge is thus resolved by sending us back to its starting-point: I know that I know nothing.

Using the terrible vantage point of Reading Gaol, Wilde looks back on his life in order to understand how his own 'soul' or self has been changed by the experience of prison. To appreciate his position, however, it is important to remember that, throughout his two years of hard labour, Wilde never came to believe that he had been guilty of a crime. Despite all the deprivation, humiliation and loneliness he had to endure, Wilde never conceded that homosexuality was a criminal or even immoral act and that there might therefore be a legitimate reason for his punishment. Never, in all his letters from prison, did Wilde express regret for his emotional and physical attachments to other men. Rejecting Douglas is the closest he got to that, but this rejection needs to be carefully qualified. Wilde believed that his moral mistake was to have allowed desire and love to blind him to the faults of Douglas's character, which he now mercilessly exposes for himself, Douglas and posterity. Wilde thus blamed himself, not for having allowed his friendship with Douglas to be debased by libido, but for having been intellectually degraded by Douglas because of the latter's lack of a real understanding of art and his extreme selfishness, of which Wilde provides many instances in the letter. The fundamentals of Wilde's allegedly criminal love and the desire it expressed are still held as ennobling for the individual. Therefore, the shame and sense of responsibility that Wilde articulates throughout the letter are the consequences, not of any crime such as society had condemned him for, but of his own faulty decision making in letting his moral integrity be subjugated by Douglas's will, in full awareness of the inferiority and insignificance of the objects of that will. His was the superior character with the superior aims, yet he let himself be controlled by an inferior character driven by inferior aims.

It is remarkable how viciously Wilde condemns Douglas's hedonistic temperament and yet, at the same time, takes perverse pleasure in associating him with the aspects of the material world that he misses in prison: beauty, 'colour and motion' as he says, food. Wilde paradoxically celebrates desire as a life-giving and life-affirming force even as he overtly strives to find a redemptive meaning in his prison experience; that is, to find a value in the deprivations of the senses enforced by the prison regime as having exercised a positive ethical influence over him. At the same time, and despite all his 'appetites', Douglas is criticised by Wilde for being fundamentally removed from experience and life itself: he is one who sees 'the strange and tragic shapes of life as one sees shadows in a crystal'. Wilde wants to teach Douglas an ethics of desire that will enable him to comprehend the complexities of experience. His scale of virtues and vices is striking in this respect. For though the words 'vice' and 'virtue', 'truth' and 'falsity' pepper the letter, Wilde is not thereby conjuring the hackneyed and pious pairs of opposites, such as 'gluttony *vs* moderation', 'studious *vs* lazy' or 'spendthrift *vs* cheapskate'. Wilde's virtues and vices are as complex and kaleidoscopic as is his profound analysis of human nature: the 'supreme vice is shallowness' he writes and its redeeming virtue is realisation: 'everything that is realised is right'. The injunction is thus not so much to be good, as to be truthful to oneself. To do this we must shine an unblinking light onto our own depth – *de profundis* – however vile what we find in there might be; in that exercise alone lies realisation, not in change or improvement. In the same way, Wilde's reflections on the deprivations of his prison life, whilst reminiscing with ekphrastic vividness over past exuberances, is the setting for a more subtle opposition between surfeit and an ideal of 'plain living and high thinking'; the 'and' in the latter formula is key. Wilde is not a convert to austerity, but he understands that true pleasure, however variegated, should include the pleasures of a higher order, the conjunction, in other words, of the satisfaction of desires of both the body and the mind, which leads to the possibility of artistic creation.

Wilde describes his time with Douglas as entirely draining of all his artistic creativity and as an infrangible obstacle to his productivity. He explains this not in practical, mundane, terms but with philosophical depth as shortcomings in his own moral character. Wilde quotes Walter Pater, a *maître à penser* since his student days,[8] saying 'failure is to form habits'. With a virtuoso sleight of hand, Wilde explains the master's thought, whilst at the same time dismissing the scholarly academy ('dull Oxford people') for not being equal to the task of understanding him and, in the same go, he gives an original and personal interpretation of Aristotelian ethics. For the habits Pater speaks of are, in essence, the opposite of the habits Aristotle encourages us to acquire: for the Greek ethicist, the formation of habit was tantamount to getting in control of one's soul, by getting used to being good and becoming thus the sculptor of one's best self. For Pater, habits are the expression of human laziness, a complacency which leads us to recognise regularity and hence be reassured by the familiarity of our surroundings where, in fact, there is variety, surprise and novelty to discover however unsettling these may be. Wilde takes the negative judgement of Pater and merges it into the Aristotelian account of character as what is in our power to mould and control if only we know how. Habits, for Wilde, are a deformation of the soul that are inflicted by regularity, by a routine which he describes with an irony which would be amusing if it were not so fatal, 'at once grotesque and tragic': for he writes thus about life with Douglas, as the daily sequence of 'luncheon, dinner, supper, amusements, hansoms, and the rest of it'. This waste of days and months on end, in a continuous and vapid flow of amusements did indeed sculpt his character, for the worse, he says, resulting in his artistic barrenness: failure; and in his moral deficiency: ruin.

Wilde wishes to instruct and his method is the compelling force of his words. He repeatedly urges Douglas to read the letter attentively: 'You must read this letter right through'; and, he insists, 'read the letter over and over again till it kill your vanity.' Just as there is a masochism in the self-imposed self-analysis to which Wilde submits himself in recounting in minute details the events of his life with Douglas, there is also a sadistic side to Wilde's desire that Douglas read and re-read the letter. No more the indulgent lover, he is now a teacher who uses, not corporal, but verbal punishment, each word meant to castigate the well-beloved student. One of the bitter historical ironies of Wilde's prison experience is that Douglas, in fact, never read his letter. Ross did send Douglas a copy (albeit not the original of the letter as Wilde had instructed him), but Douglas immediately destroyed it in a fit of rage. At least, this is what he claimed.[9] The addressee of this remarkable letter – one of the most agonising documents in the history of English literature – thus never benefited from its confessions, accusations and admonishments.

Wilde left prison in May 1897 and immediately went into voluntary exile in France, vowing never to want to see Douglas again. By the end of the summer of that same year, however, the two were reconciled and eloped together to Naples.

Oscar Wilde to Lord Alfred Douglas
Reading Gaol, January–March 1897[10]

Dear Bosie,

After long and fruitless waiting I have determined to write to you myself, as much for your sake as for mine, as I would not like to think that I had passed through two long years of imprisonment without ever having received a single line from you, or any news or message even, except such as gave me pain.

Our ill-fated and most lamentable friendship has ended in ruin and public infamy for me, yet the memory of our ancient affection is often with me, and the thought that loathing, bitterness and contempt should for ever take the place in my heart once held by love is very sad to me; and you yourself will, I think, feel in your heart that to write to me as I lie in the loneliness of prison life is better than to publish my letters without my permission, or to dedicate poems to me unasked, though the world will know nothing of whatever words of grief or passion, or remorse or indifference, you may choose to send as your answer or your appeal.

I have no doubt that in this letter which I have to write of your life and mine, of the past and of the future, of sweet things changed to bitterness and of bitter things that may be turned to joy, there will be much that will wound your vanity to the quick. If it prove so, read the letter over and over again till it kills your vanity. If you find in it something of which you feel that you are unjustly accused, remember that one should be thankful that there is any fault of which one can be unjustly accused. If there be in it one single passage that brings tears to your eyes, weep as we weep in prison, where the day no less than the night is set apart for tears. It is the only thing that can save you. If you go complaining to your mother, as you did with reference to the scorn of you I displayed in my letter to Robbie, so that she may flatter and soothe you back into self-complacency or conceit, you will be completely lost. If you find one false excuse for yourself you will soon find a hundred, and be just what you were before. Do you still say, as you said to Robbie in your answer, that I '*attribute unworthy motives*' to you? Ah! you had no motives in life. You had appetites merely. A motive is an intellectual aim. That you were '*very young*' when our friendship began? Your defect was not that you knew so little about life, but that you knew so much. The morning dawn of boyhood with its delicate bloom, its clear pure light, its joy of innocence and expectation, you had left far behind you. With very swift and running feet you had passed from Romance to Realism. The gutter and the things that live in it had begun to fascinate you. That was the origin of the trouble in which you sought my aid, and I, so unwisely according to the wisdom of this world, out of pity and kindness, gave it to you. You must read this letter right through, though each word may become to you as the fire or knife of the surgeon that makes the delicate flesh burn or bleed. Remember that the fool to the eyes of the gods and the fool to the eyes of man are very different. One who is entirely ignorant of the modes of art in its revelation or the moods of thought in its progress, of the pomp of the Latin line or the richer music of the vowelled Greek, of Tuscan sculpture or Elizabethan song, may yet be full of the very sweetest wisdom. The real fool, such as the gods mock or mar, is he who does not know himself. I was such a one too long. You have been such a one too long. Be so no more. Do not be afraid. The supreme vice is shallowness. Everything that is realised is right. Remember also that whatever is misery to you to read, is still greater misery to me to set down. They have permitted you to see the strange and tragic shapes of life as one sees shadows in a crystal. The head of Medusa that turns living men to stone, you have been allowed to look at in a mirror merely. You yourself have walked free among the flowers. From me the beautiful world of colour and motion has been taken away.

I will begin by telling you that I blame myself terribly. As I sit in this dark cell in convict clothes, a disgraced and ruined man, I blame myself. In the perturbed and fitful nights of anguish, in the long monotonous days of pain, it is myself I blame. I blame myself for allowing an intellectual friendship, a friendship whose primary aim was not the creation and contemplation of beautiful things, entirely to dominate my life. From the very first there was too wide a gap between us. You had been idle at your school, worse than idle at your university. You did not realise that an artist, and especially such an artist as I am, one, that is to say, the quality of whose work depends on the intensification of personality, requires for the development of his art the companionship of ideas, an intellectual atmosphere, quiet, peace, and solitude. You admired my work when it was finished: you enjoyed the brilliant successes of my first nights, and the brilliant banquets that followed them: you were proud, and quite naturally so, of being the intimate friend of an artist so distinguished: but you could not understand the conditions requisite for the production of artistic work. I am not speaking in phrases of rhetorical exaggeration but in terms of absolute truth to actual fact when I remind you that during the whole time we were together I never wrote one single line. Whether at Torquay, Goring, London, Florence, or elsewhere, my life, as long as you were by my side, was entirely sterile and uncreative. And with but few intervals, you were, I regret to say, by my side always.

I remember, for instance, in September [18]93, to select merely one instance out of many, taking a set of chambers, purely in order to work undisturbed, as I had broken my contract with John Hare for whom I had promised to write a play, and who was pressing me on the subject. During the first week you kept away. We had, not unnaturally indeed, differed on the question of the artistic value of your translation of *Salomé*, so you contented yourself with sending me foolish letters on the subject. In that week I wrote and completed in every detail, as it was ultimately performed, the first act of *An Ideal Husband*. The second week you returned and my work practically had to be given up. I arrived at St. James's Place every morning at 11.30 in order to have the opportunity of thinking and writing without the interruptions inseparable from my own household, quiet and peaceful as that household was. But the attempt was vain. At twelve o'clock you drove up and stayed smoking cigarettes and chattering till 1.30, when I had to take you out to luncheon at the Café Royal or the Berkeley. Luncheon with its *liqueurs* lasted usually till 3.30. For an hour you retired to White's. At tea-time you appeared again, and stayed till it was time to dress for dinner. You dined with me either at the Savoy or at Tite Street. We did not separate as a rule till after midnight, as supper at Willis's had to wind up the entrancing day. That was my life for those three months, every single day, except during the four days when you went abroad. I then, of course, had to go over to Calais to fetch you back. For one of my nature and temperament it was a position at once grotesque and tragic.

You surely must realise that now? You must see now that your incapacity for being alone: your nature so exigent in its persistent claim on the attention and time of others: your lack of any power of sustained intellectual concentration: the unfortunate accident – for I like to think it was no more – that you had not been able to acquire the 'Oxford temper' in intellectual matters, never, I mean, been one who could play gracefully with ideas, but had arrived at violence of opinion merely – that all these things, combined with the fact that your desires and your interests were in Life not in Art, were as destructive to your own progress in culture as they were to my work as an artist? When I compare my friendship with you to my friendship with still younger men, as John Gray and Pierre Louÿs I feel ashamed.[11] My real life, my higher life was with them and such as they.

Of the appalling results of my friendship with you I don't speak at present. I am thinking merely of its quality while it lasted. It was intellectually degrading to me. You had the rudiments of an artistic temperament in its germ. But I met you either too late or too soon. I don't know which. When you were away I was all right. The moment, in the early December of the year to which I have been alluding, I had succeeded in inducing your mother to send you out of England, I collected again the torn and ravelled web of my imagination, got my life back into my own hands, and not merely finished the three remaining acts of *An Ideal Husband*, but conceived and had almost completed two other plays of a completely different type, the *Florentine Tragedy* and *La Sainte Courtisane*, when suddenly, unbidden, unwelcome, and under circumstances fatal to my happiness, you returned. The two works left then imperfect I was unable to take up again. The mood that created them I could never recover. You now, having yourself published a volume of verse, will be able to recognise the truth of everything I have said here. Whether you can or not it remains as a hideous truth in the very heart of our friendship. While you were with me you were the absolute ruin of my Art, and in allowing you to stand persistently between Art and myself, I give to myself shame and blame in the fullest degree. You couldn't know, you couldn't understand, you couldn't appreciate. I had no right to expect it of you at all. Your interests were merely in your meals and moods. Your desires were simply for amusements, for ordinary or less ordinary pleasures. They were what your temperament needed, or thought it needed for the moment. I should have forbidden you my house and my chambers except when I specially invited you. I blame myself without reserve for my weakness. It was merely weakness. One half-hour with Art was always more to me than a cycle with you. Nothing really at any period of my life was ever of the smallest importance to me compared with Art. But in the case of an artist, weakness is nothing less than a crime when it is a weakness that paralyses the imagination.

    I blame myself for having allowed you to bring me to utter and discreditable financial ruin. I remember one morning in the early October of [18]92, sitting in the yellowing woods at Bracknell with your mother. At that time I knew very little of your real nature. I had stayed from a Saturday to Monday with you at Oxford. You had stayed with me at Cromer for ten days and played golf. The conversation turned on you, and your mother began to speak to me about your character. She told me of your two chief faults, your vanity, and your being, as she termed it, '*all wrong about money*'. I have a distinct recollection of how I laughed. I had no idea that the first would bring me to prison and the second to bankruptcy. I thought vanity a sort of graceful flower for a young man to wear, as for extravagance – for I thought she meant no more than extravagance – the virtues of prudence and thrift were not in my own nature or my own race. But before our friendship was one month older I began to see what your mother really meant. Your insistence on a life of reckless profusion: your incessant demands for money: your claim that all your pleasures should be paid for by me, whether I was with you or not: brought me after some time into serious monetary difficulties, and what made the extravagance to me at any rate so monotonously uninteresting, as your persistent grasp on my life grew stronger and stronger, was that the money was really spent on little more than the pleasures of eating, drinking, and the like. Now and then it is a joy to have one's table red with wine and roses, but you outstripped all taste and temperance. You demanded without grace and received without thanks. You grew to think that you had a sort of right to live at my expense and in a profuse luxury to which you had never been accustomed, and which for that reason made your appetites all the more keen, and at the end if you lost money gambling in some Algiers Casino you simply telegraphed next morning to me in London to lodge the amount of your losses to your account at your bank, and gave the matter no further thought of any kind.

When I tell you that between the autumn of 1892 and the date of my imprisonment, I spent with you and on you, more than £5,000 in actual money,[12] irrespective of the bills I incurred, you will have some idea of the sort of life on which you insisted. Do you think I exaggerate? My ordinary expenses with you for an ordinary day in London – for luncheon, dinner, supper, amusements, hansoms, and the rest of it – ranged from £12 to £20, and the week's expenses were naturally in proportion and ranged from £80 to £130. For our three months at Goring my expenses (rent of course included) were £1,340. Step by step with the Bankruptcy Receiver I had to go over every item of my life. It was horrible. *'Plain living and high thinking'* was, of course, an ideal you could not at that time have appreciated, but such an extravagance was a disgrace to both of us. (...) And though it may seem strange to you that one in the terrible position in which I am situated, should find a difference between one disgrace and another, still I frankly admit that the folly of throwing away all this money on you, and letting you squander my fortune to your own hurt as well as to mine, gives to me and in my eyes a note of common profligacy to my Bankruptcy that makes me doubly ashamed of it. I was made for other things.

But most of all I blame myself for the entire ethical degradation I allowed you to bring on me. The basis of character is will power, and my will power became absolutely subject to yours. It sounds a grotesque thing to say, but it is none the less true. Those incessant scenes that seemed to be almost physically necessary to you, and in which your mind and body grew distorted and you became a thing as terrible to look at as to listen to: that dreadful mania you inherit from your father, the mania for writing revolting and loathsome letters: your entire lack of any control over your emotions as displayed in your long resentful moods of sullen silence, no less than in the sudden fits of almost epileptic rage: all these things in reference to which one of my letters to you, left by you lying about in the Savoy or some other hotel and so produced in Court by your father's Counsel, contained an entreaty not devoid of pathos, had you at that time been able to recognise pathos either in its elements or its expression: – these, I say, were the origin and causes of my fatal yielding to you in your daily increasing demands. You wore one out. It was the triumph of the smaller over the bigger nature. It was the case of that tyranny of the weak over the strong which somewhere in one of my plays I describe as being 'the only tyranny that lasts'.[13]

And it was inevitable. In every relation of life with others one has to find some *moyen de vivre*. In your case, one had either to give up to you or to give you up. There was no other alternative. (...) I had always thought that my giving up to you in small things meant nothing: that when a great moment arrived, I could re-assert my will power in its natural superiority. It was not so. At the great moment my will power completely failed me. In life there is really no great or small thing. All things are of equal value and of equal size. My habit – due to indifference chiefly at first – of giving up to you in everything had become insensibly a real part of my nature. Without my knowing it, it had stereotyped my temperament to one permanent and fatal mood. That is why, in the subtle epilogue to the first edition of his essays, Pater says that 'Failure is to form habits'.[14] When he said it, the dull Oxford people thought the phrase a mere wilful inversion of the somewhat wearisome text of Aristotelian *Ethics*, but there is a wonderful, a terrible truth hidden in it. I had allowed you to sap my strength of character, and to me the formation of a habit had proved to be not Failure merely, but Ruin. Ethically you had been even still more destructive to me than you had been artistically.

16 A CORRESPONDENCE THEORY OF TRUTH
Mahatma Gandhi to Maganlal Gandhi
Nicholas J. Owen

M.K. ('Mahatma') Gandhi (1869–1948) was a prolific writer of letters. He wrote dozens of letters by hand almost every day of his adult life. The Sabarmati ashram, which holds the largest collection of his correspondence, has around 35,000 letters.

Gandhi also took correspondence very seriously. In his journalism, he often chided Indians for being casual about it: for failing to reply to letters or being slow to do so. He wrote – and was written to by – almost anyone. And he wrote about almost everything: not just politics but every aspect of modern life.

The letter here below was written by Gandhi in 1910 to Maganlal Gandhi, a relative of his, but not a close one. Maganlal (1883–1928) was the grandson of an uncle of the Mahatma, and he was 27 years old in 1910.

The letter was written at a decisive moment in Gandhi's life.[1] He was 41. For the previous four years he had led the passive resistance campaign in South Africa (the Transvaal) against the requirement for Indians to register for special permits for residence and work. He had been imprisoned several times. The previous year he had spent mostly in London unsuccessfully lobbying the British government to over-rule the South African government. On his return voyage to South Africa in November 1909, he had written *Hind Swaraj*, to which he refers in the letter.[2]

Hind Swaraj sets out, tellingly in the form of a dialogue, Gandhi's position on Indian freedom. It argues that India has been made unfree not by British occupation, but by Indians' acquiescence in alien rule. The cause of this acquiescence has been Indian seduction by western modernity. *Swaraj* – self-rule – meant not only self-government (political independence), but the government of the self, by each individual (self-discipline and autonomy). Politically this meant self-reliance, rather than mendicancy – the tactic of petitioning others that Gandhi had used hitherto. 'What is secured for us by others is not *swaraj* but pararaj, i.e. foreign rule.' Indians should make themselves free by resigning from government jobs, leaving western schools and colleges and boycotting British goods. They should reduce their dependence on, and admiration for, western modernity and rediscover the strengths of their own civilisation. Getting the British to leave India might take many generations. But Indians could free themselves now if they wanted. 'You and I can enjoy it even today', he tells Maganlal. 'Emancipate your own self ... Nobility of soul consists in realizing that you yourself are India.'

Gandhi's position was opposed not only to mendicancy, but also to revolutionary violence, which was the other dominant opinion among Indian anti-colonialists. Violence is mistaken because the enemy lies within and not without, but also because violence claims certainty for itself. Instead, Gandhi advocates 'truth-force' – *satyagraha* – non-violent action which is a courageous insistence on the truth: neither coercing nor begging but insisting on the truth and being willing to suffer publicly for it.

It is fair to say that when Gandhi set out this philosophy, he was not only in the minority – but almost entirely alone. To the mendicants, Gandhi seemed hostile to the most generally accepted boons of colonial influence – western medicine, legal systems, education, the railways, industrialised cotton-mills. How was India to become a modern, independent state without these things? To the revolutionaries, Gandhi's non-violence seemed quaint. Was not 'truth-force' just the sort of Hindu passivity that had made India easy to conquer in the first place?

To persuade his critics, Gandhi therefore needed to provide answers to the hundreds of questions Indians had for him. Maganlal had asked him some. How was India to become free without modernising itself on western lines? How could non-violent *satyagraha* work against violent tribes like the Pindaris?

Gandhi did have answers to these questions. Modernity was not the strength of the British, which Indians should emulate, but their weakness which Indians should reject. *Satyagraha* is not weakness. It is about not using the strength that you have.

But what is puzzling about this letter is that as well as challenging all these conventional assumptions, Gandhi has some critical things to say about correspondence itself. This is a letter which criticises letter-writing. The value of correspondence is exaggerated, Gandhi says. 'When we give up railways and such other means', he says in the letter, 'we shall not bother ourselves about writing letters'. Indeed, so far as possible, we should give these things up now. The isolated Indian village will be better off without the post office and the railway station.

So, there is an intriguing performative contradiction here. Gandhi is advocating the restriction of correspondence in a piece of correspondence. Why should Gandhi, knowing that he was almost alone in his views, wish to restrict one of the ways by which they might best be disseminated to others? Considering this puzzle also seems to speak to a central question: what can correspondence do and what can it not do?

Gandhi is concerned with truth, how to reach it, how to recognise it and how truth spreads itself. The search for truth, he says, is a personal search: you have to pursue it yourself and not receive it from others. You have to be self-reliant. But the truth for Gandhi is also many-sided and inexhaustible. Because it is inexhaustible, no one person, no matter how energetic, could ever find it all. And because it is many-sided, each individual will see a different (and small) part of it. So, dialogue between individuals – correspondence, if you like – is necessary if the truth is to be found. Each individual is uniquely constituted and must make his or her own search for truth, but the search necessarily involves seeking unity with the widest number of other human beings.

Because the truth has this character, each searcher for truth needs to be humble and aware of his or her fallibility. Correspondence is valuable to Gandhi as a way to test and correct one's own view. Correspondence can be dialogic (two-way) or instructional (effectively one-way): some letters expect answers and some do not. Gandhi's is emphatically dialogic. He asks for consideration and replies. 'Please ponder over the meaning of this statement', he writes in this letter. And right at the end: 'Please ponder over this . . . If you want to ask anything more, please do.' He always insists that his interlocutor thinks his or her words over and lets him know what he or she thinks.

This eagerness for dialogue is a deep characteristic of Gandhi's general way of proceeding, always expecting and making room for a reaction from his interlocutors. It is worth noting that Gandhi never produced a comprehensive treatise of his ideas. Instead, he developed a set of approaches which he described, somewhat misleadingly, as experimental. The title of his autobiography was 'The story of my experiments with truth'.[3] Gandhi thought that India's long civilisation was itself a form of scientific enquiry in which people had worked out, and were still working out, through observation and experiment, which moral and social practices worked, and which did not. We might well doubt that these were real experiments: they often confirmed as truth the beliefs that middle-aged male Hindus already held. But the point is that experimental testing could not be done alone. The task was too great for any single individual, so it had to be pursued by like-minded others, sharing their findings. Some lived alongside each other in ashrams, but others, in India and across the world, would share their findings through correspondence. In other words, Gandhi had, quite literally, a 'correspondence theory of truth'.

In his correspondence theory, Gandhi offers a distinctive position on three questions concerning letters and their messages. First, he has an answer to the 'problem of reach': that philosophy needs to reach large audiences, but letters only reach one or two individuals. The assumption that (unless it is published) the influence of a letter stops at its immediate recipient is something Gandhi would have denied. He thought in terms of a network of influence, in which experimenters shared their findings through correspondence with each other. He did this by reading out letters at public meetings and also by printing and publishing letters in journals which he edited himself and which, in turn, were republished as contributions to other journals, elsewhere. Something which started out as an exchange of letters – and which *needed* that channel of expression to develop, for an article would be different both in audience and tone (more finished, more authoritative) – achieved a wider circulation through republication.

What Gandhian experimenters were sharing, moreover, were their *personal* experiments. Their correspondence had impact, therefore, not *despite* the fact that it was personal, but *because* it was personal. So, we would be mistaken to assume that the personal quality of a letter diminishes its effectiveness. This is the second problem which dissolves through Gandhi's reinvention of the epistolary form. The personal dimension of a letter becomes not an impediment to the dissemination of its message but its strength. For Gandhi, the force of a view turned on whether it was practised by the individual who held it. He was very critical of people who espoused but did not live out their ideals. You can see this insistence on the importance of personal example-setting in our letter below. We should not be deterred from giving up modern practices, he says, just because we cannot end them overnight, nor because some people will never follow us. This does not matter. 'Even if one man reduces or stops their use', he writes, 'others will learn to do so'. Making 'only' a personal connection with a single individual through a letter is therefore not an impediment to spreading the truth. On the contrary: it is the best means – perhaps the only means – by which to do so.

Gandhi also has a distinct position on a third problem: the fact that letters are private yet often seek to address public matters. Gandhi draws the line between the public and private in an unconventional place. In many of his letters there is an odd mix of conventionally public and private topics. Discussions of high political developments rub up against advice on diet, health, hygiene, dress, sexual desire, marriage, child-rearing, and so on. To Gandhi, these are not incoherent juxtapositions, because his concept of freedom is one in which these supposedly 'private' matters have a profound public importance. To be politically free you have first to free yourself in ordinary life. Gandhi thought that India's subjection was a consequence of regarding its own social practices as inferior. This was what had made Indians servile and imitative. Becoming free was not just about political campaigning, but also about freeing oneself, even alone, and today, in matters of everyday life. 'In your emancipation is the emancipation of India', Gandhi writes here. 'All else is make-believe.'

So, letters can do a great deal, even if 'only' personal, even if 'only' addressed to individuals and even if 'only' private.

What, then, can letters *not* do? What does Gandhi mean when he says that it would be better if the Indian village never got a post office?

Gandhi feared that Indian rural localities would be overwhelmed by western modernity. This was not because he romanticised the condition of the traditional Indian village. Nor was it that he wanted to keep new ideas out. He thought Indian culture had always been open to and influenced by the ideas that came from outside it, which it absorbed, traditionalised and Indianised, to remain true to itself. The trouble with western modernity was that, unlike earlier religious incursions such as Buddhism and Islam, it was spiritually impoverished. It had made Indians indifferent to the cultural resources they already possessed and anxious to imitate alien ones. The ironic consequence of greater openness to communication, therefore, is that people became more alienated from their own identities; hence the world becomes more, not less, fragmented.

Letters, therefore, cannot substitute for what Gandhi identifies as the 'local'. Correspondence connects people across distance, but in doing so, it also distracts people from locality. For Gandhi, living under colonialism, the alien had displaced the indigenous, and this had happened not only by invasion and coercion but by the dangerous seductions of western modernity, which had stimulated desire – as he says in the letter, we have to beware of our desires – but which pushed aside duties to others and which alienated them from the local, the situated, the familiar, the timely. 'The English have not taken India', he wrote in *Hind Swaraj*. 'We have given it to them.' 'They are not in India because of their strength, but because we keep them.'

The trouble with modern communications was not only that they carried spiritually dead cargo. We also have to remember that Gandhi was trying to reach a largely illiterate society. The Indian literacy rate was about 5% in 1910. There were around 200 languages spoken across India. So written correspondence in English or even Hindi, could never have been enough for him. The traditional information order in India relied less on printed or written materials and more on relayed news, storytelling, dramatic production, song. Gandhi was suspicious that the prioritisation of the written form would displace these non-written and even sometimes non-verbal symbolic modes of communication. So, letters cannot substitute for non-written and non-verbal communication.

Modern communications also worked too fast. They failed to respect the pace at which human lives could sensibly be lived. Letters, especially pouring in at modern rates, cannot substitute for consideration. While Gandhi rejected the idea of monkish withdrawal from the world, he thought that everyone should engage in daily meditation, without distraction, to reflect on things and compose one's own thoughts. One can have too much correspondence, too many demands on one's attention which lead to dispersal and ultimately slackening and apathy.

Letters, furthermore, cannot substitute for the face-to-face. Gandhi sets great store by the change of heart: the connection that is made when you speak with others directly and without mediation. He thought, for example, that it was harder for us to lie face-to-face than it is when we write to each other. He thought too, that people were more likely to change when they directly witnessed truth-force, rather than read about it. In India, especially in the Gandhian ashram, much of ordinary life was carried out in full view of everyone else. So, though the fact that letters are private does not preclude their having wider influence, the most valuable forms of influence are exerted face-to-face in local communities, such as ashrams and villages.

Gandhi's largest objection to mass communication concerned the way that it rendered the individual a passive recipient and echo for others' ideas. Correspondence cannot substitute for action. 'It is not enough merely to profess [humility] ... it should stand the test when the occasion comes.' So, it is not enough for the lawyer to boast of his altruism or spirituality: 'let him learn his livelihood through physical labour and carry on his legal practice without charging anything for it'. Indeed, it is telling that Gandhi, although a prolific correspondent, did not much value the physical letter itself. He took care with correspondence, but did not take care of his letters. He did not preserve them or refer to them or regard them as in any permanent way, defining his view. They were needed only for the moment: for the impact they might have on people's thinking or action.

So, in colonial conditions, like other aspects of western modernity, modern correspondence was double-edged. It was both the means by which an alternative to colonialism might be articulated and also the means by which it had come under colonial rule in the first place. This is an instance of a wider dilemma for Gandhi, which was how to fight a battle against western modernity without relying on the weapons of western modernity.

Like other such dilemmas, this expressed itself in terms of opportunities and vulnerabilities. One interpretation of what Gandhi is saying in this letter is that natural leaders may continue to correspond, provided their heads are not turned by this practice, but the Indian villagers will be too easily corrupted; they are too vulnerable and so must not be permitted it. '*Swaraj* is for those who understand it', Gandhi writes. There's a double meaning in that. First, anyone can be free: once you have understood, you are free. But you need to understand what it means before you can use it. 'You and I can enjoy it today', Gandhi says to Maganlal. 'All the others will have to learn to do likewise.' There's a tension here between autonomy and liberation, on the one hand, and slowly acquired self-discipline on the other.

But there is also opportunity. The British Empire was governed through correspondence. The post is, paradoxically, one of its enabling weaknesses. How had Gandhi corresponded with Maganlal? He had bought a stamp with King Edward's head on it and used the imperial postal service. In order to govern a far-flung empire, the British had developed a system of postal communication. And in order that it should work cheaply and in depth, the system was not reserved for the governors, but could be used by anyone who could afford a stamp. This meant that it could be exploited by anyone.

Indeed, 20 years after the date of this letter, Gandhi was able to plan a nationwide campaign of civil disobedience, which the British struggled to control by censorship because the flow of propaganda and conspiracy through the postal systems they had themselves introduced was so great.

In that campaign, Gandhi wrote another letter, to the Viceroy of India, on the eve of his famous Salt March. He could have issued a press statement, but he sent a letter. Addressing the Viceroy as 'Dear friend', rather than the expected 'Your Excellency', Gandhi claimed the level status of friendship. He did not beg or make threats: on the contrary, he informed his 'friend' of his plans and asked for his views.

Gandhi's letter to the Viceroy can usefully be contrasted with the written communicative forms generally used by other Indians when addressing the British. It differed both from the *petition*, which Gandhi had used himself when a mendicant and the *demand*, made by the revolutionaries.

The petition comes from below: it concedes a position of superiority to authority and defers to the recipient's conceptions of what is right and just. Demands, on the other hand, are violent. To impose your own view on others is a form of violence, made from above, from omniscience. In Gandhi's correspondence, by contrast, you can set out your own views and you can try and persuade, or even educate, your readers. But you cannot compel them. And you must not beg.

This sort of communication-on-the-level was very destabilising to the British. They knew what to do with petitions from below. They met them not with rejection, but perpetual deferral – always holding out the prospect that they might meet them one day. They knew too what to do with threats: they fought back or they gave in. But the personal letter – 'Dear Friend' – had a strange forcefulness they could not easily reject. Friendship with Indians was, as E.M. Forster saw, incompatible with imperial relationships, in which the office defined the man and the personal and the official were kept firmly apart.[4]

So firm was this separation, indeed, that the British actually separated the correspondence they received into distinct categories – official, demi-official, private – precisely so that they could file letters appropriately, for fear that the private and the personal might corrupt the public and official. Gandhi's letters could not be filed properly. He broke the rules of correspondence and he did so using correspondence as his weapon.

Mohandas K. Gandhi to Maganlal Gandhi

2 April 1910[5]

Chi Maganlal,

Your letter to hand. I return it to you so that you can understand my reply to it.

I shall try to answer the questions you have raised. But even then you may not understand thoroughly. You will perhaps find the explanations you have sought from [Hind] *Swaraj* itself if you read it afresh once or twice.

There is no doubt that we shall have to go back to the extent to which we have imbibed [modern] civilization. This part of the task is the most difficult one, but it will have to be done. When we take a wrong path there is no alternative but to go back. We have got to free ourselves from attachment to the things we are enjoying. For this it is necessary that we begin to feel disgust for them. Whatever means and instruments appear to us to be beneficial are not going to be given up. Only he who realizes that there is more harm than the apparent benefit from a particular thing will give it up. I personally feel that no benefit has been derived from our being able to send letters quickly. When we give up railways and such other means we shall not bother ourselves about writing letters. A thing which is really free from fault may be used to a certain extent. We who are engulfed in this civilization may avail ourselves of postal and other facilities as long as we are so engulfed. If we make use of these things with knowledge and understanding we shall not go crazy over them, and instead of increasing our preoccupations we shall gradually reduce them. He who will understand this will not be tempted to take the post or the railway to the villages which do not have these. You and I should not remain passive and increase the use of steamers and other evil means for fear that these things cannot be abolished forthwith and that all the people will not give them up. Even if one man reduces or stops their use, others will learn to do so. He who believes that it is good to do so will go on doing so irrespective of others. This is the only way of spreading the truth; there is no other in the world.

It is very difficult to get rid of our fondness for Parliament. It was no doubt barbarous when people tore off the skin, burned persons alive and cut off their ears or nose; but the tyranny of Parliament is much greater than that of Chengiz Khan, Tamerlane and others. Hence it is that we are caught in its meshes. Modern tyranny is a trap of temptation and therefore does greater mischief. One can withstand the atrocities committed by one individual as such; but it is difficult to cope with the tyranny perpetrated upon a people in the name of the people. It seems to have happened in the past that some rulers were like King Foolishman while others turned out to be wise. Had Edward alone been our ruler it would not have been so objectionable; but every Englishman is ruling over you and me. Please ponder over the meaning of this statement. I do not refer here to people's fondness for this world. The common man in India at least believes that the Parliament is a hoax. Even an extraordinarily intelligent man, caught in the meshes of this civilization, loses his sanity in Parliament. By saying that mercy cannot have any effect on the Pindaris you have denied the very existence of the soul or its [essential] attribute. Lord Patanjali has emphasized the greatness of mercy, etc., in such a way that we feel delighted even while thinking of those virtues. The real fact is that fear has taken deep root in us and consequently truth, mercy and such other virtues do not develop. And then we think that mercy has no effect on cruel people. If we show mercy to the person who shows mercy to us it is no mercy; it is only the return for mercy.

We should be considered weak if someone protects us free of charge or even if we pay him for doing so. If we have to seek outside help to be free from the menace of the Pindaris, etc., we are unfit for swaraj. If we would subdue them with physical force, we shall have to develop that force in ourselves. We shall not then have to pay blackmail or tribute. A woman seeks her husband's protection as a matter of right; but she is considered an *abala* (weak) after all.

Swaraj is for those who understand it. You and I can enjoy it even today. All the others will have to learn to do likewise. What is secured for us by others is not *swaraj* but *pararaj* (i.e., foreign rule, whether they be Indians or Englishmen).

In calling the cow-protection societies cow-killing societies, I have but stated the truth; for their object is to rescue the cow or protect her by bringing pressure on Mussalmans [muslims].

To rescue the cow by paying money is no protection of the cow; it is a way to teach the butcher to be deceitful. If we try to coerce the Mussalmans they will slaughter more cows. But if we persuade them or offer satyagraha against them they will protect her. No cow-protection society is necessary for doing this. That body should be for teaching Hinduism to the Hindus. It is better to kill an ox by a single blow of the sword than to kill it by starving it, by pricking it, by over-working it and thus torturing it.

It would be very confusing to take the examples of Shri Ramachandra and others literally. I have never imagined the possibility of a Ravana in the physical form of a man with ten heads and twenty arms. But to imagine that he was a huge passionate senseless animal and that he was killed by Shri Ramachandra representing the divine essence may appeal to the intellect. Tulsidasji has described Ramachandraji as the forces of the Sun who is the destroyer of pride, infatuation, and the darkness of the night of excessive attachment. Do you think we shall have the least desire left in us to destroy anybody when we are rid of all pride, infatuation and attachment? If you say 'no', how could Ramchandraji who was free from pride, infatuation and attachment and who was an ocean of mercy destroy Ravana? However, let us first attain his stage, like Lakshmana give up sleep and observe *brahmacharya* for fourteen years and then see where physical force could be used.

I want to say that everything is achieved by humility. The example you gave of the Transvaal is quite appropriate. It is not enough merely to profess orally to have the above sentiment; it should stand the test when the occasion comes. Think of the numberless adversities Harishchandra had to face before his [devotion to] truth was proved. Think of the suffering Sudhanva had to undergo before his *bhakti* (devotion) was proved to be genuine. We may not consider these as mere legends. It may be that the names and forms were different; but they who have composed these stories have given their own experiences through them. Even in the Transvaal the babblings of persons like me are being put to the test. Also bear in mind that many who were regarded as satyagrahis have proved to be insincere demagogues. Who, then, should be regarded as true satyagrahis? Of course, they who possess virtues like compassion, etc. Nowhere has it been said that suffering may not have to be undergone. And what does suffering after all mean? It is the mind, says the *Gita*, which is the cause of our bondage as well as of our freedom. Sudhanva was thrown into boiling oil. The person who got him thrown into it thought that he was inflicting suffering on Sudhanva; but for the latter it was a grand opportunity to show the intensity of his devotion.

It will never happen that all are equally rich or equally poor at the same time. But if we consider the good and evil aspects [of the various professions] it seems that the world is sustained by farmers. Farmers are of course poor. If a lawyer would boast of his altruism or spirituality, let him earn his livelihood through physical labour and carry on his legal practice without charging anything for it. You will not easily realize that the lawyer is lazy. Just as a sensuous man, even when exhausted by indulging in passions, remains engrossed in sensual pleasures, so a lawyer, even when he is exhausted, goes on straining his nerves to the breaking point in his practice in the hope of getting wealth and attaining to greatness and later on passing a life of luxury and comfort. This is his objective. I am conscious that there is a little exaggeration in this; but, what I have said above is true for the most part.

What service will an army of doctors render to the country? What great things are they going to achieve by dissecting dead bodies, by killing animals, and by cramming worthless dicta for five or seven years? What will the country gain by the ability to cure physical diseases? That will simply increase our attachment to the body. We can formulate a plan for preventing the growth of disease even without the knowledge of medical science. This does not mean that there should be no doctors or physicians at all. They will always be with us. The point is that many a young man who gives an undue importance to this profession and wastes hundreds of rupees and several years qualifying for it, ought not to do so. We must know that we are not, nor are we going to be, benefited in the least by allopathic doctors.

I hope I have replied to all your questions. Please do not carry unnecessarily on your head the burden of emancipating India. Emancipate your own self. Even that burden is very great. Apply everything to yourself.

Nobility of soul consists in realizing that you are yourself India. In your emancipation is the emancipation of India. All else is make-believe. If you feel interested, do persevere. You and I need not worry about others. If we bother about others, we shall forget our own task and lose everything. Please ponder over this from the point of view of altruism, not of selfishness. If you want to ask anything more, please do.

Blessings from

Mohandas

17 DISPELLING THE TOWER OF FEAR
Rainer Maria Rilke to Lotte Hepner

Charlie Louth

Rainer Maria Rilke (1875–1926) is sometimes taken to be a philosophical poet. He has attracted the attention of a number of philosophers (Heidegger, Gadamer, Agamben) and he is often read alongside them.[1] But 'philosophy' and 'philosophical' are words he hardly, perhaps never, used, even in letters; he showed no interest in acquiring philosophical knowledge: like almost everyone else of his generation, he read Nietzsche, and he also read some Kierkegaard and a little Bergson. But to sit down and study Plato, say, or Kant or the Pre-Socratics, never seems to have crossed his mind. So, if we are looking for philosophy in Rilke, what we will find is something very different from what a classical understanding of philosophy might be; it draws not on any philosophical canon, but on writers like Tolstoy and on the discoveries of his own writing. Above all, it is practical: to do with the business of how we lead and make sense of our lives.

Rilke must qualify as one of the great letter writers of the early twentieth century. He wrote letters nearly every day, sometimes several at a sitting and saw himself as belonging among 'those old-fashioned people who still regard the letter as one of the most beautiful and productive means of communicating' (to Lisa Heise, 2 August 1919).[2] But he also spoke of the way his letter-writing worked as a preparation for his poetic work – in clearing his desk he also seemed to be opening up the terrain for the poems which, particularly in the relatively long period between beginning the *Duino Elegies* in 1912 and completing them in 1922 were always elusive and hard to summon, always being solicited, striven towards, willed into possibility by an elaborate establishing of the right conditions, of which letter-writing, fulfilling the debt laid on him by his many correspondents, was a crucial part. It took him towards a clearing, towards an uncluttered space in which he could write, but it also, perhaps, functioned as a warming up of his language, a working into expressiveness, an approach to the 'zone'. It seems clear that it was essential to his *modus operandi* as a writer and that in writing his letters, he was often already writing his work, coming into writing, making discoveries, losing certainties, finding formulations which revealed the make-up of things, improvising a sense of life. The Expressionist poet Franz Werfel, recipient of several of these letters but probably not the best of them, questioned whether they were really to be considered letters at all: 'Hardly a page on which there is not some bright treasure of insight, of something suddenly understood, of being; and again and again the extraordinary analogies, the marvelous and terrifying glimpses... These are not letters, but poems, which only because they were subject to a little less pressure have not turned into crystal.'[3] In fact, Rilke is always supremely attentive to his correspondents, at least on the face of it; in that way, the essential nature of the letter is respected. It is by writing *to* someone that Rilke works out his ideas.

He wrote thousands of letters, probably well over 10,000, not all of which have been published. There are letters to lovers, to his publisher and to his translators, to the many people unknown to him who wrote having read his work, to patrons, politicians and sometimes other poets. A very high proportion of his correspondents are women.[4] Publication, which he expressly did not want to stand in the way after his death, 'since I have long been accustomed to channel a part of my productivity into letters' began with the quickly famous *Letters to a Young Poet* in 1929, originally written in 1903–1904 (with a straggler from 1908) to a young man who had written to him for advice on his own poems (but on much more besides) having read Rilke's own early work.[5] The letter selected here also belongs among the first to be published: in 1933 it appeared alongside a fictional letter, the *Letter from the Young Worker* (which Rilke wrote in 1922 right in the middle of completing the *Duino Elegies*) as *Über Gott: Zwei Briefe* (*On God: Two Letters*). It has long been recognised as a significant letter and, much more recently, has been singled out by Paul Bishop as the 'philosophical text' among Rilke's writing.[6]

Many of Rilke's letters could be called 'philosophical' in the sense that they represent an attempt to work out the basic elements of life, to offer some practical advice, to venture, in conversation with another and usually in response to questions and troubles raised by his correspondent, an attitude to life, a 'philosophy of life', what in German is called a 'life-practice'. Rilke certainly used his letters – and the occasion of writing them – as a space for thinking. Again and again, with a multitude of different correspondents, many of whom wrote to him out of the blue, he took it upon himself to think through the conditions and premises of his own life; to examine the grounds of existence; to talk through, in particular, its difficulties, what gets in the way of living life properly. Because of some quality in his published writings, his correspondents often came to him with their problems, after bereavement, after separation, at points of crisis. As Rilke responded, he seemed to think these things through in a way which made them his own, so that he was writing at once for his interlocutor and for himself, answering what had been put to him, but also appearing to discover the truth of what he is saying in the writing, extending the reach of his own understanding. What comes out most clearly is an attentiveness to the world on the one hand and an extraordinary facility and felicity with language on the other; it sometimes seems as if the richness and subtlety of the language actually *produces* the insights that the letters offer up as born of experience. The letters are a place where experience and expression are brought together in the desire to respond to another human being: the result seems bright with insight and curiously provisional at the same time. Rilke knew that his letters were worth preserving and he kept copies of key passages in his notebooks.

We do not know anything about Lotte Hepner, the addressee of this letter, but it is clear that she had written to Rilke after reading his (only) novel, *The Notebooks of Malte Laurids Brigge* (1910), a book which, because it focuses squarely on the difficulties of living one's life, provoked a good number of letters from readers whose own troubles had been touched on – perhaps in some cases exacerbated by – Malte's. *Malte* provides the starting-point for the letter and it seems that it had provoked Hepner into a series of fundamental questions, what Rilke calls the 'great question dynasties', which he sets out to address while acknowledging that they can never be answered or, at least, that they never *have* been answered. These dynasties, as they are inherited in *Malte*,[7] Rilke sums up in his letter as: '*this*: How is it possible to live if the elements of this life are completely unfathomable? If, the whole time, we are inadequate in love, uncertain in decision and incapable in face of death, how is it possible to exist?' A bit further on, he talks of his astonishment at the fact that 'for thousands of years people have been dealing with life and death (not to mention God) and, for all that, in face of these first, most immediate and strictly speaking *only* tasks (for what else is there for us to do?), still stand here today (and for how much longer?) like novices without a clue, caught between terror and excuse, pitiful. Is this not incomprehensible?'

So, Rilke starts at the beginning, with the 'elements' of life and, by noting how little we know about the fundamental aspects of existence. We are as much beginners now as we always were. To live one's life means to live amid insoluble questions, questions which we can neither ignore nor answer. This leads to 'a kind of horror', but beyond that lies something so intense that 'my senses are not able to tell me whether it is red-hot or ice-cold'. This is the first sketch of a figure which will be familiar to readers of Rilke's poetry, a figure of inversion when, through intensity, a phenomenon flips or comes to the point of flipping, into its opposite. Rilke's first image is one he had used before in another letter about *Malte*, suggesting the book might be seen as a mould or form 'whose every groove and furrow were pain, disconsolation and direst insight; but that the cast, if it was possible to produce one (like the positive figure that emerges when making a bronze), would perhaps be happiness, assent; – most exact and surest felicity'. That is, though negative itself, something positive might come of it. At the end of the letter the figure returns in the form of the difficult idea that the strength involved in building up the *Angstturm*, the tower of fear Tolstoy raises at the thought of death, is displaced into what surrounds it as, acknowledging how much effort has been spent on this fear, it can suddenly inhabit everything that is not the tower, the 'firm ground, its landscape and sky and the wind and a flight of birds'.

A related image is the odd one, which draws on a passage in *Exodus* (33:18-23), that has us standing *behind* the gods, so they have their backs to us and we are 'separated from their elevated radiant faces by nothing but themselves'. That is, we are in close proximity to something we shall never get to see, but are somehow 'at one' with the gods in that we are looking in the same direction. God and the gods are thus brought into the letter in a rather sudden move, seemingly not prepared by anything Hepner may have said in her own letter since Rilke more or less asks for her forgiveness in broaching the matter. He embarks on a kind of anthropological explanation of religion according to which the gods are a creation made of all the aspects of our existence we fear and cannot deal with. All the things that belong to us (intimately) but cannot easily be integrated into our everyday lives and which we shunt off into another place, thereby estranging ourselves from ourselves. An act of repression (Rilke uses the Freudian word), except that the things do not become unconscious, they become the supernatural. What ought to be part of and inside us, is located outside us, 'part of the human spirit that has never been taken up, a part that has always been put off, saved for later'. Out there, it gradually becomes more than we can cope with.

Rilke transposes this line of thought onto death. (It seems that in doing this he is responding to something Hepner had brought up in her letter.) Death too has been 'expelled'. Instead of being considered part of us, part of life, it becomes its opposite, 'something external, held further off day by day, lying in wait somewhere in the void ready to attack at random, out of malice' – the antithesis of life. Without God and without death – they have been 'othered' – we lead severely reduced lives, lives emptied of meaning, but made manageable. Perhaps this wouldn't matter so much, Rilke suggests, if it weren't for the fact that nature knows nothing of this extraction: 'all around us death is at home still and looks at us from out of the cracks in things'. Death is still with us, but we have no means of dealing with it since we have excised it from what we think of as our own. Though Rilke does not put it this way, there is a mind and body problem. Our bodies still die, but we spend our time convincing ourselves that they do not. We undergo death, but we do not live it or admit it into our experience.

Love, as something which 'takes no heed of our partitions but tears us, trembling, into an unending consciousness of the whole', can join together what we have split apart. Lovers are said to be '*full of death in that they are full of life*'. Love is presented as an intense form of experience and it is implicitly in our experience, which Rilke sets against speech or talk, that some sort of answer to the initial questions about how to live is to be sought, though Rilke does not make this at all explicit. Experience is 'a mystery that is sure of itself, that stands open like a temple'. It is a kind of open secret. It can't be described, but it can be a place in which what we tend to separate out might be joined together again, where mind and body can (again) seem to be aspects of the same thing.

From there, via references to unnamed things that Hepner has undergone, we come to Tolstoy. His tip about *The Death of Ivan Ilyich* is one he gave to several correspondents. Tolstoy is presented as someone who could think and write 'out of a sense of the whole', for whom death is indeed an aspect of life. In ending the way it does, with the idea of how fear shifts into a kind of security and the tower becomes what surrounds it, the letter is quite openly speculating, inventing a moment of reversal for Tolstoy which is probably intended to be a comfort to Hepner. But it was also a comfort Rilke is convinced of the importance of believing in, and he is convincing himself of it as he writes.

Rainer Maria Rilke to Lotte Hepner

Munich, 8 November 1915[8]

There are so many points in your letter, L.H., that one might pick up from, almost every sentence seems to invite ten letters in reply. Not that all it contains in the way of question (and what in it is not question?) could be met by an answer, no, but then all are the kinds of questions which have forever been covered up by yet more questions or, at best, displaced by the arrival of other luminous questions. They are the great question dynasties: who has ever been able to answer them? What finds utterance, no, what is endured in *Malte Laurids Brigge* (forgive me if I mention this book again, since it is after all what has brought us together), is in the end only *this*, using every means and starting again and again and using every scrap of evidence, this: *this*: How is it possible to live if the elements of this life are completely unfathomable? If, the whole time, we are inadequate in love, uncertain in decision and incapable in the face of death, how is it possible to exist?

I did not manage, in this book which was done under deep inner compulsion, to put wholly into words my astonishment at the fact that for thousands of years people have been dealing with life and death (not to mention God), and for all that, in face of these first, most immediate and strictly speaking *only* tasks (for what else is there for us to do?), still stand here today (and for how much longer?) like novices, without a clue, caught between terror and excuse, pitiful. Is this not incomprehensible? My amazement at it, each time I give myself up to it, drives me first into great dismay and then on, into a kind of horror. But even behind the horror there is something else, and then something beyond that, something so intense that my senses are not able to tell me whether it is red-hot or ice-cold. Years ago, to someone who was appalled at the book, I once tried to say of *Malte* that, myself, I sometimes thought of it as a hollow mould, a negative whose every groove and furrow were pain, disconsolation and direst insight; but that the cast, if it was possible to produce one (like the positive figure that emerges when making a bronze), would perhaps be happiness, assent; – exactest and surest felicity. Who knows, I wonder whether we don't always come out as it were *behind* the gods, separated from their elevated radiant faces by nothing but themselves, very close to the expression we long for but on the other side, at its back. But what does that mean other than that our visages and the divine face are looking out in the same direction, at one? And how, this being so, can we approach the god from the space that lies in front of him?

Does it bewilder you that I say God and gods and for the sake of completeness come to speak of these institutions (exactly as with ghosts) in the belief that these words must mean something to you too? But assume that a realm beyond the senses exists. Let's agree that from the earliest beginnings mankind created gods in whom everywhere were contained only death and menace and destruction and terror, violence, anger, supernatural lethargy, knotted together, so to speak, into a dense, malignant compaction: the Other, if you like, but an Otherness that to an extent allows that we have taken cognizance, tolerated it, even acknowledged it for a certain mysterious affinity and relevance: *we were also this*, only at the outset we didn't know where to begin with these aspects of our experience. They were too big, too dangerous, too multi-faceted, they grew out beyond us into an excess of meaning; it was impossible, alongside the many pressing demands of an existence set up for utility and achievement, always to take these unwieldy and unfathomable matters with us and so we settled on the idea of occasionally placing them outside, taking leave of them. – But as they were so abundant, the strongest things, precisely *too* strong; vast, not to say violent; incomprehensible and often monstrous –: how, gathered together in one place, were they ever not going to exert an influence, have an effect, make their power and superiority felt? And now, of course, from outside. Couldn't the history of God be treated, so to speak, as a part of the human spirit that has never been taken up, a part that has always been put off, saved for later and finally missed out on, for which there was a time – the resolve and composure – and which out there, where it had been driven, repressed, gradually grew until it had a tension against which the initiatives of the individual heart, ever distracted and trivially employed, barely figure?

And you see, it was no different with death. Experienced and yet not experienceable by us in its reality, growing out beyond us all the time and yet not properly acknowledged, harming and overtaking the meaning of life from the first, it too was expelled, forced outward, so that it couldn't constantly interrupt us in our search for meaning. Death, which is probably so near to us that we cannot establish the distance between it and the inner centre of our lives, death became something external, held further off day by day, lying in wait somewhere in the void ready to attack at random, out of malice. More and more the suspicion arose that death was the contradiction of everything, the adversary, the invisible antithesis in the air, what makes our joys perish, the perilous glass of our happiness from which we might be spilt at any moment.

God and death were now outside, were the Other, and inside was our life, which in exchange for this removal, this rejection, now seemed to become human, familiar, possible, manageable – in a confined sense we could call it our own. But because in what was a sort of beginners' course in life, a life pre-school, there were countless things that still needed to be ordered and understood, and because it was never possible to make clear distinctions between problems that had been resolved and those that had just been skipped over for the time being, the result, even in this restricted version, was not straightforward and reliable progression, but rather we lived from a mixture of real returns and miscalculations, and from every result, as a basic error, there inevitably emerged once more precisely that condition which was the premise and foundation of this whole attempt at existence. As God and death seemed to have been deducted from every meaning that was put into use (as not belonging here and now, but for later, elsewhere and other), the reduced circuit of the merely here accelerated more and more. And so-called progress became an occurrence in a world caught up in itself which forgot that despite all its efforts it was always, from the beginning, exceeded and surpassed by death and by God. Now, this could have led to a kind of contemplation, had we been capable of keeping God and death at a remove in our minds, simply as ideas. But Nature knew nothing of this repression we had somehow performed: when a tree blossoms it is as much the blossoming of death as of life, and the field pushing a rich expression of life up from its recumbent face is full of death, and the animals go patiently from one to the other – and all around us death is at home still and looks at us from out of the cracks in things, and a rusty nail sticking up out of a plank somewhere does nothing but delight in it day and night.

And love too, which scrambles the numbers between us to inaugurate a game of proximities and distances in which we always behave as if the universe were full and the only space were in us – love too takes no heed of our partitions but tears us, trembling, into an unending consciousness of the whole. People in love don't live out of the sequestered Here and Now. As if no separation had ever taken place, they tap into the vast assets of their hearts; of them one can say that God is nourishment to them and death can do them no harm: *for they are full of death in that they are full of life*. But it is not for us to speak about experience, it is a mystery, not one that shuts itself off, not one that seeks to be hidden, it is a mystery that is sure of itself, that stands open like a temple whose entrances glory in being entrances, singing between immense columns that they are the way in.

But (and here I am back with your letter again) how can we prepare ourselves properly for the experience, which cannot fail to take hold of us one day in our personal relations, in our work, in our suffering and for which we cannot be approximate because experience itself is exact, so exact that we encounter one another and ourselves as we come up against it, never by chance. You have discovered several paths of learning for yourself, and one senses that you have gone along them contemplatively and with attention. And so the shocks and upheavals of which you write have shaken you down into something more compact and have not buried you – I should like as far as I can to help you in your study of death, both from the biological perspective (by suggesting Wilhelm Fließ and his remarkable investigations: I'll be sending a little book of Fließ's in the next day or two) and by pointing you towards a few important writers who have reflected on death more quietly, calmly and magnificently than most. For now: Tolstoy.

He has a story called *The Death of Ivan Ilyich*. On the evening your letter came I felt a strong urge to reread these extraordinary pages. – I did so and, with you in my thoughts, I all but read out loud to you. The story is in the seventh volume of the collected edition published by Eugen Diederichs, together with *Walk in the Light while there is Light* and *Master and Man*. Can you get hold of it? It would be good if you could lay your hands on lots of Tolstoy, the two volumes of autobiography, *The Cossacks*, *Polikushka*, *Kholstomer*, *Three Deaths*. His enormous faculty for experiencing Nature (I can hardly think of anyone so passionately part of

Nature) enabled him to think and write to a startling degree out of a sense of the whole, out of a feeling of life and being alive that was so interpenetrated by death in its finest ramifications that it seemed to be everywhere part of its texture, a peculiar spice in the strong taste of life. But precisely for that reason this man would take fright, deep and utter fright, when he became aware of an instance of pure, neat death, the flask full of death or that ugly cup with the broken handle and the meaningless script 'Faith Hope Charity' from which someone had been forced to drink the bitterness of undiluted death. This man observed in himself and in others many kinds of mortal fear, for it was also given to him by his natural constitution to be the observer of his own fear, and right until the end his relationship with death will have been a grand pervasive fear, as it were a fugue of fear, a vast edifice, a tower of fear with passages and stairways and unprotected ledges and drops on every side – only that the very strength required to experience and acknowledge his fear at the last moment, who knows how, veered into unapproachable reality, suddenly became this tower's firm ground, its landscape and sky and the wind and a flight of birds around it.

18 THE EPIC SIDE OF TRUTH

Walter Benjamin to Gershom Scholem

Daniela Helbig

'You should know from the outset that this letter will be entirely reserved for this subject, which is of profound concern to us both. For news of me, you'll have to be patient for a day or two', the German-Jewish émigré from National Socialist Germany, Walter Benjamin opens thus his letter, written in Paris in 1938, to his old friend Gershom Scholem in Jerusalem. The question of Benjamin's increasingly precarious financial situation, of his fragile health, of a meeting during Scholem's next trip to Europe or, above all, of Benjamin's ever-deferred plans for his own emigration to Palestine will have to wait. The more urgent subject of profound concern to both friends is Max Brod's new biography of Franz Kafka, and since Scholem asked for Benjamin's views, he will give them – and make short shrift of Brod's work, which lacks all 'ability to gauge the tensions that must have permeated Kafka's life'.[1] His own reflections follow. They may be dense and 'dangerously foreshortened in perspective' within the space of a few pages, but Benjamin declares his confidence that he can rely on his friend's ability to follow, and to place these reflections in the context of his earlier work on Kafka. This degree of confidence reflects their long-standing relationship of intellectual exchange through letters and reading each other's published writings, keenly and as soon as they could get their hands on them. If Kafka's friendship with Brod, across the intellectual and temperamental unevenness that seems so apparent to Benjamin, is a 'question mark which he chose to ink in the margin of his life', his own friendship with Scholem is one of the few remaining constants of Benjamin's life. From 1923, when Scholem emigrates to Palestine, this friendship becomes an epistolary one, punctuated by few brief encounters in person. But as this letter testifies, the paper base of this friendship and the rhythm of postal exchange provided the space and material format for some of Benjamin's most insightful thoughts.

One of the reasons why we find those thoughts in the form of letters is pragmatic. As a Jew writing in German, from the mid-1930s Benjamin was increasingly denied publication opportunities in Germany, leaving him without much of an income and without the audience his work deserved. However, for Benjamin, the proper form of expression was inseparable from a text's content, a genuine concern permeating all his work. What material would take the shape of an essay or letter, book or radio broadcast? Within a given text, how should one relate citations from other writers and one's own comments on those? For Benjamin, the relationship to such text fragments was personal, charged with responsibility. He insisted that citations should never be subordinated to an argument, abused as mere proof of the commentator's opinion, but should instead be given a voice of their own. As he put it famously and picturesquely in his 1928 *One-way Street*: 'Quotations in my work are like wayside robbers who leap out, armed, and relieve the idle stroller of his conviction.'[2] Even during a time when the conventional modern formats of writing philosophy –chains of sentences argumentatively connected into scholarly articles or books – were challenged by figures as different as Ludwig Wittgenstein and Martin Heidegger, Benjamin's idiosyncratic approach was beyond the grasp of most of his academic contemporaries, who did not see his major book on the Baroque, *Origin of German Tragic Drama*, proudly conceived as a mosaic of quotations, fitting into any existing disciplinary divisions. Benjamin's choice of journalistic formats, as well as letters, reflects his unwillingness to adopt formal conventions that impose a separation of what counts as philosophical content from questions of personal experience. The tensions that permeate lives, to him, were part and parcel of the abstract thoughts that arise within the same lives. The letter was a format that did justice to this inseparability, speaking to the thoughts that moved Benjamin in the existentially difficult years of exile and flight.

An instance of a wayside robber quote opens Benjamin's discussion of Kafka: a long passage, quoted verbatim, by the British astrophysicist Sir Arthur Stanley Eddington. Eddington was a distinguished scientist, a Quaker and pacifist, foremost advocate of Einstein's work on both special and general relativity in Great Britain, and a gifted writer whose popular works on modern physics quickly found a broad audience. It might still come as a surprise that Benjamin should pick a physicist's passage to address Franz Kafka's fiction, but as he declares in his letter: 'If you read the following passage from Eddington's *Nature of the Physical World*,[3] you can virtually hear Kafka speak.' What follows is Eddington's description of the attempt to cross a doorstep, fictionally projecting both microscopic and cosmic-scale scientific knowledge onto the length scale of our everyday perceptual world. As we try to step onto them, big holes appear within the atoms and molecules that make up the wooden doorstep; our heads are dragged around by an 'ether-wind' as the surface of the earth rushes about in space. This kind of description had drawn criticism from some of Eddington's contemporaries on the British side of the Channel, including friends such as Bertrand Russell, who accused Eddington of dangerous linguistic confusion. Ordinary language as Eddington used it here, they argued, was simply unsuitable to render the strange and unintuitive results of modern, mathematical physics intelligible. Worse, it was bound to mislead the common reader into believing 'that facts are not facts and things are not what they seem.'[4] Not so for Benjamin. Rather than a case of confusion, the passage captures crucial aspects of 'the most recent of experiential worlds'.

Just how does it do so? According to Benjamin's reading of the passage, by defying its author's intentions. The passage concludes the final chapter of the *Nature of the Physical World*, titled 'Science and Mysticism' and it is likely that Benjamin picked up the book to learn about a physicist's view of this relationship. However, his letter to Scholem leaves unmentioned the lengthy discussion introducing the doorstep passage where Eddington takes pains to explain that the passage is a comical absurdity, an illustration of a bizarre loss of the 'sense of proportion' that helps to distinguish between a world described by science and a world distinct from that which is the world of ordinary experience.[5] Our ordinary conceptions, such as that of the solidity of wood, may be crude compared to scientific terms, but they reliably suffice to move about that world of ordinary experience. Rutherford's recent experimental demonstration that atoms mainly consist of empty space, Eddington seeks to reassure his readers, is irrelevant to our day-to-day experience of safely stepping on a wooden plank. But, like other writer-readers of Eddington's in his day, such as Virginia Woolf, things do not quite seem that clear-cut to Benjamin.[6] To him as well as Woolf, the new possibilities of representing an elusive 'reality' matter all the more precisely because the scientific articulation of that reality does not sit easily in ordinary language, while at the same time that scientific articulation increasingly gains in prestige and authority to speak to what is real. Rather than being a comical absurdity that remains irrelevant to everyday experience, Eddington's description strikes a chord with his reader Benjamin. Benjamin had long argued that human experience is not just the ahistorical product of the human animal's perceptual and cognitive makeup, but that experience itself is historicised. It is structured by our changing ways of representing reality. For that reason, the possibility of writing about a doorstep in Eddington's way, fictional but nevertheless grounded in new empirical, scientific findings, goes to the heart of capturing what Benjamin calls 'the experience of the modern city-dweller'.

Benjamin is precise about what he means by that 'modern city-dweller': 'On the one hand, I speak of the modern citizen, who knows he is at the mercy of vast bureaucratic machinery, whose functioning is steered by authorities who remain nebulous even to the executive organs themselves, let alone the people they deal with. On the other hand, by modern city-dwellers I am speaking of the contemporary of the modern physicist.' In his earlier essay on Kafka, published in 1934, Benjamin had already discussed the 'vast bureaucratic machinery'; in this letter, Eddington's passage leads him into a discussion of the 'contemporary of the modern physicist.' In an intriguing turn, Benjamin argues that what conveyed this 'most recent of experiential worlds' to Kafka, who worked as a clerk in an insurance agency but certainly not as a physicist, was his familiarity with the Jewish mystical tradition or Kabbalah. Benjamin owed much of his own knowledge of that tradition to Scholem's life-long research on the topic, begun during their joint days as students before and during the First World War. Scholem describes the structure of mystic experience in the words of Thomas Aquinas as *cognitio dei experimentalis*: 'experiential knowledge of God'.[7] Aquinas is referring to the Book of Psalms: 'Taste and see that the Lord is good.' Mystical experience is identical with knowledge rather than being extraneous to it. But, or so Benjamin's historical argument in his letter goes, for centuries before Kafka, such alleged mystic identity of knowledge and experience had already become a thing of a possibly never actual past. What was passed on was its epic representation until, eventually, the 'consistency of truth' was lost, as Benjamin puts it here: the tales of past mystic experience started to lose their plausibility in the face of the modern, scientifically described world. In his 1936 essay 'The Storyteller', Benjamin had already written about the decline of storytelling as a sign of the lost ability to convey lived experience; here, he connects that diagnosis explicitly not just with a new language of information rather than storytelling as he had done previously, but with modern science. In the face of its results, it no longer seemed possible to construe experience and knowledge as potentially being identical. What Eddington's passage brings out is just this: the absurdity of thinking of lived experience and theoretical knowledge as identical.

Eddington asserts, reassuringly, a separation between such lived experience and scientific knowledge, a conceptual separation that supposedly guarantees that his projection of the scientifically known into the sphere of lived experience is not much more than a comical absurdity. Despite this assertion, for Benjamin, the comical mode is mixed with the tragic when he insists with Kafka that the passage represents the experience of the modern city-dweller. His own, historicised understanding of human experience resists the neat distinction between the scientifically known and the ordinarily lived. Thanks to representations of reality such as those by Kafka and Eddington, that ordinary, lived experience now includes, crucially, the awareness of the modern dividing line between the scientifically known and the ordinarily encountered. According to this view, the narratively conveyed sense of contingency of our everyday world – the gesture shared by Kafka and Eddington – counts as an actual experience rather than a comical absurdity. As long as this experience remains confined to encounters with the merely theoretical aspects of '*that* reality of ours which is projected theoretically, for example, in modern physics, and practically in the technology of warfare', it is so subtle an historical change that its perception and articulation remain rare and have as their prerequisite Kafka's extraordinary ability to listen to the faint traces of the mystical tradition, 'eavesdropping' on it. However, it seems obvious to Benjamin, in his Paris exile from Nazi Germany, that the tragic and collective aspects of this experience will become apparent soon enough in further encounters with the technology of warfare. His sober prediction that 'the experience that corresponds to that of Kafka as a private individual will probably first become accessible to the masses at such time as they are about to be annihilated' is not the end point of his analysis, but the opening to his true subject of profound concern: Kafka's rare ability to turn into stories the tensions permeating his life and to take those stories seriously in their existential significance. They inevitably become '*more* than parables', not only reflecting changing historical realities but raising 'a mighty paw' against any pretence that what counts as the given way can remain untouched by the new realities. The sense of 'folly' that, according to Benjamin, is the only remnant of the lost 'consistency of truth' besides the 'rumours' of past wisdom in Kafka's work (i.e. the accumulation of hushed up 'obsolete' knowledge), had long characterised his descriptions of his own life. The ideological positions he found himself debating with friends, Zionism and Communism, he deemed deeply inadequate; as a personal question, an identification with what he saw as the remnants of the Jewish tradition, aligned with the question of his emigration to Palestine, seemed fraught with contradiction and hypocrisy. Back in his 'production plant' in West Berlin in 1931, he had portrayed himself being in a place of desperate folly, as 'a castaway who drifts on a wreck by climbing to the top of an already crumbling mast. But from here he has a chance to give a signal leading to his rescue'.[8]

If it weren't for Benjamin's closing paragraph, we might be tempted to read the 1938 letter as a sign of hope in dark times. After all, Benjamin chooses to devote the letter format's room for intimacy and earnestness not to the looming personal and collective catastrophes he rightly expected, but to the discussion of what he deemed a more truthful representation of his and his contemporaries' reality that might enable change. And yet, his concluding quote of Kafka's is that there is an 'infinite amount of hope, but not for us'. Kafka is a 'figure of failure', he insists in his final few sentences, leaving it to his reader to draw a parallel to Benjamin's diagnoses of his own failure or his own fervor in emphasising it. In contrast to Kafka's inky question mark, Benjamin pulls his reflections back into the letter format by placing his warmest, '*herzlichste*', greetings to Scholem at their centre.

Walter Benjamin to Gershom Scholem

Paris, 12 June 1938[9]

Dear Gerhard.

At your request. I'm writing you at length what I think of Brod's Kafka. After that, you will find some of my own reflections on Kafka.

You should know from the outset that this letter will be reserved entirely for this subject, which is of profound concern to us both. For news of me, you'll have to be patient for a day or two.

Brod's book is characterized by the fundamental contradiction that obtains between the author's thesis, on the one hand, and the attitude he adopts, on the other. The latter serves rather to discredit the former, not to speak of the other reservations that must be made about it. The thesis states that Kafka found himself on the path to saintliness.[10] But the attitude taken by the biographer is one of supreme bonhomie. Its lack of detachment is its most salient feature.

The *very fact* that *this* attitude could avail itself of *this* opinion of the subject robs the book of its authority from the outset. *How* this has been done is illustrated, for instance, by the turn of phrase that introduces 'our Franz' to the reader via a photograph (p. 127). Intimacy with the saintly has its own special appellation in the history of religion: Pietism. Brod's attitude as a biographer amounts to a pietistic stance of ostentatious intimacy – in other words, the most irreverent attitude imaginable.

This slovenliness in the work's economy is underscored by habits the author may have acquired in the course of his professional activities. At any rate, it is virtually impossible to overlook the traces of his journalistic hackwork, down to the very formulation of his thesis: 'The category of saintliness ... is truly the only correct category in which Kafka's life and work can be considered' (p. 49). Is it necessary to state that saintliness is an order reserved for life, and that artistic creation does not belong to it under any circumstances? And does it need to be pointed out that the epithet of saintliness is nothing more than a novelist's empty phrase when used outside a traditionally established religious framework?

Brod lacks the merest sense of that pragmatic circumspection which should be required of a first biography of Kafka. 'We knew nothing of deluxe hotels and were nevertheless happy as larks' (p. 103). On account of the author's striking lack of tact, of a feeling for thresholds and distances, feuilletonistic clichés have seeped into a text that should have been obliged to exhibit a certain dignity, given its very subject. This is not so much the reason for, as evidence of, the extent to which Brod has been denied any authentic vision of Kafka's life. This inability to do justice to his subject becomes especially scandalous where Brod discusses the famous instructions in Kafka's will (p. 198), in which the latter charges Brod with the task of destroying his papers. There if anywhere would have been the ideal place to broach fundamental aspects of Kafka's existence. (He was obviously unwilling to bear responsibility to posterity for a work whose greatness he was well aware of.)

The question has often been considered since Kafka's death: one might have done well to let the matter rest for once. That would have meant some soul-searching on the part of the biographer, of course. Kafka presumably had to entrust his posthumous papers to someone who would be unwilling to carry out his last wishes. And neither the testator nor his biographer would be harmed by looking at things in this way. But that would require the ability to gauge the tensions that permeated Kafka's life.

That Brod lacks this ability is demonstrated by the passages in which he sets out to comment on Kafka's work or style. He doesn't get beyond dilettantish rudiments. The singularity of Kafka's being and his writing is certainly not merely an 'apparent one', as Brod would have it, any more than you come near to Kafka's depictions with the insight that they 'are nothing but true' (p. 52). Such digressions on Kafka's work are of a kind that render Brod's interpretation of Kafka's *Weltanschauung* problematic from the very start. When Brod says of Kafka that he more or less followed Buber's line (p.198), this amounts to looking for a butterfly in the net over which it casts its fluttering shadow. The 'as it were realistic-Jewish interpretation' of *The Castle* suppresses the repulsive and horrible features with which Kafka furnishes the upper world in favour of an edifying interpretation which the Zionist ought to be the first to view with suspicion.

Occasionally, such smugness, so out of keeping with its subject, divulges itself even to a reader who is not all that punctilious. It remained up to Brod to illustrate the intricate difficulties of symbol and allegory, which he considers important for the interpretation of Kafka's work, by the example of the 'tin soldier', which constitutes a valid symbol because it not only 'expresses much ... that extends into infinity', but also touches us 'through the story of his fate as a tin soldier, in all its detail' (p. 194). One might like to know how the Star of David would look in the light of such a theory of symbols.

Brod's awareness of the deficiency of his own Kafka interpretation sensitizes him to the interpretations of others. It makes one uneasy to see the way he brushes aside the surrealists' by no means foolish interest in Kafka, as well as Werner Kraft's in some measure significant interpretations of the short prose pieces. Beyond that, he is clearly making an effort to belittle any future writing on Kafka: 'Thus one could go on and on explaining (and some will indeed do so), but necessarily without coming to an end' (p. 53). The emphasis on the words in parentheses is obvious.

That 'Kafka's many private, accidental failings and sufferings' contribute more to the understanding of his work than do 'theological constructions' (p. 174) is unwelcome coming from a man who is resolute enough to base his own presentation of Kafka upon the concept of saintliness. The same dismissive gesture is used against everything that Brod found disturbing in his acquaintanceship with Kafka – psychoanalysis as well as dialectic theology. It allows him to contrast Kafka's style with Balzac's 'fraudulent exactness' (p. 52) – and all he has in mind here are those transparent rodomontades that cannot possibly be separated from Balzac's work and its greatness.

None of this originates in Kafka's intentions. Brod all too often misses the assurance, the equanimity so peculiar to Kafka. There is no man alive – as Joseph de Maistre said – who cannot be won over with a moderate opinion. Brod's book does not win one over. It oversteps moderation both in the way in which he pays homage to Kafka and in the familiarity with which he treats him. Both presumably have their prelude in the novel for which his friendship with Kafka served as the subject.[11] The inclusion of passages from that novel by no means represents the least of this biography's improprieties. By his own admission, the author is surprised that outsiders could believe that the novel contained an affront to the piety due the deceased. 'This was misunderstood just as everything else is ... People failed to remember that Plato, in a similar, albeit much more comprehensive way, wrested his friend and teacher Socrates away from Death, all his life seeing him as a companion who continued to live, work, and think by his side, and making him the protagonist of almost every dialogue he wrote after Socrates' death' (p. 64).

There is little chance that Brod's Kafka will someday rank among the great standard biographies of men of letters, in a class with Schwab's *Hölderlin* or Bächtold's *Keller*. It is all the more memorable as a text documenting a friendship that is not among the smallest mysteries of Kafka's life.

You will see from the preceding, dear Gerhard, why an analysis of Brod's biography – even if only in a polemical way – seems to me unsuitable as a vehicle to offer a glimpse of my own image of Kafka. It remains to be seen, of course, whether the following notes will succeed in sketching that image. In any case, they will introduce you to a new aspect, one that is more or less independent of my earlier reflections.

Kafka's work is an ellipse with foci that lie far apart and are determined on the one hand by mystical experience (which is above all the experience of tradition[12]) and on the other by the experience of the modern city-dweller. When I speak of the experience of the city-dweller, I subsume a variety of things under this notion. On the one hand, I speak of the modern citizen, who knows he is at the mercy of vast bureaucratic machinery, whose functioning is steered by authorities who remain nebulous even to the executive organs themselves, let alone the people they deal with. (It is well known that this encompasses one level of meaning in the novels, especially in *The Trial*.) On the other hand, by modern city-dwellers I am speaking of the contemporary of today's physicist. If you read the following passage from Eddington's *Nature of the Physical World*, you can virtually hear Kafka speak.

> I am standing on the threshold about to enter a room. It is a complicated business. In the first place I must shove against an atmosphere pressing with a force of fourteen pounds on every square inch of my body. I must make sure of landing on a plank travelling at twenty miles a second around the sun – a fraction of a second too early or too late, the plank would be miles away. I must do this while hanging from a round planet heading outward into space, and with a wind of ether blowing at no one knows how many miles a second through every interstice of my body. The plank has no solidity of substance. To step on it is like stepping on a swarm of flies. Shall I not slip through? No, if I make the venture one of the flies hits me and gives a boost up again; I fall again and am knocked upward by another fly; and so on. I may hope that the net result will be that I remain about steady; but if unfortunately I should slip through the floor or be boosted too violently up to the ceiling, the occurrence would be, not a violation of the laws of Nature, but a rare coincidence ...
>
> Verily, it is easier for a camel to pass through the eye of a needle than for a scientific man to pass through a door. And whether the door be barn door or church door it might he wiser that he should consent to be an ordinary man and walk in rather than wait till all the difficulties involved in a really scientific ingress are resolved.[13]

In all of literature I know of no printed passage that exhibits the Kafkaesque *gestus* to the same extent. One could effortlessly match almost every passage of this physical *aporia* with sentences from Kafka's prose, and much speaks in favour of the fact that the 'most unintelligible ones' would he among them. If I were to say, as I just did, that there was a tremendous tension between those of Kafka's experiences that correspond to present-day physics and his mystical ones, this would only amount to a half-truth. What is actually and in a very precise sense *folly* in Kafka is that this, the most recent of experiential worlds, was conveyed to him precisely by the mystical tradition. This, of course, could not have happened without devastating occurrences (which I am about to discuss) within this tradition. The long and the short of it is that clearly an appeal had to be made to nothing less than the forces of this tradition if an individual (by the name of Franz Kafka) was to be confronted with that reality of ours which is projected theoretically, for example, in modern physics, and practically in the technology of warfare. What I mean to say is that this reality can scarcely still be experienced by an individual, and that Kafka's world, frequently so serene and so dense with angels, is the exact complement of his epoch, an epoch that is preparing itself to annihilate the inhabitants of this planet on a massive scale. The experience that corresponds to that of Kafka as a private individual will probably first become accessible to the masses at such time as they are about to be annihilated.

Kafka lives in a *complementary* world. (In this he is precisely on the same level as Klee, whose work in painting is just as essentially solitary as Kafka's work is in literature.) Kafka was aware of the complement without being aware of what surrounded him. If one says that he perceived what was to come without perceiving what exists in the present, one should add that he perceived it essentially as an *individual* affected by it. His gestures of terror are given scope by the marvellous *field for play* which the catastrophe will not entail. But his experience was based solely on the tradition to which Kafka surrendered: there was no farsightedness or 'prophetic vision'. Kafka eavesdropped on tradition, and he who listens hard does not see.

The main reason why this eavesdropping demands such effort is that only the most indistinct sounds reach the listener. There is no doctrine that one could learn and no knowledge that one could preserve. The things one wishes to catch as they rush by are not meant for anyone's ears. This implies a state of affairs that negatively characterizes Kafka's works with great precision. (Here a negative characterization probably is altogether more fruitful than a positive one.) Kafka's work represents tradition falling ill. Wisdom has sometimes been defined as the epic side of truth[14]. Such a definition marks wisdom off as a property of tradition; it is truth in its aggadic consistency.

It is this consistency of truth that has been lost. Kafka was far from being the first to face this situation. Many had accommodated themselves to it, clinging to truth or whatever they happened to regard as such, and, with a more or less heavy heart, had renounced transmissibility. Kafka's real genius was that he tried something entirely new: he sacrificed truth for the sake of clinging to transmissibility, to its aggadic element. Kafka's writings are by their nature parables. But that is their misery and their beauty, that they had to become more than parables. They do not modestly lie at the feet of doctrine, as *aggadah* lies at the feet of *halakhah*. When they have crouched down, they unexpectedly raise a mighty paw against it.

This is why, in the case of Kafka, we can no longer speak of wisdom. Only the products of its decay remain. There are two: one is the rumour about the true things (a sort of theology passed on by whispers dealing with matters discredited and obsolete); the other product of this diathesis is folly – which, to be sure, has utterly squandered the substance of wisdom but preserves its attractiveness and assurance, which rumour invariably lacks. Folly lies at the heart of Kafka's favourites – from Don Quixote via the assistants to the animals. (Being an animal presumably meant to him only to have renounced human form and human wisdom owing to a kind of shame – as shame may keep a gentleman who finds himself in a disreputable tavern from wiping his glass clean.) This much Kafka was absolutely sure of: first, that someone must be a fool if he is to help; second, that only a fool's help is real help. The only uncertain thing is: can such help still do a human being any good? It is more likely to help the angels who could do without help. Thus, as Kafka puts it, there is an infinite amount of hope, but not for us. This statement really contains Kafka's hope; it is the source of his radiant serenity.

I leave you this image, somewhat dangerously foreshortened in perspective, with all the more ease as you may clarify it by means of the views I have developed from different aspects in my Kafka essay in the *Jüdische Rundschau*. What prejudices me most against that study today is its apologetic character. To do justice to the figure of Kafka in its purity and its peculiar beauty, one must never lose sight of one thing: it is the figure of a failure. The circumstances of this failure are manifold. One is tempted to say: once he was certain of eventual failure, everything worked out for him *en route* as in a dream. There is nothing more memorable than the fervour with which Kafka emphasized his failure. His friendship with Brod is to me above all else a question mark which he chose to ink in the margin of his life.

That seems to bring us back to where we started from, and I place the kindest regards to you at its centre.

Yours, Walter

19 'A SHIT ON A PEDESTAL'

François Truffaut to Jean-Luc Godard

Antoine de Baecque

François Truffaut (1932–1984) and Jean-Luc Godard (born in 1930) met in 1949. They would go to the same cinemas, hanging out at the same film clubs, socialising in the same crowd of misfit film-lovers. Godard was 19, Truffaut, two years younger. A spontaneous, youthful complicity arose between them, though their backgrounds could not be more different. Godard was to the manor born, so to speak: his father was a doctor at a private clinic in Switzerland, on the banks of lake Leman. He grew up in a large family, with all material comforts and surrounded by art and culture. His mother belonged to the Monod family, a well-established Protestant dynasty of intellectuals and, in her branch of the family, of bankers. Her father, Julien Monod, Jean-Luc's grandfather, was one of the founders of the Bank of Paris and Netherlands. The young Godard was quick to rebel against his family: he went to Paris, chose films over studies and stole constantly from his family. He made his own decisions about his life, against the wishes of his family. François Truffaut, by contrast, was an auto-didact: reading and seeing films were his life-support. From a humble background, he was a street-boy from the *rue des Martyrs* in the ninth *arrondissement* in Paris; his childhood was difficult – he was an unloved bastard child. He left school early, moving from one odd job to the next, and all the while going avidly to the cinema. As a teenager, he launched a film club, but he had to steal to pay the debts incurred for what he had dubbed his 'Cinemaniac Circle'; as a consequence, his adopted father denounced him to the police.¹ He was arrested and sent to a reform school for delinquent minors. He enlisted in the army, and subsequently deserted, to be arrested once again. Jean Genet, the playwright and poet, who met him during that period, in 1950, wrote in a dedication to him: 'My dear Francois, do not be offended, but when I saw you, I had the feeling of seeing myself in some sort of hallucination, of when I was nineteen years old. I hope you will keep for a long while still to come, that grave look, and that simple and somewhat sorrowful way of expressing yourself.'²

In many ways, these two young men were polar opposites, yet they find themselves thrown together, gripped by *cinephilia*, the all-invasive passion of the time. To be a cinephile, a fanatic of film, is to be in love with the darkness of the picture house; the feeling of entering a kingdom of shadows, with a touch of underground secrecy. It is a form of resistance against the establishment, against the adults, against all the pretensions of the serious people. There, sitting in front of the screen, side by side, real life began. They saw hundreds of American and Italian films, and a French film here and there. They also joined forces at the *Cahiers du Cinema*, the film journal in which the new generation of cinephiles learnt the ropes of film criticism. They were soon known as 'the Young Turks' or the 'Hitchcocko-Hawksians' in honour of their devotion to Alfred Hitchcock and Howard Hawks, the two masters of American cinema. Eric Rohmer was the leader of the group, with Jacques Rivette and Claude Chabrol in his wake, as well as the duo Godard-Truffaut.³

The duo shared similar taste and ideas on what was good and bad in film. They admired the same masters and together, made a short film, *A Story of Water* which Truffaut directed and for which Godard wrote the dialogue and which he edited.⁴ They fell in love with the same girls and frequented the same brothels. After the younger of the two became a film director, with *The 400 Blows*, which triumphed at the Cannes festival in 1959, he naturally helped his friend to move on to a full-length film by giving him a three-page-long film treatment, which would become *Breathless*, written and directed by Godard in 1960.

The success of their two first films launched their careers as film directors, but also marked the end of their cinephilic friendship – a friendship which they would come to regret for ever more. From then on, they became isolated one from another, each working on his own films, often using the same actors, actresses, technicians and producers such as the cinematographer Raoul Coutard or the New Wave's pet actor Jean-Pierre Léaud. For Godard, judging by the letters exchanged at the time, there was a great nostalgia for that friendship. He wished, at all costs, to keep it alive, though everything in life and work made that impossible. Two letters from Godard to Truffaut say as much: '*Caro* Francesco – he writes in 1962 – I too feel completely lost. I'm roaming a strange zone. I feel that there is something very beautiful which is hovering around me. But each time I tell Coutard to quickly pan over it to catch it, it's disappeared.' In December 1961, he had written to Truffaut: 'We never see each other anymore, it's stupid. Yesterday I went to see Claude [Chabrol] on set, it's terrible, we've got nothing to say to each other. [. . .] We've moved on, each alone, to his own planet; we don't see each other in close-ups anymore, as we used to, all we see are long shots. The girls we sleep with only separate us more by the day instead of bringing us closer together. It's not normal.'[5]

But what really divides the two friends is politics. Around May 1968, Godard enrolled in the revolution and started to make militant films, whereas Truffaut persisted in making the same kind of films, as if nothing had changed. The break-up is violent.

After seeing Truffaut's *Day for Night* from 1973, Godard comes out of it sickened to his core. The film recounts the goings-on on a film set in which the challenges of making a film are entangled with the criss-cross love affairs between members of the crew. Godard writes to Truffaut, at the end of May 1973:

> It's unlikely anyone will call you a liar, so I will. It's not more of an insult than calling someone a fascist, it's a critique – and what I'm complaining about, with films like yours, or those of Chabrol, Ferreri, Verneuil, Delannoy, Renoir etc.,[6] it's that these films you make leave no place for critique. You say: a film is like getting on a night train, but who takes this train? Which class? And who's driving it with the 'snitch' from the executive board sitting beside him? Those people also make train-films. (. . .) You're a liar, because the shot of you and Jacqueline Bisset from the other night at *Francis'* [a restaurant near the Place d'Alma in Paris] is not in your film, and one wonders why the director is the only one who doesn't get laid in *Day for Night*. And I come now to a more material point. I need five or ten million francs to make *A Simple Film*. Given *Day for Night*, you should help me, so that audiences won't think that there only are films like yours around. If you want to talk about it, okay.[7]

A few days later, Truffaut replied to Godard. This hand-written letter of over 20 manuscript pages is extremely violent. Truffaut does not think he has any moral lessons to learn from Godard, who has gone too far. He rips apart the attacks and poses of his ex-friend, leaving no stone unturned. He thereby also unmasks the hypocrisies and arrogance, both political and moral, of the supposedly superior militant stance. He starts with their respective relationships with Jean-Pierre Léaud, whom both use as an actor in their films. Truffaut had discovered and 'invented' the character of Léaud-Doinel in *The 400 Blows*. The character developed through what became known as the series of Doinel films which follow the character, Antoine Doinel, played by Léaud, in his life adventures.[8] Truffaut reproaches Godard for having insulted Léaud at a time when he was particularly fragile. Godard had written to the actor, upbraiding him for starring in *Day for Night* and in other films made by people he calls 'capitulators', for having yielded to popular demands and tastes. Not unlike in his letter to Truffaut, Godard also ended his letter to Léaud by asking him for money. 'I send you back your letter to Jean-Pierre – writes Truffaut – I read it and find it simply disgusting. It is because of that letter that I feel it is time to tell you, in as long as it takes, that, as far as I'm concerned, you behave like a shit.'

It is hard not to hear in that stark condemnation, in that 'disgusting' which Truffaut throws at Godard, the echo of the famous last dialogue in Godard's first film, *Breathless* in which the hero, Michel Poiccard, played by Jean-Paul Belmondo, is shot to the ground and says, expiring – literally breathless: 'It's disgusting', to which Patricia (who had betrayed him to the police), played by Jean Seberg, says: 'What did he say?' and a policeman answers: 'He says that you are really disgusting', and Patricia then retorts: 'What is "disgusting"?'.[9] It is that equivocation, between the 'it' and the 'you', which gives this short dialogue all its spice and subtlety in which the human condition, the inexorability of fate, guilt and indifference all converge in a cataclysm of both understanding and non-understanding which made Godard, from that first film to this day, one of the greatest cinema writers and directors of all times.

But when Truffaut writes to Godard that his letter to Léaud 'is simply disgusting', it is all that subtle equivocation which is shattered; there is no more play on words and syntax, no possibility to explain away guilt and wrong-doing as matters of fate and inescapability as Godard makes his heroes, Michel and Patricia in the film, claim. It is not because of fate that one behaves badly; it is he, Godard, who has acted in this way and he must bear the responsibility of his actions. In this way, Truffaut demystifies the very essence of Godard's artistic and intellectual persona by bluntly showing him that he is hiding behind a fake ethics, all the while giving other people lessons in morality. The whole of Truffaut's letter is one long argument directed at showing Godard that one is indeed responsible for one's actions – precisely what Michel and Patricia in *Breathless* are shirking away from – just as Godard is in real life.

An even deeper question arises however, about Truffaut himself, who all his life and throughout his films and writings was obsessed with the question of whether cinema is more important than life. In *Day for Night* over which his friendship with Godard imploded, he has one of the characters, the assistant on the film set, played by Natalie Baye, say: 'I could leave a guy for a film, but I could never leave a film for a guy.' But that is what the assistant says; the director, who is played by Truffaut himself, says something rather different, mentioning the night trains (which Godard had so objected to in his letter), the character of the director says: 'Real life moves with a limp, films are more harmonious than life; there are no traffic jams, no down-times, films move like trains in the night.' Films, Truffaut seems to be acknowledging, are better than life, one would want to escape into a film, but life, makes other demands on us, and is, in fact, inescapable. In his letter to Godard, Truffaut thus also faces his own internal nagging question, between life and film.[10] In exposing Godard's own unacknowledged way of hiding behind his films as not so much behind a screen, but as a pseudo-moral scrim, he deepens his own moral dilemma, acknowledging the weight of reality over one's desires for escape into film.

Truffaut decries Godard's arrogance and contempt, his superior airs, 'this knack for passing off as a victim, [...] a victim of Pompidou, of Marcellin,[11] of censorship, of cut-throat film distributors, when in fact you always manage perfectly well to do what you want, when you want, as you want, and most importantly, you get to preserve that pure and tough image of yourself, which you want to maintain, even at the expense of people who have no means of defending themselves against you'. The self-moulded image of the revolutionary struggling artist does not hide Godard's poses and affectations in Truffaut's eyes: 'a shit on a pedestal', he calls Godard. And he repeats this violent rebuke, insisting on 'the behaviour of a shit' as a leitmotiv in his letter, which is all the stronger for the clash with the classicism and reserve of Truffaut's general style. Truffaut tries to frame Godard and his profoundly elitist manners in contradiction with his political purity. He recalls how he had thought Godard a coward when, in 1970, they had all gone out in the street, alongside Jean-Paul Sartre, Simone de Beauvoir, Patrice Chereau and many other intellectuals and artists, to sell the *Cause du Peuple*, a Maoist paper, which had been banned from publication for its provocative and extremist views. Truffaut had rallied to the cause out of admiration for the moral integrity of Sartre and in the name of free speech and free press, not particularly because of leftist commitments.[12] But Godard, who proclaimed precisely such leftist commitments, was nowhere to be seen: 'I have not felt anything else towards you other than contempt – writes Truffaut in 1973 – when I saw the scene in *Wind from the East* about 'how to make a Molotov cocktail',[13] and that a year later, you got cold feet when they asked us to distribute *La Cause du Peuple* in the street [with Sartre]. The idea that all men are equal is theoretical with you, not heartfelt.'

Finally, having gone through a whole series of base and petty affairs punctuating their relationship throughout the ten preceding years, Truffaut tells Godard that he is a manipulative egoistical obsessive: 'you like to razzle-dazzle and make big declarations, [...] you are still in 1973 ensconced on your pedestal, indifferent to others, incapable of devoting a few disinterested hours to help someone out. Between your interest for the masses and your narcissism, there is room for nothing and no one. [...] I have always been under the impression that real political militants were like cleaning ladies, with a thankless task on their hands, day in day out, necessary. But you, you're more on the Ursula Andres' side of things,[14] a four-minute appearance, a few flash photos, two or three well-booted witticisms and you vanish, back to that self-promoting mysteriousness.' It would be a mistake to read Truffaut as defending his own sincere political commitments against Godard's spoof 'all talk and no action'. Truffaut's attack articulates a more subtle moral stance, one which characterises his cinematic work as a whole and which shines a light on the contradictions of Godard's engagement as an artist in politics. For Truffaut proves to Godard that it is, in fact, impossible to be an artist and to live out at the same time, one's political anti-bourgeois, anti-establishment commitments. For part of what those revolutionary commitments imply is to expose the artifices of society: but cinema is artifice, everything about it is a spectacle, including the promotion and commentary on one's cinematic art.

Truffaut himself has no pretension to be a pure defender of political rights or equality for all, but we can see what counts for him: 'helping one person', coming to be aware of the daily drudgery of a cleaner. It is thus not only the lack of humility which Truffaut condemns, but also the hypocrisy of seeming to think that it is enough to be an artist shrouded in 'mystery' to fulfil the political engagement for which Godard claims to sacrifice his artistic persona: his provocative one-liners, brief public appearances, and his requests for 'truth' in Truffaut's film serve only himself and not any noble cause at the service of which he claims to be. It is a deep critique which goes beyond the feud with Godard, but touches the nerve of artistic expression and political and philosophical demands for the truth: whose truth? Of which moment? Godard is despite all, a great artist, as is Truffaut, though they both tell a different kind of truth and neither tell, or can tell, *the* truth, if such a thing ever existed, which is also what Truffaut is saying.

The last, and perhaps cruellest attack on Godard, is Truffaut's insistence on the falsity and pretension of the director of *Wind from the East*, Godard's revolutionary film from 1969: 'You are a fraud. A dandy. You've always ever only been a dandy, when you sent a telegram to De Gaulle for his prostate, [...], when you called Chauvet corrupt because he was the last, the only one to resist you,[15] a dandy when you mix and merge: Renoir-Verneuil, *tomahto tomayto* and you're a dandy still today when you claim you will show the truth about cinema, about the people who make it happen, away from the limelight, badly paid etc.' Godard has so entrenched himself in his artistic and leftist intellectual superiority that there is him on one side and everyone else on the other, even putting Henri Verneuil, the director of popular films the New Wave critics had lambasted, side-by-side with Jean Renoir, the director they had hailed as one of the greatest cinematic geniuses.[16]

Truffaut concludes his letter as Godard had concluded his: 'If you want to talk about it, okay.' They would never talk about it and would never see one another again – Truffaut's untimely death, in October 1984, put an end to any possible reconciliation. The break-up this time was irrevocable.

Neither Godard nor Truffaut can conceal from themselves a certain hard fact. It is a fact that became inescapable for the people around them at the time and which often led to people falling out with either one or the other, or sometimes with both. For many people at the time, Godard was indeed 'a shit human being'. Truffaut, on the other hand, was regarded as someone who would not give up on his comfortable situation and, as such, is seen as a social climber, a 'bourgeois' who would be hard pressed to risk his films by exploring freer or more adventurous modes of expression. From the time of the letter onwards, the two friends of 25 years would have to live with this moral and social rift between them.

Though, of course, these two depictions, of the callous revolutionary on the one hand, and the bourgeois compromiser on the other are both equally false. They are caricatures that the very violence of their break-up helped to consolidate and which has changed the way critics and viewers have viewed their films ever since.

This friendship and this fall-out constitute the embodied history of French cinema. They say so much about film, and more generally about France. Almost all film directors in the world, and many viewers have had to decide at some point where they stand with regard to this friendship and this duel: Truffaut or Godard? Which means: classical or modern? Matisse or Picasso? The craftsman or the artist? The plotline or abstraction? Being sensible or being outrageous?

François Truffaut to Jean-Luc Godard
May–June 1973[17]

Jean-Luc.

So that you needn't read this unpleasant letter to the end, I'll begin with the essential point: I shall not co-produce your film.

Next, I give you back the letter you sent to Jean-Pierre Léaud: I have read it and think it is disgusting. It is this letter which makes me feel that the moment has come for me to tell you, at length, that according to me, you behave like a shit.

Regarding Jean-Pierre, who has been having such a difficult time since what happened to Marie *la grande*[18] and, more recently with work, I find it disgusting your preying on the weak as you do; simply disgusting to try to extort money by intimidation from someone who is fifteen years younger than you, whom you paid less than a million francs when he was the central actor of the films which earnt you thirty times more.

Jean-Pierre has certainly changed since *The 400 Blows*, but I can tell you that it is when I saw him in *Masculin Feminin*[19] that I realised for the first time, that being in front of the camera could make him anxious and not happy. The film was good, and he was good in the film, but that first scene, in the café, was oppressive for someone who was looking at him as a friend and not like an entomologist.

I never said a thing against you in front of Jean-Pierre who admired you so much, but I know that you often told him all sorts of rubbish about me, like when someone says to a child: 'so, is your father still as a drunk as a fish?'

Jean-Pierre is not the only one to have changed in fourteen years; if we were to screen *Breathless* in the same night as *All's Well*,[20] the latter's disillusioned and overcautious aspects would be bewildering and sad.

I couldn't care less about what you think of *Day for Night*. But what is pathetic is for you to still go and see films like that, when you know in advance what they're like and that they fit neither your idea of how to make films nor your idea of how to live. Would Jean-Edern Hallier write to Daninos to tell him that he does not agree with his latest book?[21]

Your life has changed, your mind too, and still, you continue losing hours of your life at the cinema, ruining your eyes. For what? To feed your contempt for all of us, to strengthen your new found certainties?

It is my turn to tell you, that you are a liar. At the beginning of *All's Well*, someone says: 'to make a film, you need film stars'. What a lie. Everyone knows that it is you who insisted on getting Jane Fonda,[22] who was trying to get out of doing the film, when your investors told you, you could take anyone. As for your star couple, you've treated them like Clouzot would:[23] 'since you're lucky enough to work with me, a tenth of your salary will do' and all that. Karmitz, Bernard Paul, sure, they need film stars,[24] you do not, so, again, liar. And then in papers we read: he was 'forced' to take film stars. And here's another lie about your new film: you don't mention the very generous advance you asked for, and subsequently got, and which should be more than enough for you, even if Ferreri,[25] as you so brazenly accuse him, has spent the money which had been 'reserved' for you. Who does he think he is – right? – this Italian macaroni eating our bread, this immigrant stealing our jobs, he should be deported via Cannes!

You've always had the knack for passing yourself off as a victim, like Cayatte, Boisset or Michel Drach[26] – a victim of Pompidou, of Marcellin,[27] of censorship, of cut-throat film distributors, when in fact you always manage perfectly well to do what you want, when you want, as you want and, most importantly, you get to preserve that pure and tough image of yourself, which you want to maintain, even at the expense of people who have no means of defending themselves against you, as for example Janine Bazin.[28] Six months after that Kiejman story,[29] her two TV shows were cancelled, in a cleverly delayed retaliation. Kiejman could not talk about politically engaged cinema without an interview with you, but the role you chose to play – and really it's all only ever a role – was to maintain your subversive image; so what you gave him was one of your well-chosen cutting aphorisms. You deliver your line, and you know that either you get away with it and your witticism is sharp enough that no one could suspect you of becoming soft, or it's too much and then, that's just wonderful because everyone says: that Godard though, he sticks to his guns! And all that.

Things go as expected: the show gets censured and you, you get to stay on your pedestal. And no one realises that your little aphorism, is just another lie. Pompidou may be making a joke out of this country, but you, you're making a joke out of the Communist Party and the Unions by using means (too complicated for the 'masses') like circumlocutions, irony and derision, in *All's Well* – a film which was meant to be widely distributed.

The reason I withdrew from the debate after the screening of *Fahrenheit 451*, at the time, was because I was trying to help Janine Bazin and certainly not out of solidarity with you; and that's why I never returned your call at the time.[30]

And with all that, Janine was in the hospital last month, after being knocked down by a car whilst filming, with knee surgery (she'd been limping since her teens, ugh! etc.) and there she is, in hospital, with no job and no money and of course, no news from Godard who only descends from his pedestal to entertain Rassam from time to time.[31] So let me tell you this: the more you love the masses, the more I love Jean-Pierre Léaud, Janine Bazin, Patricia Finaly (who's just come out of hospital, her too, and has got to harass the Cinémathèque who owes her six months' salary), Helen Scott, whom you bumped into at the airport and don't even say hello to, why? because she's American or because she is my friend?[32] That is the behaviour of a shit. A girl from the B.B.C. calls you to talk about political films in a programme about me; I warn her in advance that you'll say no, but you do one better and hang up on her before she even finishes her sentence! Pompous behaviour, shit behaviour, just as when you agree to go to Geneva, London or Milan and then don't turn up, and why? to astound, to surprise, like Sinatra, like Brando, the behaviour of a shit on his pedestal.

For some time right after May 68, no one heard anything from you, only mysterious rumours: he's working in a factory, he's created a group, that sort of thing, and then, one Saturday, there's a radio announcement saying you'll be speaking with Monod on R.T.L. radio station.[33] I stay at the office to listen, to have some news from you in a way; your voice falters, you sound very moved, you announce that you are going to shoot a film called *The Death of My Brother*, about a sick black worker who was left to die in the basement of a factory manufacturing televisions; and as I listen to you, despite your faltering voice, I can just feel: (1) that the story is not exactly true, it's in any case manipulated; (2) that you will never make this film. And then I thought: what if that man had a family, and that family would be living now in the hope that this film will get done? There was no role for Montand in that film, nor for Jane Fonda,[34] but, for quarter of an hour, you gave the impression of 'doing the right thing', like Messmer when he promises the right to vote at 19.[35] You're a fraud. A dandy. You've always ever only been a dandy, when you sent a telegram to De Gaulle for his prostate, when you called Braunberger a dirty Jew on the phone,[36] when you called Chauvet corrupt (because he was the last, the only one to resist you),[37] a dandy when you mix and merge: Renoir-Verneuil, *tomahto tomayto*[38] and you're a dandy still today when you claim you will show the truth about cinema, about the people who make it happen, away from the limelight, who are badly paid etc.

But those times when you would get the tech crew to prepare a set for you, in a garage or a shop and that you would arrive and say: 'I have no ideas today, no filming' and the crew would have to dismantle everything, did it ever occur to you that the workers were feeling totally useless and disregarded? Just like the sound engineers who waited all day in the empty auditorium at Pinewood studios for Brando who didn't show up.

Why am I telling you all this today and not three, five or ten years ago?

For six years, like everybody else, I saw you suffer because of (or for) Anna[39] and all that was abhorrent about you, we all forgave you because you were suffering.

I knew that you had made a pass on Liliane Dreyfus (David) by telling her: 'François doesn't love you anymore, he is in love with Marie Dubois who is in his film'[40] and I thought that it was pitiful but touching, yes, that's right, let's go as far as that, touching! I knew that you'd been going to see Braunberger telling him: 'let me do the sketch that Rouch is supposed to shoot, instead of him'[41] and I thought that was ... let's say, pathetic. And when I'd walk with you on the Champs-Elysées, and you'd say: 'I hear that *Bébert et l'Omnibus* isn't doing well, serves them right',[42] I'd say: 'Oh come on ...'

In Rome, I even had an argument with Moravia because he was asking me to make *Contempt*;[43] I was there with Jeanne,[44] to present *Jules and Jim* and your last film wasn't doing very well, so Moravia wanted to change horses in midstream.

And it was again out of solidarity with you that I quarrelled with Melville who could not forgive you for helping him make *Léon Morin, Priest* and who was trying to harm you.[45] It was in the same period that you were humiliating Jeanne either wilfully or to please Anna (along the lines of *Eva*[46]), and you were trying absurdly to blackmail Marie-France Pisier (about Hossein,[47] or Yugoslavia and more than once at that . . . or about 'the alliance'), etc. You got Catherine Ribeiro,[48] whom I had sent to you, to act in *The Carabineers* and then, you jumped on her like Charlie Chaplin on his secretary in *The Dictator* (the comparison is not from me). I list all these things to remind you not to forget a single thing in your film about the truth in cinema and sex. Instead of showing the bottom of miss X . . . and the lovely hands of Anne Wiazemsky against the windowpane,[49] you could do the opposite now that you know that not only men, but women as well are equal and that also goes for actresses. Every shot of X . . . in *Weekend* was a little poke to the old boys:[50] that little whore wants to make a film with me, look at how I treat her. There are those who are whores and then there are the poetical girls.

I'm telling you all this today because, for all the dandyism, which was made worse by the bitterness that came out from a few of your statements, I thought that you had changed quite a bit; well, I could have thought so *before* reading your letter to Jean-Pierre Léaud. If you had sealed it, I would have given it to him without reading it and I would have regretted it – perhaps you were giving me the possibility of not giving it to him . . .?

Today you're strong, you're meant to be strong, you're no longer the suffering lover; like everyone else, you prefer yourself to anyone else and you know that you prefer yourself; you know the truth about life, about politics, about activism, about cinema, about love, all of that is very clear to you and anyone who does not think like you do is a rotten bastard, even if what you say in June is not what you say in April. We're in 1973, your prestige is intact, that means that when you come into the office, people look at your face to figure out if you're in a good mood or if they'd better stay clear from you; sometimes you agree to laugh or smile; first names have replaced more formal address but the intimidation stays the same, insulting comes easy to you as well and terrorism (that's your way of brown-nosing in reverse). What I mean, is that I'm not worried about you, there are enough rich kids in Paris, who feel guilty for having their first car at eighteen and who will be happy to atone by saying: 'yes but I'm producing the next Godard'.

When you wrote to me, at the end of 68, asking for eight or nine thousand francs that, in fact, I didn't owe you at all (even Dussart was shocked![51]) adding: 'anyway, we have nothing more to say to one another', I took all of that literally. I sent you the money and, with the exception of two moments when my heart softened (one for myself, unhappy in love, the other for you, lying in hospital[52]), I have not felt anything towards you other than contempt: when I saw the scene in *Wind from the East* about how to make a Molotov cocktail[53] and that a year later, you got cold feet when they asked us to distribute, for the first time, *La Cause du Peuple* in the street...

The idea that all men are equal is theoretical with you, not heartfelt, that's why you can't love anyone, nor help anyone, other than throwing some cash on the table. Someone, Cavanna or someone like that,[54] once said: 'Money should be disregarded, especially small change.' I never forgot how you'd get rid of your pennies by shoving them down the back of the bistro booth seats. Unlike you, I never uttered a single negative statement about you in public, on the one hand, because you were being attacked for stupid reasons and rather 'beside the point' as to the real issues, and then, because I've always hated those public quarrels between writers or painters, with those dubious score-settlings in the newspapers; and then, also because I've always felt you were both jealous and envious, even in your good periods – you are super competitive whereas I'm not, or almost not at all – and then, as far as I'm concerned, I admired you, I admire easily, you know that, and I wanted us to be friends since you'd been upset by something I'd said to Claire Fischer about the change in our relationship after (for me) the army and (for you) Jamaica. I don't usually make statements about things because I'm never absolutely certain that the opposite couldn't also be correct, but if I state that you are a shit, it is because, when I see Janine Bazin in the hospital, or your letter to Jean-Pierre, there is no room for doubt on this matter. I'm not crazy: I'm not saying Janine was in hospital because of you; but losing her job after ten years with the television, that is directly tied to you, and you couldn't care less. You like to razzle-dazzle and make big declarations, you're haughty and high-handed and you are still in 1973 ensconced on your pedestal, indifferent to others, incapable of giving a few disinterested hours of your time to help someone. Between your interest for the masses and your narcissism, there is room for nothing and no one. Who was it that called you a genius no matter what you did, if not that old-world elegant left from Susan Sontag to Bertolucci via Richard Roud, Alain Jouffroy, Bourseiller, Cornot;[55] and even if you appeared to be impervious to vanity, it's because of them that you started mimicking the good and greats of this world: de Gaulle, Malraux, Clouzot, Langlois.[56] You were keeping up the mythology, that dark, inaccessible side, temperamental (as Scott would say[57]), which would subjugate everyone around you. You need to play a role, and you need that role to be prestigious. I have always been under the impression that real political militants were like cleaning ladies, with a thankless task on their hands, day in day out, necessary. But you, you're more on the Ursula Andres's side of things,[58] a four-minute appearance, just enough for a few flash photos, two or three well booted witticisms and you vanish, back to that self-promoting mysteriousness. At the complete opposite of you, there are the *humble* men, from Bazin to Edmond Maire, via Sartre, Buñuel, Queneau, Mendès France, Rohmer, Audiberti – people who ask other people how they're doing, who help them fill in a social security form, reply to letters; what they all have in common is that they easily forget themselves and that, above all, they are more interested in what they are doing than in what they are and in how they appear.

Now, what is written can also be said, that is why I end as you do: if you want to talk about it, okay.

François

'Had I, like you, failed to keep the promises of my ordination, I would have preferred the reason to be the love of a woman rather than what you call your intellectual evolution.'
Diary of a Country Priest[59]

20 A PHILOSOPHY OF DANCE

Ada Bronowski

Maurice Béjart (1927–2007) was one of the greatest choreographers and dance innovators of the twentieth century. He was also one of its great humanists, a twentieth-century Renaissance man, the author of a novel, *Mathilde or Lost Time* from 1963, based on a love triangle between the composer Richard Wagner and a married woman, the poet Mathilde Wesendock (1828–1902) – and which he would later, in 1965, transpose into a ballet, *Wagner Ou l'Amour Fou*, (*Wagner or the Folly of Love*) – he also wrote a series of memoirs, overflowing with anecdotes from his encounters with the most influential and important artists and intellectuals of the twentieth century, from the American choreographer Martha Graham to Italian film director Federico Fellini to the actor and theatre director Jean-Louis Barrault, singer-songwriter Barbara, composer Nino Rota or film director Jean-Luc Godard. His memoirs are also filled with deep and insightful commentaries and analyses of texts from writers and philosophers past and present, who nourished his work from Goethe, Nietszche or Rilke, to Molière, Baudelaire or Jean Genet. He also invented a literary genre, the dialogue with a dead man's diary, in his book *La Mort Subite: Journal Intime* (*Sudden Death: A Diary*),[1] in which he establishes a conversation between himself and fragments of his late father's personal diary. His own memories serve to reconstruct the background to the entries from the diary which he found after his father, the philosopher Gaston Berger (1896–1960), died, conjuring also, amidst this dialogue with the dead, the imagined contributions of his mother who had died when Béjart was only seven years old.

Death is always at the door in Béjart's world of curiosity and motion, we extend our arms to it, our fingertips are always just missing it – until, of course, one day, we seize it or it seizes us. Béjart is principally a creator of dance, which for him means a thinker in dance. That movement of the extended arm and outstretched fingers is one of his signature gestures, which appears in almost all of his many choreographies, most notably in his *Boléro* from 1961, set to the eponymous music by Maurice Ravel, considered as one of his masterpieces and which is regularly performed across the world.[2] In it, the extended arms of the dancers encircling a podium express unstoppable energy but also direct the gaze upwards towards an ungraspable and foreboding otherness, which in other works is more explicitly spelt out as the other side of death. This is the case, for instance, in Béjart's *Ballet for Life* from 1997, an anguished celebration of those who die young, in direct homage to Freddie Mercury, the founder of the group Queen, and Béjart's star dancer, Jorge Donn, who both died from AIDS at 45; the ballet is set to a mix of music from Queen and Mozart, who also died at a trailblazing young age.

Béjart's work is an ever-continued reflection on the possibilities and modes for dialogue: dialogue with death, with past selves, with the audience, between the choreographer and the dancer, between the bodies of the dancers, between the dancer and the floor. Whether in his writing – he also published a series of dialogues, or *Conversations* with friends[3] – in his films,[4] or exponentially in his choreographies of which there are over 300, Béjart's main preoccupation is with creating the conditions for an original dialogue, between people, between different art forms, between traditions and times.

His uniqueness in the cultural and intellectual landscape of the twentieth century consists in this, that his research focuses on putting in contact things which do not or should not or cannot be put in contact. Such a meeting creates a tension which is resolved in a form of transcendence: it is the special event which is the performance, neither repeatable nor fully describable. The aim each time is to create a unicity in the experience, by drawing on all the art forms to make up a total work of art. However, in contrast to Wagner, the model and inventor of the *Gesamtkunstwerk*, the total work of art, for whom it is the music which unifies and justifies all the other participant art forms in the work, for Béjart, it is the dance. Béjart harboured a life-long admiration for Wagner, saying in an interview that he 'was born Wagnerian'. As mentioned, he wrote a novel about him, and choreographed several pieces to music by

Wagner.[5] But the shift in centre of gravity from the music to the dance changes everything about the conception of totality in a work of art and, of course, changes everything about the kind of dance.

Béjart is the twentieth-century's thinker of the sublime, rebooted to grapple with the weight and horrors but also the astonishing innovations and potentialities of the century's modernity. His greatest discovery was that dance was the artistic – but also philosophical – form capable of ingesting and expressing this new sublime, through the liberation of the body on the one hand, but also because only the body was capable of taking stock of the twentieth century's complexity, there to be expressed. This complexity derives from the weight of centuries of culture and thought and the necessity to know all of it because there is no possible excuse not to. Béjart brings to realisation what Lucian of Samosata had theorised in the second century about the role of the dancer, in his *On Dance*, namely that a dancer 'must know what is, what will be and what was, in such a way that nothing escapes him, having a faultless memory (...) He must know everything'.[6] To know everything in the twentieth century is to accept the impossible clash between the capacity for natural beauty of the body and the ineffable horrors of the tragic human condition. The sublime in Béjart is the expression, in dance, of that impossible, unutterable meeting. This is why it is so important for him, as he explains in the letter presented here, that the experience of a performance be unique and ephemeral.

His task, he says, is that of creating an unrepeatable event; he speaks of the creation of a '*fête*', a party, which he defines as the opposite of anything that all forms of media have to offer, which he describes as a 'diarrhoea of the senses'. This is not so much a critique as it is the incitement to the challenge of creation in the age of the reproducibility of art, which Walter Benjamin had captured so matter-of-factly in his *The Work of Art in the Age of Mechanical Reproduction*, from 1935.[7] The consumerist means by which a work of art or a performance can be repeated only means that the new art must overcome those pitfalls. Ultimately, modern technologies which regiment and make more extensively available the range of sights and sounds, merely up the game for the artist. Béjart thus gives a more profound sense to the word 'party', as an experience not only for the senses but also one that makes us intellectually aware of its unicity. Dance is the art form capable of producing this double effect, in which the physicality of the mind is made manifest on stage by the dancer and, in their seat, for the audience.

In the year 2000, a new dancer entered Béjart's Swiss-based company, the Béjart Ballet Lausanne, by the name of Octavio de la Roza, originally from Argentina and whom Béjart had spotted a few years earlier on tour in South America. He had invited the young dancer to join his dance school first, the Ecole-Atelier Rudra, before making him one of the principal dancers of his company. Béjart, at 73, was thus a mentor and Pygmalion to this burgeoning and still-raw dancer whose Argentinian roots perhaps also reminded him of Jorge Donn (1947–1992), a pivotal figure in the life and work of Béjart, who had joined Bejart's then Brussels-based company Ballet du XXe Siècle in 1963 never to leave Béjart until his untimely death. At the dawn of de la Roza's career, and at the twilight of the great master's life, Béjart writes a series of letters to a young dancer, dedicated to 'Nahuelt', an Amerindian name which is both a nickname of endearment for Octavio de la Roza, but which also echoes his other South American muse, and beyond both these figures, addresses not one real person but an idea of an addressee, in whom inexperience is mixed with the desire to learn. It is, in other words, the prototypical setting for the unequal exchange nurtured by trust and familiarity, between an experienced wise figure and a disciple, in yet another configuration of Béjart's cherished form, the dialogue. It is precisely that kind of dialogue to which Béjart refers in the first letter of the correspondence, presented here, in which he evokes with ironic nostalgia the bond between the craftsman and his apprentice at a time where there were no artists but only craftsmen.

How to pass down knowledge? How to share experience? Béjart's *Letters to a Young Dancer* are just as much a nod to Rilke's *Letters to a Young Poet* in which finding one's voice is intrinsically related to learning to engage with the world (see Chapter 17 in this volume), as they are to the premises of that tradition, begun in ancient Greece with Epicurus and the latter's humble summarising of doctrine for the benefit of the philosophical novice (see Chapter 1 of this volume), and amplified with Seneca's *Letters to Lucilius*, which are written for posterity (see Chapter 2). But Béjart reimagines the problem of transmission not as what there is to know, but rather, as how to work, when there is so much to learn. The letters become, for him, the format in which to discuss his philosophy of dance.

Béjart begins his letter to Nahuelt with a Socratic declaration, that the more he searches for answers, the more he realises he does not know anything. It is dance which brings this constant unquenchable desire for knowledge and which also makes it impossible to satisfy. The solution, then, is to cling to the basics, to what one can grab hold of: in dance, the answer to that is, in a way, easy: it is the body. Where the tools of abstract thought are themselves abstract – Socrates' famous and elusive 'dialectic' – dance has this advantage, that its primary material is supremely malleable. But the difference is purely superficial: just as for Socrates, the problem and the solution lie in one and the same tool, namely language, so it is for the choreographer, for whom the problem and the solution are to be found in and with the body. The body is thus both the mystery and the basic material from which questions arise.

Socrates famously roots his inquiries in the simple questions, so as all the better to explode conventions and truisms: What does shape mean? Doesn't everyone want good things? Is justice good? – are some of his famous 'innocent' questions. But it is the same with the choreographer, who appeals to the simple things about the body. Dance has a routine and a discipline which are the essential conditions for its development. Is this a truism, a 'common-place' as Béjart says self-deprecatorily? To get anything done, one must go back to the basics and do the everyday, seemingly uninspiring work. In dance, this is epitomised by the daily exercises at the barre. Béjart thus turns around the notion of a common-place, by making its literal meaning re-emerge – in true Socratic fashion: the barre is a common place, a shared place where all dancers come to, and from which all work evolves. The abstract common place, which one forgets to remember, becomes concrete: it is a place, the barre, a time, the routine where the primary material, the body, is shaped and kneaded.

Béjart says there is no difference for him between life and dance and to understand what this means beyond a mere declaration of the artist's commitment, body and soul, to his art, we must delve deeper into his analysis of what the work of dance-making involves. He says that he does not see himself as a choreographer, that is, as the creator of a particular sequencing of steps which makes up a beginning, middle and ending of a dance piece; rather, again in an uncanny echo to Socratic thought, he says his work is more akin to that of a midwife of the dance. Whereas Socrates had used refutation and Socratic irony to help his interlocutor find in himself the means to reach truth, Béjart's midwifery consists in a discovery through dance of what is inside the dancer, bringing him or her to a higher realisation of themselves.

He writes humorously that dance-making, like love-making needs two people and is perhaps even orgiastic when the audience enters into the game as well. Joking aside, there is here too, a deeper insight into the kind of dialogue established between a dancer – and through him or her, the choreographer – and the audience: for unlike in a performance where there are words (opera or theatre or a traditional ballet based on a story) around which everyone will agree the piece is about, what is communicated in dance is dependent on the means of reception which are necessarily individual and personalised for each member of an audience. Each of us is called upon to tie a personal relationship to the dance, intensifying thereby the unicity of the event. That something does get communicated is part of the mystery of dance.

There is, in Béjart's writing generally – and all the more so in the benevolent effusion in his letters to Nahuelt – a tone which is always light-hearted, full of cheekiness and fun, all the while harbouring a deep reflection about the always-almost seriousness of life, art and dance. He encourages Nahuelt to open his mind and his dance to all forms of dance across traditions. For wisdom lies in the hybridisation of cultures. He says of himself in another letter to Nahuelt that he is: 'contemporary, post-African, pseudo-classical, Japo-minimalist, Argentinian-modernist, folk-retro, and Indo-Petipa*tist*.' It is not only inspiration that Béjart draws from the different cultures; he also had life-long fascinations with: going regularly to India to learn more about 'real yoga' and Indian dance, spending time in Japan, deepening his practice of zen and his love of kabuki dance-theatre, cultivating his Senegalese roots (his great-grandmother was Senegalese), all the while broadening his knowledge and practice of classical dance, placing Marius Petipa (1818–1910) at the forefront, with his neologism 'Petipatist'. In one of his many brilliant verbal portraits, Béjart describes Petipa, his 'colleague', as 'the Meliès and the Griffith of choreography'.[8] Born, like Béjart, in Marseille, Petipa ended up in St Petersburg, via Brussels, creating the great ballets of the classical canon together with Tchaikovsky. Béjart's fraternal apostrophe to 'his colleague' Petipa is just one of a myriad of such emotional and intellectual identifications he expresses with all practices and traditions, arts, and cultures, which Béjart cannot but embrace fully.

It is these capacities for love and curiosity and the humility that comes with them, with which Béjart infuses his letter to the young dancer. He ends with a quotation from his father, the philosopher Gaston Berger, on the state of this poor humanity of ours which is torn between thinking that it knows and realising, through science, that it still has everything to learn. It is at heart Socrates' mantra revisited, that he knows he knows nothing, turned now into a scientific discovery which, 'backed by science', is harder than ever to brush aside. Though Béjart leaves it open, he intimates with a casual 'it is not without relevance', that one way to face the crisis is to pretend it does not exist – the age-old reaction to Socratic admonitions – but another way is to open our minds to a philosophy of reciprocal mixture of all forms of expression, of all cultures. Dance does not accompany this realisation, but rather is the place in which such a mixture can effectually occur.

Maurice Béjart to Nahuelt
Christmas 2000[9]

Thank you for your last letter. I've been slow in replying, forgive me but you ask so many questions! I've been mulling them over in my head, trying to find answers, but each question was generating other questions, which themselves generated others and so on; no answers. But are there any answers? We keep moving forward in our lives and doors pop up out of nowhere in front of us, we open one searching for an answer, for a way through, a way out, but each door opens up onto a corridor filled with new doors, and we must go on, choose again, proceed ... but, perhaps, this is what it is to be alive: to ask questions. And the only answer, so close and yet which seems to us always so remote, is death.

You see, forgive me, I am far away from dance ... I am, and I am not. Dance is my life, and dance asks me questions every morning, and the more I live, the less I know. Of one thing I am sure: I must go on. Of one thing I am utterly convinced: I must work.

> 'Cent fois sur le métier remettez votre ouvrage'[10]
> 'A hundred times over put your craft to the test'

Oh, old school memories! ... but what I like in this line, are the words 'craft', 'test'.

Art was created by craftsmen; only later, much later, there came the *artists* and almost always the artists killed the art, in any case, they distorted its deepest sense. Craftsmen used to learn their *craft* slowly from a master; and then, by the very act of building, painting, sculpting, singing, writing, they would pass on their techniques to an apprentice.

Work! Someone once declared (many in fact could have said so): genius is ten per cent inspiration and ninety per cent perspiration. Yes, you know it well, it's a common-place, but there's nothing like repeating to oneself every morning before breakfast a number of common-places ... on this point, the exercises at the barre are a wonderful common place.

Craft. If I think about it, what is my craft?

In a book once, I wrote at the start of the first chapter: 'I am a choreographer because I cannot do anything else.'[11] The truth is, I'm not even sure that I am a choreographer ... in fact, I'm quite sure the opposite is true ... first, because choreography in itself does not interest me (in that very same book, I had also written: 'in a ballet, the most important is not the choreography but the dancer').

What is wonderful for me is to discover an interpreter, and then to be inside the interpreter, and then to play the midwife, and deliver this being of him or herself, of what he or she is deep down without knowing, and to help them give birth to what the dance has revealed of their true personality ... next to that, what are steps, however beautiful or innovative ... mere bagatelles!

After the dancer (I wrote again in that same book: 'it takes two to make a choreography just as it takes two to make love', but I'm getting on your nerves with this pedantic and continuous self-quoting ...) stop ... so yes, after the dancer, comes the audience ... ah! you're laughing, it's a threesome now, it takes three to make a choreography! No, because I go away. I've given what I had to give already, but you, you stay on your own, with *your* audience. Of course, I love them too, I loved them when I created you, when I built you, but now, it's your turn to show what you've got.

As for the audience, I don't look for success, but I love the joy, I love shows which are not 'works of art', but a party, an event, an explosion ... yes, *a party*, that is the right word, my work is to organise parties, and we need them so much in a world in which permanent and controlled pleasure (a diarrhoea of the senses) has killed the one-off party.

When you have time, or the opportunity to do so, have a look at traditional dances ... or what is left of them ... you better hurry!

I learnt all I know from Spanish dances, African, Indian etc. They are so complex no amateur can grasp them and yet, and that is genius! it is amateurs who dance them ... or rather, no, they are 'artisans' (I like this term of artisan). The President Leopold Sedar Senghor told me once: 'All great civilisations come, in a deep sense, from hybridization. Purity (like distilled water) only generates death.'

Try to learn your dance together with the other dances; the barre is a means, not an end.

But time passes, here I am, talking and the rehearsal awaits; keep asking me questions, that'll mean that you're asking yourself questions, therefore that we are alive, you and I. I end with a quote from my father Gaston Berger . . . which is not without relevance:

'Humans thought they hailed from an established noble lineage, but they realise that they might, at best, be the descendants of apes who got lucky; that is why they have the arrogance and anxieties of upstarts.'

See you soon!

Salve.

LIST OF CONTRIBUTORS

Delphine Antoine-Mahut, Professor of Early Modern Philosophy, École Normale of Lyon (original French text translated by A. Bronowski).

Ada Bronowski, Fellow in Philosophy, University of Strasbourg, Institute of Advanced Studies.

Alberto Camerotto, Associate Professor in Classics, University of Ca' Foscari, Venice. (original Italian text translated by A. Bronowski).

Luigi Capitano, Research Fellow, University of Palermo (original Italian text translated by A. Bronowski).

Máire Fedelma Cross, Professor of French Studies, University of Newcastle.

Antoine de Baecque, Professor of Film Studies, École Normale of Paris (original French text translated by A. Bronowski).

Stefano Evangelista, Associate Professor of English, Trinity College, University of Oxford.

Rick Anthony Furtak, Associate Professor of Philosophy, Colorado College.

Gweltaz Guyomarc'h, Associate Professor in Ancient Philosophy, University of Lyon III-Jean Moulin.

Katherine Harloe, Associate Professor of Classics, Reading University.

Daniela Helbig, Senior Lecturer in History and Philosophy of Science, University of Sydney.

Sarah Hutton, Professor of Philosophy, University of York.

Charlie Louth, Associate Professor of German, The Queen's College, Oxford University.

Dalia Nassar, Senior Lecturer in Philosophy, University of Sydney.

Nicholas J. Owen, Associate Professor of Politics, The Queen's College, Oxford University.

Marie-Frédérique Pellegrin, Professor of Philosophy, University of Lyon III-Jean Moulin (original French text translated by A. Bronowski).

Kelsey Rubin-Detlev, Assistant Professor of Slavic Languages and Literatures, University of Southern California.

Catriona Seth, Marshal Foch Professor of French Literature, All Souls College, University of Oxford.

Christelle Veillard, Associate Professor in Ancient Philosophy, University of Paris-Nanterre (original French text translated by A. Bronowski).

ACKNOWLEDGEMENTS

The editor would like to thank the following publishers, editors and all owners of copyright for permission to use and translate the sources included in this book:

Lisa Shapiro and Chicago University Press for permission to reproduce Lisa Shapiro's translation of the letters of Descartes and Elisabeth of Bohemia.

The Library of Christ's College Cambridge and Oxford University Press for permission to reproduce the letter by Anne Conway to Henry More.

Oxford University Press for permission to use K. Rubin-Detlev's translation of Catherine the Great's letter to the Prince de Ligne.

Professor Stephane Michaud, owner of copyright for the letters of Flora Tristan in S. Michaud, (2003) *Flora Tristan, La Paria et son rêve*, with a preface by Mario Vargas Llosa, Paris: Presses Sorbonne Nouvelle, for permission to translate a letter from his edited corpus.

Mr Merlin Holland, owner of the copyright of the letters of Oscar Wilde, for the text and permission to reproduce an extract of Oscar Wilde's *De Profundis*.

Penguin Random House for permission to reproduce the translation of the letters of Walter Benjamin.

Eva, Laura and Josephine Truffaut for permission to translate a letter by François Truffaut.

The Fondation Béjart and Actes Sud editions for permission to translate a letter from Maurice Béjart's *Lettres à un Jeune Danseur*.

Every effort has been made to trace copyright holders. In the event of errors or omissions, please notify the publisher in writing of any corrections that will need to be incorporated in future editions of this book.

NOTES

Introduction

1. On the Early Modern constitution of the Republic of Letters, see P. Hazard, *The European Mind: The Critical Years, 1680–1715*, trans. J. Lewis May (1953), New Haven: Yale University Press, (repr. as *The Crisis of the European Mind, 1680–1715*, (2013), New York: NYRB), esp. part two 'The War on Tradition', and on the eighteenth-century open battlefield of the Republic of Letters, see A. Goldgar (1995), *Impolite Learning: Conduct and Community in the Republic of Letters, 1680–1750*, New Haven: Yale University Press.
2. In R.M. Rilke, (1908), 'Archaïscher Torso Apollos' in *Der Neuen Gedichten: Anderer Teil*, Leipzig: Insel, trans. in R.M. Rilke (2015), *New Poems*, L. Krisak (trans.), New York: Camden House, 173.

1 Be Present!

1. Diogenes of Oenoanda, Frag. 124–126 in M.F. Smith, (ed.) (1993), *The Epicurean Inscription Fragments*, Naples.
2. The dissemination of Epicurean doctrine thanks to his letters as a triumph over time and the tribulations of textual transmission was already celebrated in antiquity, as highlighted by the Roman philosopher Seneca (first-century AD) who claims he is emulating Epicurus by writing his own letters to a friend (see Chapter 2, p. 20 in this collection) and Diogenes Laertius (third century AD) who bases most of his presentation of Epicurus in his *Lives of the Eminent Philosophers*, P. Mensch, trans. and J. Miller, ed. (2018), Oxford: Oxford University Press, on a selection of Epicurus's letters.
3. See Plutarch, *That Epicurus Actually Makes a Pleasant Life Impossible*, 1100A-B, in B. Einarson and P.H. De Lacy (eds) (1967), *Plutarch's Moralia*, vol. xiv, Cambridge, MA: Loeb Classical Library.
4. Diogenes Laertius, *Lives* ... 10.13–14. And see on this specificity of Epicurus: B. Inwood (2007), 'The Importance of Form in the Letters of Seneca the Younger' in R. Morello and A. Morrison (eds) (2007), *Ancient Letters: Classical and Late Antique Epistolography*, Oxford: Oxford University Press, 143.

5 The references to Epicurus's letter to Herodotus indicate the text found in Diogenes Laertius's book 10, thus *Her*.35 = D.L. 10.35.

6 The English words mirror the original Greek play on '*mellein*' and '*meletan*', respectively 'being about to happen, but not yet' and 'actually paying attention to something here and now'. Epicurus urges his friend to pay attention to the present things (*meletan*), and not dwell on the ungraspable future (*mellein*).

7 On the paradoxical simplicity of the formula, see J. Warren (2004), *Facing Death: Epicurus and his Critics*, Oxford: Oxford University Press.

8 See for instance, Plato's *Charmides* in Plato, *Early Dialogues*, C. Emelyn-Jones, (ed.) (2005), London: Penguin, 177–211.

9 See G. Canguilhem (1989), *The Normal and The Pathological*, C.R. Fawcett and R.S. Cohen (trans.), Urzone: MIT Press, Part I, chapter 4.

10 See Plato, *Republic* IX, 581C, in Plato, *The Republic*, D. Lee (trans.) (1987), Penguin. Aristotle *Nicomachean Ethics* I.5, 1095b17–19, in Aristotle, *Nicomachean Ethics*, J.A.K. Thompson, H. Tredennick and J. Barnes, (trans. and ed.) (rev. 2004), London: Penguin.

11 Epicurus, *Letter to Menoeceus*, in H. Usener (ed.) (1887), *Epicurea*, Leipzig: Teubner, 57–66. Translated from the Greek by Ada Bronowski.

12 Epicurus quotes a line from the sixth-century BC poet Theognis (l.427) (in D.E. Gerber (ed.) (1999), *Greek Elegiac Poetry*, Cambridge, MA: Loeb Classical Library), which Sophocles famously echoes in the chorus from his *Oedipus at Colonus* (ll.1225–1228) (in Sophocles, *The Theban Plays*, R. Fagles (trans.) (1984), London: Penguin), beginning, 'Not to be born is best . . . second best, once a man has seen the light of day, is to go back where he came from, as fast as he can'.

2 The Price of Time

1 A complete edition of the *Letters to Lucilius* in Latin and English is found in Seneca, *Ad Lucilium Epistulae Morales*, R.M. Gummere (ed. and trans.) (1917–1925), 3 vols, Cambridge MA: Loeb Classical Library, abridged as *Luc*.

2 Seneca, *Natural Questions*, pref. iv^a, §20, in H.M. Hine (trans.) (2010), Chicago: Chicago University Press.

3 On Marcus Aurelius's appreciation of the benefits of philosophy, see Chapter 3 in this volume.

4 In Seneca, *Ad Lucilium Epistulae Morales*, R.M. Gummere (ed.) (1917), vol. 1, Cambridge, MA: Loeb Classical Library. Translated from the original Latin by Ada Bronowski.

3 The Self-Punishing Student of a Doting Teacher

1 See Chapter 2 in this volume.
2 See *Ad M. Caes.* 1.4 and 1.5 = pp. 90–98, Haines vol. 1. The correspondence is published in C.R. Haines (1919), *The Correspondence of Marcus Cornelius Fronto*, 2 vols, edition with translation, Cambridge, MA: Loeb Classical Library. References here are made first to the first nineteenth-century editor's group titles in abbreviated Latin form (e.g. *Ad M. Caes.*) with a specific numbering, followed by the corresponding pages in Haines's edition.
3 See *Ad M. Caes.* 3.16 = pp. 104–107, Haines vol. 1.
4 See *Ad Ver.* 2.8 = pp. 238–239 Haines vol. 2, on the kiss they exchange as the mark of Lucius Verus's cultivated education, as also the numerous appeals to their love: *Ad Ver.* 2.5 = pp. 236–237 Haines vol. 2, *Ad. Ver.* 2.10 = pp. 234–237 Haines vol. 2, or missing one another: *Ad. Ver.* 2.4 = pp. 236–237 Haines vol. 2.
5 See, for example, A. Richlin (ed., trans., with intro and comm.) (2006), *Marcus Aurelius in Love: The Letters of Marcus and Fronto*, Chicago: University of Chicago Press.
6 *Ad M. Caes.* 3.11 = pp. 12–14 Haines vol. 1.
7 *Ad M. Caes.* 3.15 = pp. 100–103 Haines vol. 1.
8 *Ad M. Caes.* 3.17 = p. 106 Haines vol. 1.
9 *Ad M. Caes.* 3.12 = p. 14 Haines vol. 1.
10 See S. Bartsch (2017), 'Rhetoric and Stoic Philosophy', in M.J. MacDonald, (ed.) (2017), *The Oxford Handbook of Rhetorical Studies*, Oxford: Oxford University Press.
11 See C. Gill (2011), 'Introduction', *esp.* pp. viii–xiii, in Marcus Aurelius, *Meditations*, R. Hardy (trans.) (2011), Oxford: Oxford University Press.
12 *Ad M. Caes.* 3.15 = pp. 100–103 Haines vol.1.
13 *Ad Amicos* 1.2 = pp. 286–289 Haines vol. 1.
14 *Ad M. Caes.* 3.12, see n. 9 above.
15 *Ad Fer. Als.* 4 = pp. 18–19 Haines vol. 2.
16 *Ad Ver.* 2.7.6 = pp. 154–155 Haines vol. 2.
17 Marcus Aurelius, *Ad. M. Caes.* 4.13 in C.R. Haines (1919), *The Correspondence of Marcus Cornelius Fronto*, 2 vols, Cambridge, MA: Loeb Classical Library, pp. 214–218. Translation from the original Latin by Ada Bronowski.

4 A Philosophy for the Poor from a Cynical God

1. The manuscript tradition of the works of Lucian of Samosata places this correspondence within a series of other texts by Lucian devoted to Kronos and grouped under a Greek title which translates as 'All about Kronos' (*Ta Pros Kronon*), usually referred to under its Latin title, *Saturnalia* abridged as *Sat.*, and which is found in Lucian, *The Works of Lucian of Samosata*, H.W. Fowler and F.G. Fowler (trans.) (1905), Oxford: Oxford University Press (repr. by Forgotten Books in 2007), vol. 4, pp. 624–638. The first text of the *Saturnalia* is an interview of the god of the Saturnalia festival; it is followed by a pseudo-archival document of laws been set out by Kronos, now a legislator like Solon and who acquires the splendid name of Kronosolon. The *Saturnalia* ends with our epistolary exchange.

2. For a general overview, see J. Bompaire (1958), *Lucien écrivain. Imitation et création*, Paris: E. de Boccard, pp. 293ff. And more recently, F. Vettorello, 'I *Saturnalia* di Luciano. Struttura e contesti', in *Lexis* 33 (2015): 418–431, esp. 417–422.

3. On otherness in satire which opens a different perspective from which to observe reality, see A. Camerotto (2014), *Gli occhi e la lingua della satira. Studi sull'eroe satirico in Luciano di Samosata*, Milano: Mimesis Edizioni, pp. 74–76. As for Kronos as a paradigm of a faraway world, see Lucian, *The Rhetorician's Vade Mecum* 10, in *Works ... cit.* vol. 3, and Aristophanes, *Clouds*, l.929, in Aristophanes, *Lysistrata and Other Plays*, A. Sommerstein (trans. and ed.) (2002), London: Penguin. And see more in Bompaire n. 4 at 256.

4. See Chapter 1 in this volume, Epicurus's *Letter to Menoeceus*, 123–124.

5. For a definition of the satiric hero, see Camerotto (2014), n. 3 at 105–107. Other gods in the Lucianic Olympus belong to this class of satiric heroes, such as Momus, who appears in other dialogues (e.g. Lucian's *Nigrinus*, or his *Hermotimus*, in *Works ...* vols. 1 and 2).

6. Aeschylus in his *Prometheus Unbound*, l.182, in Aeschylus, *The Persians and Other Plays*, A. Sommerstein (trans.) (2009), London: Penguin, has the chorus say to Prometheus that 'you speak too freely (*eleutherostomeis*)', which Lucian, in his *Prom.* 4 (*Prometheus on the Caucasus* in *Works ...* vol. 1) transforms into 'you are the most ingenious when it comes to speeches'.

7. See Chapter 2 of this volume.

8. For instance, by Hesiod, in *Works and Days*, ll.109–119, in Hesiod, *Theogony and Works and Days*, M.L. West (trans. and ed.) (2008), Oxford: Oxford World Classics, who evokes the Golden Age under the rule of Kronos.

9. Crates's poem is quoted in Diogenes Laertius, *Lives of the Eminent Philosophers*, P. Mensch (trans.) and J. Miller (ed.) (2018), Oxford: Oxford University Press, 6.85. On the Cynics's ideal city, see D. Dawson (1992),

Cities of the Gods: Communist Utopias in Greek Thought, Oxford: Oxford University Press, pp. 111-222 and also A. Camerotto (2018), 'Vite da cani. Utopie e distopie ciniche in Luciano di Samosata', in *Quaderni Urbinati di Cultura Classica* 148(2018): 105-126.

10   See the giant ants from India in Herodotus, *The Histories* 3.102-105, R. Waterfield (trans.), C. Dewald (ed.) (1998), Oxford: Oxford World Classics.

11   Thus Bompaire (n. 4) at 293 describes this letter as 'a seeming defence of the rich which in fact nails down their condemnation'.

12   Thus, on Crates's imaginary island, *Pera*, once all riches are taken away, so all reasons for hate and war amongst men also disappear, see Crates in *Diogenes Laertius* (n. 9) at 6.85.

13   See more on the social context in C.P. Jones (1986), *Culture and Society in Lucian*, Cambridge: Cambridge University Press, pp. 87-88, and B. Baldwin (1973), *Studies in Lucian*, Toronto: Hakkert, pp. 109-110.

14   On the spectacle of riches and its critique, see F. Vettorello (2017), 'L'ostentazione è l'anima della ricchezza. La lezione dei Saturnalia lucianei', in A. Camerotto and S. Maso (eds) (2017), *La satira del successo. La spettacolarizzazione della cultura nel mondo antico: tra retorica, filosofia, religione e potere*, Milano-Udine: Mimesis, pp. 413-438.

15   See Lucian *Nigrinus* 12f, in *Works* (n. 1), vol. 1, and Thomas More, *Utopia* 2.123-134, Part 129, D. Baker-Smith (trans. and ed.) (2012), London: Penguin Classics. See further, I. Gassino (2010) 'Fiction, parodie et utopie: les *Histoires vraies* de Lucien et *l'Utopie* de Thomas More', in *Morus* 7(2010): 43-57.

16   On the afterlife for Lucian as the only possible utopia, with all the cynical aspects this entails, see A. Camerotto, 'L'utopia dell'aldilà in Luciano di Samosata', in *Annali Online Ferrara-Lettere* 11(2) (2016): 9-26. Available at: http://annali.unife.it/lettere/article/view/1398; P. Gómez (2016) 'Voces del Hades, decretos del más allá: la consulta a los muertos en Luciano', in *Revista de Estudios Clásicos* 43 (2016): 97-128.

17   In Lucian of Samosata, *Luciani Samosatensis Opera*, K. Jacobitz (ed.) (1896), Leipzig: Teubner, vol. 3, *Sat.* 25-29. Translation from the original Greek by Ada Bronowski.

5   Real Philosophy for Real People

1   Seneca, *On the Happy Life*, in Seneca, *Dialogues and Essays*, J. Davie (trans.) and T. Reinhardt (ed.) (2007), Oxford: Oxford World Classics, pp. 85-111. On Seneca, see Chapter 2 in this volume.

2   In R. Descartes, *Oeuvres*, C. Adam and P. Tannery (eds) (1897-1909), Paris: Cerf, in vol. iv, pp. 281-287. Translation by Lisa Shapiro, in L. Shapiro, (ed. and trans.) (2007), *The Correspondence between Princess Elisabeth of*

Bohemia and René Descartes, Chicago: University of Chicago Press, reproduced here with the permission of L. Shapiro and Chicago University Press.

6 Good Intentions and the Resistance of Reality

1 R. Descartes, *A Discourse on the Method*, I. Maclean (trans.) (2008), Oxford: Oxford World Classics, pp. 5–6.
2 R. Descartes, *Principles of Philosophy*, in J. Cottingham, R. Stoothoff, D. Murdoch (eds and trans.) (1985), *The Philosophical Writings of Descartes*, Cambridge: Cambridge University Press, pp. 177–292.
3 R. Descartes, *The Passions of the Soul*, in J. Cottingham, R. Stoothoff, D. Murdoch (eds and trans) (1985), *The Philosophical Writings of Descartes*, Cambridge: Cambridge University Press, pp. 325–404.
4 R. Descartes, *Discourse of the Method* (n. 3) at p. 14.
5 In R. Descartes, *Oeuvres*, C. Adam and P. Tannery (eds) (1897–1909), Paris: Cerf, vol. iv, pp. 287–290. Translation by Lisa Shapiro, in L. Shapiro, (ed. and trans.) (2007), *The Correspondence between Princess Elisabeth of Bohemia and René Descartes*, Chicago: University of Chicago Press, reproduced here with the permission of L. Shapiro and Chicago University Press.

7 'No. Colours are real.'

1 A sample from the correspondence between Descartes and Elisabeth can be found in this volume in Chapters 5 and 6.
2 This correspondence ranges well beyond philosophy. Of the 39 extant letters, only a handful are on philosophical themes. A full list of the letters is available at *Early Modern Letters Online*. Available at: http://emlo.bodleian.ox.ac.uk/forms/advanced?people=Anne+Conway.
3 See *Conway Letters*, ed. Marjorie Hope Nicolson, revised by Sarah Hutton (Oxford: Clarendon Press, 1992), 18, p. 51. Hereafter cited as *Conway Letters*. Subsequently her brother, John Finch, sent her three copies of Descartes' *Principles* (*Conway Letters* 486, n. 2). More was one of the first to advocate the inclusion of Cartesianism in the university curriculum. See H. More (1662), *Of the Immortality of the Soul*. Preface, printed in *A Collection of Several Philosophical Writings*, London.
4 For more detail, see S. Hutton, (2004), *Anne Conway. A Woman Philosopher*, Cambridge: Cambridge University Press, chapter 2.

5   Conway Letters, p. 487. The lost letter apparently discussed Descartes' claim that the universe is indefinite in extent (Principles 2, para. 21). Both are topics raised by More in his first letter to Descartes. This correspondence, dating from 1648–1649, is printed in Clerselier's 1657–1667 Paris edition of Descartes' letters and in More's (1662), *A Collection of Several Philosophical Writings*, London: James Flesher for William Morden.
6   This distinction is more familiar to philosophers today in the Lockean formulation of 'primary and secondary qualities'.
7   *Conway Letters*, 24a, p. 493.
8   *Conway Letters*, 22a, p. 490.
9   *Conway Letters*, p. 493.
10 *Conway Letters*, 53.
11 Conway, *Principles* p. 52.
12 The original letter is held at Christ's College Cambridge, Henry More's College, (MS Fellows' Papers 21, No. 1). It is transcribed here with the kind permission of the College Library. It is printed in full in Hope Nicolson, M., revised by Hutton, S. (eds), *The Conway Letters*, Oxford: Clarendon Press, 1992, pp. 493–494; it also appears in part in A. Gabbey (1997) 'Anne Conway et Henry More', in *Archives de Philosophie*, xl (1977) 379–404. Spelling has been modernised in this transcription. It is reproduced here with the permission of Christ's College Library and Oxford University Press.
13 being in physick] undergoing medical treatment.
14 sending to me] sending a letter to me.
15 similitudinary] similar.
16 without] outside.
17 The astronomer Johannes Kepler (1571–1630) now chiefly remembered for the three laws of planetary motion named after him.
18 Sir Henry Wotton (1568–1639), diplomat whose embassies took him to Prague and Venice. He reports his meeting with Kepler in his *Reliquiae Wottonianae* (1651), which contains the letter to Francis Bacon describing the *camera obscura* experiment, which is Conway's source.
19 *eidolum*] eidolon; image, especially an insubstantial one.
20 Early intromission theories of vision explained sight as the efflux of continuous streams of immaterial particles or species from the object of sight to the eye. See David Lindberg (1976), *Theories of Vision from Al Kindi to Kepler*, Chicago: University of Chicago Press. Kepler was among those who subscribed to such a view.
21 *globuli*] globules; particles.

8 A Philosopher-Empress in a Revolutionary World

1. D. Beales (2006), 'Philosophical Kingship and Enlightened Despotism', in M. Goldie and R. Wokler (eds) (2006), *The Cambridge History of Eighteenth-Century Political Thought*, Cambridge: Cambridge University Press, pp. 497–524.
2. Voltaire, *Dictionnaire Philosophique*, ed. C. Mervaud, in T. Besterman *et al.* (eds) (1968–ongoing), *The Complete Works of Voltaire*, Geneva and Banbury, Oxford: Voltaire Foundation, vol. 36, p. 433. All translations are by the author unless otherwise indicated.
3. D. Diderot and J. Le Rond D'Alembert (eds) (1751–1772), *Encyclopédie, ou dictionnaire raisonné des sciences, des arts et des métiers, etc.*, 17 vols, Paris: Briasson, David, Le Breton, Durand, vol. 12, p. 510. On this article's complex history, see H. Dieckmann (1948), *Le Philosophe: Texts and Interpretation*, St Louis: Washington University Studies.
4. She reflected on this evolution in a letter to the German doctor and writer, Johann Georg Zimmermann, in April 1787: 'I remember how, in 1740, even the least philosophical minds pretended to be philosophers. At least reason and common sense did not suffer for it.' In Eduard Bodemann (ed.) (1906), *Der Briefwechsel zwischen der Kaiserin Katharina II. von Russland und Joh. Georg Zimmermann*, Hannover and Leipzig: Hahn, p. 44.
5. Prince Charles-Joseph de Ligne, *Correspondances russes*, Alexandre Stroev and Jeroom Vercruysse (eds) (2013), 2 vols, Paris: Honoré Champion, vol. 1, p. 193.
6. Montesquieu, *Considérations sur les causes de la grandeur des Romains et de leur décadence*, Françoise Weil at al. (eds) (1998–ongoing), in *Œuvres complètes de Montesquieu* Oxford, Naples, Lyon and Paris: Voltaire Foundation, Istituto Italiano per gli Studi Filosofici, ENS Editions, Classiques Garnier, vol. 2, p. 91.
7. Montesquieu, *The Spirit of the Laws*, A.M. Cohler, B.C. Millerand and H.S. Stone (eds. and trans.) (1989), Cambridge: Cambridge University Press, p. 55.
8. The letter is found in A. Kahnand and K. Rubin-Detlev (eds. and trans.) (2018), *Catherine the Great, Selected Letters*, Oxford: Oxford University Press, pp. 317–320; it is translated by K. Rubin-Detlev and reproduced with permission from Oxford University Press. Peterhof is an imperial residence on the Gulf of Finland near St Petersburg. Catherine uses the Julian calendar retained in Russia until 1917; in the eighteenth century it was eleven days behind the Gregorian calendar employed in the rest of Europe.
9. Catherine was awaiting the conclusion of the second Russo-Turkish War of her reign (1787–1791). After many failed attempts at negotiations, the final peace treaty was concluded in late December 1791.

10 Against Catherine's wishes, de Ligne had allowed one of her previous letters to be published in the newspapers. When Catherine rebuked him, de Ligne disavowed responsibility for the leak, claiming that some acquaintances to whom he had read the letter had, unfortunately, remembered it verbatim.

11 The published letter contained a satirical tableau of the political situation around the world, including the effects of the French Revolution.

12 Catherine is reacting to de Ligne's claim that he and others with pro-royalist and pro-Russia sentiments had found encouragement in the letter he had published.

13 Catherine alludes to the Hungarians, who had offered her some troops.

14 By promulgating the Constitution of 3 May 1791, the Great Sejm (the Polish parliament) attempted to create a stronger constitutional monarchy in Poland; this move alarmed Catherine, who had an interest in keeping Poland weak and subject to Russian influence and intervention.

15 Holy Roman Emperor Joseph II (1741–1790).

16 A character in Voltaire's *The Café, or the Scotswoman* (1760), who in the final scene asks why one would separate people who want to come to blows.

17 In the letter to which Catherine is responding, de Ligne said he wished England and Prussia had followed through on their threats to attack Russia so that he could have seen Catherine vanquish them.

18 In 1791, Catherine had six grandchildren: two boys and four girls. The eldest was the future Emperor Alexander I of Russia (1777–1825); the next eldest, Constantine, later relinquished his right to succeed his childless brother (1779–1831).

19 The grand equerry is Lev Naryshkin (1733–1799), courtier, highly amusing conversationalist, and favourite satirical target in Catherine's writings.

20 Charles-Joseph-Antoine de Ligne, the addressee's son, to whom in March 1791 Catherine awarded the Russian Order of St George for his valour at the capture of the Ottoman fortress of Izmail.

21 In his previous letter, de Ligne mentioned Joseph II's promise that Catherine's former lover and most trusted subordinate, Grigory Potemkin, would soon receive from him the Habsburg Order of the Golden Fleece, which he never did.

22 Catherine was offended by Frederick the Great's negative comments about Russia.

23 The French ambassador, Count Louis-Philippe de Ségur (1753–1830), arrived in Russia in 1785 and soon became part of Catherine's inner circle. He left Russia for good at the start of the French Revolution in 1789.

24 In March 1791, Ségur was named the French Revolutionary government's envoy to the Holy See.

25 Reference to the flight to Varennes in June 1791, when Louis XVI and Marie Antoinette tried to escape Revolutionary France; members of the municipal government of Sainte-Menehould recognised the royal family, captured them, and brought them back to Paris. The event severely shook public confidence in the monarchy.

9 From Exile with Love

1 G. de Staël (1813), *Reflections on Suicide*, translated from the French (London: Longman, Hurst, Rees, Orme, and Brown).

2 The letter is in the public domain; the original manuscript letter can be found in the James M. Olin Library, Cornell University, Ithaca, NY, in the Tessé file of the Arthur H. and Mary Marden Dean Lafayette Collection. It has also been reproduced in J.F. Marshall (1967), 'Madame de Staël et Madame de Tessé', in *Revue d'histoire littéraire de la France* (1967), Jan.–Mar., pp. 114–122 and subsequently in Madame de Staël, *Correspondance. De « Corinne » vers « De l'Allemagne » 9 novembre 1805–9 mai 1809*, B. Jasinski (ed.) (1993), vol. 6, Paris: Klincksieck, p. 106. Translated here by Catriona Seth.

10 Erotic Affinities

1 J.W. Goethe, *Sämtliche nach Epochen seines Schaffens, Müncher Ausgabe* (*MA*), in 33 vols (1985–1998), vol. 6:2, Munich: Carl Hanser Verlag, p. 188.

2 J.J. Winckelmann, *Briefe an seine Freunde in der Schweiz*, L. Usteri (ed.) (1778), Zurich, which include letters to the painter Johann Caspar Füssli. The letter presented here to Leonhard Usteri appears as number 39, pp. 119–120. For the omissions in it see discussion below.

3 Usteri died in 1789, aged 48, after a period of illness which was presumably brought on by overwork, as is suggested in his article in the *Allgemeine Deutsche Biographie* (1895) vol. 39. Available at: https://de.wikisource.org/wiki/ADB:Usteri,_Leonhard_(P%C3%A4dagoge).

4 Claude-Henri Watelet was a patron of the arts, (erstwhile patron of Jean-Baptiste Greuze), writer and art critic and pioneer in garden design and aesthetics, who contributed articles on aesthetics (notably on etching, 'Gravure', in vol. 7) to the *Encyclopédie*, under the general editorship of D. Diderot and J. D'Alembert (1751–1772).

5 On this opposition, see further K. Harloe, (2013) *Winckelmann and the Invention of Antiquity: History and Aesthetics in the Age of Altertumswissenschaft*, Oxford: Oxford University Press, p. 69ff.

6   In J.J. Winckelmann, *Briefe, Kritisch-historische Gesamtausgabe*, W. Rehm and H. Diepolder, (eds), (1952–1957), 4 vols, Berlin: De Gruyter, vol. 2, letter 488, 9 June 1762.

7   In J.J. Winckelmann, *Essays on the Philosophy and History of Art*, C. Bowman, (ed. and trans.) (2001–2005), 3 vols, Bristol: Thoemmes Press, vol. 1, pp. xxi–xlvii.

8   *Ibid* at p. xxvi.

9   In J.J. Winckelmann, *Briefe*, (n.6) vol. 3, letter 868, 27 June 1767. Leonhard Usteri published this letter, this passage included, in his 1778 edited collection (see (n. 2) pp. 182–186). It appears to have inspired Wilhelm von Humboldt and Goethe, see W. Daniel Wilson, (2013) 'Höhere Begattung, höhere Schönheit': Goethe's Homoerotic Poem 'Selige Sehnsuch', *Goethe Yearbook* 20 (2013) 117–132 at 124–126.

10 '[O]ur intellectual harmony became known to me when I first saw you. Your form allowed me to infer what I was looking for, and I found in a beautiful body a soul constituted for virtue, a soul endowed with a sentiment for the beautiful ... Let this essay be a monument to our friendship, which, for my part, is free of all imaginable motives and remains faithfully maintained and dedicated to you.' See Winckelmann, *Essays on the Philosophy and History of Art* (n. 7), p. xxi (translation modified slightly).

11 See the discussion on 'The Essentials of Art', in J.J. Winckelmann (1764), *Geschichte der Kunst des Altertums*, translated as *History of the Art of Antiquity*, by H. Lodge (1873), Boston, part 1, chapter 4, section 2.

12 See Winckelmann (n. 6) vol. 2, letter 591. Translation by Katherine Harloe.

11 Rational Empiricism?

1   From *The Correspondence Between Schiller and Goethe* 1794 to 1805, George H. Calvert (trans.) (1845), New York and London: Wiley and Putnam, letter 414.

2   Schiller and Goethe wrote such '*xenia*' from the Greek: poisoned gifts in the shape of short poems, in which they would even scores with critics. Schiller is probably referring to a *xenion* enclosed in Goethe's previous letter.

3   Friedrich Wilhelm Gotter (1746–1797) wrote and translated for the theatre. He adapted Shakespeare's *The Tempest* on the basis of Friedrich von Einsiedels's version for the libretto of *Die Geisterinsel* (*The Enchanted Isle*) which would be set to music by Johann Friedrich Fleischmann (1766–1798) and produced in Weimar under the aegis of Goethe in 1798.

4   *Die Horen* was a monthly journal which ran from 1795 to 1797. Edited by Schiller, most of the prominent figures of the day wrote for it: the Schlegel brothers, Fichte, the Humboldt brothers and many more.

12 'What then is happiness, my dear friend?'

1. G. Leopardi, *Canti*, trans. J. Galassi (2010), Penguin Classics; G. Leopardi, *Moral Fables*, trans. J.G. Nichols, (rev. ed.) (2017), Alma Classics; G. Leopardi, *Zibaldone*, M. Caesar and F. D'Intino (eds.) (2015), New York: Farrar, Straus and Giroux.
2. The correspondence is collected in G. Leopardi, *Epistolario*, F. Brioschi and P. Landi (eds) (1998), Turin: Bollati Boringhieri, 2 vols (referred to hereafter as *Ep.*).
3. On the reception of Leopardi's poetry in England (developing also a parallel with Shelley), see D. Cerimonia, (2015) *Leopardi and Shelley: Discovery, Translation and Reception*, Cambridge/New York: Legenda: Modern Humanities Research Association, pp. 45–101.
4. A. Brilli (2000), *In viaggio con Leopardi*, Bologna: Il Mulino.
5. L. Capitano (2016), *Leopardi. L'alba del nichilismo*, Napoli-Salerno: Orthotes.
6. Leopardi had met Jacopssen probably at the house of the Minister from Holland in the Pontifical State, see S. Verhulst (2008), 'André Jacopssen e Giacomo Leopardi, fra testi e contesti del Gran Tour', in *Studi e problemi di critica testuale*, n. 76 (2008), pp. 187–189.
7. We do not know if it was purposefully destroyed (by stipulation of Jacopssen's will) or whether it was simply lost, see S. Verhulst (2005), 'Leopardi e Roma', in S. Verhulst (ed.) (2005), *La 'stanca fantasia'. Studi leopardiani*, Milan: Franco Angeli, pp. 141–142.
8. C.G. da Filicaia (2006), *Fuori di Recanati io non sogno. Temi e percorsi di Leopardi epistolografo*, Florence: Le Lettere, pp. 148–149.
9. Leopardi evokes a similar yearning in a dialogue, *Malambruno and Farfarello*, in which Malambruno, a Faustian epigone, asks for a single moment of happiness in exchange for his soul, in *Moral Fables*, n. 1, pp. 32–34.
10. See entries *Zib.* 3241; 3269, 23 August 1823; with far-reaching consequences at *Zib.* 4418; and 4492–4493.
11. On Jacopssen's travels, S. Verhulst (ed.) (2008), *André Jacopssen. Itinéraires d'un Brugeois en Italie et en Sicilie (1821–1823)*, Geneva: Droz.
12. F. Pessoa, *The Book of Disquiet*, M. Jull Costa (trans.), M. José de Lancastre, (ed.) (1991), London: Serpent's Tail, p. 76: 'Why travel? In Madrid, in Berlin, in Persia, in China, at the North and South Poles, where would I be other than inside myself, feeling my particular kind of feelings?'
13. In the 'Notes to "To His Lady"' as yet untranslated in G. Leopardi (1997), *Annotazioni alle dieci canzoni. Alla sua Donna* in *Tutte le poesie e tutte le prose*, L. Felici and E. Trevi (eds.), Rome: Newton Compton.

14 J-J. Rousseau, *Julie or the New Heloise*, P. Stewart and J. Vaché (trans. and ed.) (1997), Dartmouth College Press, p. 569 (translation modified here). And see Leopardi's notes on this passage in *Zib.* 4500, 4502. Leopardi used an edition of Rousseau's *Pensées* from his father's library from 1786, published in Amsterdam, vol. II, pp. 206–207. The passage from Rousseau was evoked by Leopardi's brother, Carlo, in a letter to Giacomo from 12 December 1822 (in *Ep.* (n. 2), I, p. 588).

15 G. Leopardi, *Canti*, J. Galassi (trans.), 'To Angelo Mai', ll.169–170: 'O my Victorio, this was not for thee/The fitting age, or land.'

16 G. Leopardi, 'To His Lady', *Canti*, ll.17–20, translation by Ada Bronowski.

17 In G. Leopardi, *Epistolario*, P. Viani (ed.) (1849), Florence: Felice Le Monnier, in vol. 1, n. 183, pp. 302–305. Translated from the original French by Ada Bronowski.

18 Franceso Cancellieri (1751–1826) was an erudite bibliophile and librarian in Rome.

13 A Philosophy of Love

1 The letter is numbered 180 out of 224 in the first ever published work dedicated to a chronological classification of Flora Tristan's scattered letters in Stéphane Michaud (1980), *Flora Tristan Lettres*, collected, presented and annotated by S. Michaud, Paris: Seuil, pp.182–183. He subsequently published two further editions of Tristan's correspondence with the text of other letters added, including those sent to Flora Tristan, which meant a change in the numbering of this letter. See S. Michaud (1995), *Flora Tristan. La paria et son rêve*, Fontenay/Saint Cloud: E.N.S Editions, 1995, no. 107, pp. 167–168 and S. Michaud (2003), *Flora Tristan. La paria et son rêve* Paris: Presses Sorbonne Nouvelle, no. 112, pp. 202–204. For his contextual commentary on her epistolary writings see Stéphane Michaud (1979), 'Flora Tristan: Trente-Cinq Lettres', *International Review of Social History*, 24(1): 80–125; see also Máire Fedelma Cross, *The Letter in Flora Tristan's Politics 1835-1844*, Houndmills, Basingstoke: Palgrave, 2004, pp. 9–19; 80–81.

2 See N.J. Andrews (2006), *Socialism's Muse: Gender in the Intellectual Landscape of French Romantic Socialism*, Lanham, MD and Oxford: Lexington Books; J. Billington (1980), *Fire in the Minds of Men: Origins of the Revolutionary Faith*, London: Maurice Temple Smith, Chap. 8, 'Prophecy: The Emergence of an Intelligentsia', pp. 208–42; J. Beecher (2001), *Victor Considerant and the Rise and Fall of French Romantic Socialism*, Berkeley, Los Angeles and London: University of California Press, pp. 157–159.

3 For published translations of Flora Tristan's brochure *Nécessité*, see Máire Cross's translation, 'On the need to provide hospitality for women travellers' in F. Gordon and M. Cross (1996), *A Passion for Liberty, Early French*

Feminisms, 1830–1940, Cheltenham: Edward Elgar, pp. 27–44; of *Pérégrinations*, see Flora Tristan, *Peregrinations of a Pariah*, J. Hawkes (trans., ed. and intro.) (1986), London: Virago.

4   For published translations of Flora Tristan's *Promenades dans Londres*, see F. Tristan, *The London Journal of Flora Tristan* (1842 edition), J. Hawkes (trans., annotated and intro.), London: Virago, 1982; and of *L'Union Ouvrière*, F. Tristan, *The Workers' Union*, B. Livingston (trans. with intro.), Urbana, Chicago and London: University of Illinois Press, 1983 and 2007.

5   See S. Michaud, 'Flora Tristan' (n. 1) at p. 94.

6   For further discussion about Flora Tristan's social performance as an activist see S. Grogan (2000), 'Playing the Princess: Flora Tristan, Performance, and Female Moral Authority during the July Monarchy', in an acclaimed volume, J. Burr Margadant (ed.) (2000), *The New Biography: Performing Femininity in Nineteenth-Century France*, Berkeley, Los Angeles and London: University of California Press, pp. 72–98. For a full translation of her journal, published posthumously, see *Flora Tristan's Diary: The Tour of France, 1843–1844*, trans. and intro. by Máire Fedelma Cross (2002), Oxford: Peter Lang.

7   C. Moran (2013), 'Theatricality, Irony and Artifice in Gustave Courbet's Self-portraits', *Journal of Romance Studies*, 13(2): 41–62. For a discussion of performativity in a critique of Judith Butler see G. Boucher (2006): 'The Politics of Performativity: A Critique of Judith Butler', *Parrhesia*, 1: 112–41.

8   A. Lucas, *Le Club des Clubistes* (1851), Paris: E. Dentu, Libraire éditeur, p. 154.

9   C. Fillieu: *Le Barde gaulois*, drame en 2 actes, en vers, Paris: Michel Lévy frères, 1860. Available at: http://catalogue.bnf.fr/ark:/12148/cb30436203q, last accessed 20 December 2018; C. Fillieu, *Chant de gloire*, dédié à S.A.R. Monseigneur le prince de Joinville, Paris: Imprimerie de H. Fournier (1844). Available at: http://catalogue.bnf.fr/ark:/12148/cb304362042, last accessed 20 December 2018; C. Fillieu, *Plus de partis* (Chant), Imprimerie de E. Challuau (Chinon), 1859. Available at: http://catalogue.bnf.fr/ark:/12148/cb30436205d, last accessed 20 December 2018.

10 In S. Michaud (2003), *Flora Tristan, La Paria et son rêve*. Correspondence established by S. Michaud, Preface by Mario Vargas Llosa, Paris: Presses Sorbonne Nouvelle, pp. 201–204. Translated by Ada Bronowski, with the kind permission of Professor Stéphane Michaud.

14 Just the Magnificence of Reality

1   H.D. Thoreau, *Walden; or, Life in the Woods*, J.S. Cramer (ed.) (2004), New Haven, CT: Yale University Press, Chapter IX. Hereafter, all citations of *Walden* will be given in parentheses, with chapter number indicated

in Roman numerals, to make references independent of any particular edition.

2   Cf. Thoreau, *Walden*, II: 'A man is rich in proportion to the number of things which he can afford to let alone.'

3   See R.F. Fleck (ed.) (1974), *The Indians of Thoreau: Selections from the Indian Notebooks*, Albuquerque, NM: Hummingbird Press.

4   B. Torrey and F.H. Allen (eds.) (1962), *The Journal of Henry D. Thoreau*, New York: Dover Publications. All references to the journal are cited parenthetically by date of entry.

5   See, e.g. Aristotle, *Nicomachean Ethics*, 1159a, in J.A.K. Thompson, H. Tredennick and J. Barnes (trans. and ed.) (rev. 2004), London: Penguin.

6   In H.D. Thoreau, *Essays and Other Writings of Henry David Thoreau*, W.H. Dircks, (ed.) (1891), London: Walter Scott Ltd.

15 *De Profundis*: A Philosophical Letter

1   Wilde to Douglas [? January 1893], in *The Complete Letters of Oscar Wilde*, ed. by M. Holland and R. Hart-Davis (2000), London: Fourth Estate, p. 544.

2   The most recent editor of the letter, Ian Small, provides a detailed account of the history of composition and publication in his introduction. Wilde, *De Profundis, 'Epistola: In Carcere et Vinculis'*, ed. by I. Small (2005), Oxford and New York: Oxford University Press. The information about the manuscript's history comes from Small.

3   In A. Carson, transl. (2002), *If not, Winter: Fragments of Sappho*, New York: Knopf, fragment 130, p. 265. Sappho describes Eros as a 'sweetbitter unmanageable creature who steals in'.

4   Wilde, 'The Portrait of Mr W. H.', in *The Artist as Critic*, ed. by Richard Ellmann, New York: Random House (1969), pp. 152–220 (p. 211).

5   *The Trials of Oscar Wilde: Transcript Excerpts from the Trials at the Old Bailey, London, during April and May 1895*, London: Stationery Office, (2001), p. 148.

6   Wilde, *Complete Letters* (n. 1) at p. 729.

7   *Ibid* at p. 753.

8   On the relation of Wilde and Pater, see S. Evangelista (2009), *British Aestheticism and Ancient Greece: Hellenism, Reception, Gods in Exile*, New York: Palgrave Macmillan, pp. 130–134.

9   On this episode, see N. Frankel, *Oscar Wilde: The Unrepentant Years*, Cambridge, MA and London: Harvard University Press, 2017, pp. 68–69.

Frankel gives a detailed and sensitive reassessment of Wilde's post-prison years, in which he seeks to rehabilitate the figure of Douglas.

10 ©Merlin Holland. Extract from 'Oscar Wilde to Lord Alfred Douglas, January–March 1897', in *Selected Letters of Oscar Wilde*, R. Hart-Davis (ed.) (1962), pp. 152–159, text established by Merlin Holland and reproduced here with his kind permission.

11 John Gray (1866–1934) poet and translator of French poetry, in the Decadent style, later was ordained a Catholic priest, was associated with Wilde in the early 1890s. Pierre Louÿs (1870–1925) French writer of Symbolist, precious and libertine style, to whom Wilde dedicated his *Salomé* in 1891.

12 Over half a million pounds on a contemporary scale of value.

13 From Oscar Wilde's play *A Woman of No Importance*, Act III.

14 See W. Pater (1873), 'Conclusion', in *The Renaissance*, A. Phillips (ed.) (1986), Oxford: World Classics.

16 A Correspondence Theory of Truth

1 J.M. Brown (1989), *Gandhi: Prisoner of Hope*, New Haven: Yale University Press.

2 A.J. Parel (ed.) (1997), *Gandhi: 'Hind Swaraj' and Other Writings*, Cambridge: Cambridge University Press.

3 M.K. Gandhi, *An Autobiography, or, The Story of My Experiments with Truth*, translated from the original Gujerati by M. Desai, with an introduction by S. Khilnani (2001), London: Penguin.

4 E.M. Forster (1924), *A Passage to India*, London: E. Arnold & Co.

5 Mohandas K. Gandhi to Maganlal Gandhi, 2 April 1910, from *The Collected Works of Mahatma Gandhi* (New Delhi, 100v., 1958–) vol. 10, pp. 473–477. Translated from the Gujarati Gandhiji-ni Sadhana by Raojibhai Patel, and Mahatma Gandhiji-na Patro, edited by Dahyabhai Patel.

17 Dispelling the Tower of Fear

1 See A. Phelan (2010), 'Rilke and His Philosophical Critics', in K. Leeder and R. Vilain (eds) (2010), *The Cambridge Companion to Rilke*, Cambridge: Cambridge University Press, pp. 174–188.

2 In R.M. Rilke, *Briefe*, K. Altheim (ed.) (1950), Wiesbaden: Insel, p. 586. My translation.

3   In Franz Werfel's letter to Marie Taxis of 1 February 1929, in R.M. Rilke and M. von Thurn und Taxis, *Briefwechsel*, R. Kassner (ed.) (1951), 2 vols, Zurich: Max Niehans, in vol. 2, p. 966. Translation by Charlie Louth.
4   See Rilke's correspondence with Lou Andreas-Salomé, trans. E. Snow and M. Winkler (2008) *A Love Story in Letters*, New York: Norton.
5   R.M. Rilke, *Letters to a Young Poet & The Letter from the Young Worker*, trans. C. Louth (2011), London: Penguin.
6   P. Bishop (2010), 'Rilke: Thought and Mysticism', in *The Cambridge Companion to Rilke* (n. 1), pp. 159–173 at 167.
7   See R.M. Rilke, *The Notebooks of Malte Laurids Brigge: A Novel*, trans. S. Mitchell (1982), New York: Vintage International, pp. 22–24.
8   R.M. Rilke (1950), *Briefe* K. Altheim (ed.), from the Rilke-Archiv in Weimar, and in collaboration with R. Sieber, Wiesbaden: Insel-Verlag, pp. 510ff. Translated by Charlie Louth.

18 The Epic Side of Truth

1   All unattributed quotes are from the letter.
2   Walter Benjamin (1928), *Einbahnstrasse*, Berlin: Rowohlt, p. 71.
3   Benjamin quotes the German translation by M.R. von Traubenberg and H. Diesselhorst (1931), *Das Weltbild der Physik und ein Versuch seiner philosophischen Deutung*, Braunschweig: F. Vieweg & Sohn.
4   Norman Campbell (1931), 'The Errors of Sir Arthur Eddington,' *Philosophy* 6(22): 180–192 at 189.
5   A.S. Eddington (1928), *The Nature of the Physical World*, Cambridge: Cambridge University Press, p. 341.
6   On Woolf's reception of Eddington, see G. Beer (1995), 'Eddington and the Idiom of Modernism', in H. Krips, J.E. McGuire and T. Melia (eds) (1995), *Science, Reason, and Rhetorics*, Pittsburgh: University of Pittsburgh Press, pp. 295–316 and pp. 303–305.
7   G. Scholem (1957), *Die jüdische Mystik in ihren Hauptströmungen*, Frankfurt am Main: Alfred Metzner Verlag, p. 4.
8   Letter to Scholem, 17 April 1931, in G. Scholem (1981), *Walter Benjamin. The Story of a Friendship*, Philadelphia: Jewish Publication Society, p. 233.
9   From *The Correspondence of Walter Benjamin and Gershom Scholem, 1932–1940*, edited by G. Scholem, trans. G.Smith and A. Lefevere, translation and introduction copyright © 1989 by Penguin Random House LLC. Used by permission of Schocken Books.
10 See M. Brod (1937), *Franz Kafka: Eine Biographie*, Prague: Heinrich Mercy Sohn and in translation, M. Brod (1963), *Franz Kafka: a Biography*, trans.

G. Humphreys Roberts and R. Winston, New York: Schocken, here p. 49 (all further page references are to this translation).

11 M. Brod's 1928 novel *Zauberreich der Liebe*, Berlin: P. Zsolnay, translated in 1930 as *The Kingdom of Love*, E. Sutton (trans.), London: M. Secker.

12 W. Benjamin's use here of the term 'tradition' has technical connotations from its being the literal translation of the Hebrew word 'Kabbalah', on which Scholem is an expert.

13 A.S. Eddington (1929), *The Nature of the Physical World*, New York and Cambridge: Cambridge University Press, p. 342.

14 A definition found in W. Benjamin, 'The Storyteller', in W. Benjamin (1968), *Illuminations*, H. Zohn, trans., H. Arendt ed. & introd., New York: Schocken Books, see p. 87.

19 'A Shit on a Pedestal'

1 On the fate of the '*Cercle Cinémane*', or 'Cinemaniac Circle', see A. De Baecque and S. Toubiana (1999), *Truffaut: A Biography*, C. Termerson (trans.), Berkeley: University of California Press, pp. 36–39.

2 On Truffaut's relation to Genet, see A. De Baecque and S. Toubiana, *ibid.*, pp. 60–62.

3 See André Bazin's analysis of the specific appreciation for '*mise en scène*', staging, of the new critics of the Cahiers in A. Bazin, 'Comment peut-on être Hitchcocko-Hawksien?', in *Cahiers du Cinema* (1955) 44, February: 17–18.

4 *Histoire d'Eau*, a short film written and directed by François Truffaut and Jean-Luc Godard in 1958.

5 These letters are reported and commented on in A. De Baecque and S. Toubiana (n. 1) at pp. 171–173.

6 Claude Chabrol (1930–2010) French film director, member of the French New Wave; Marco Ferreri (1928–1997), Italian film director, who made the decadent and provocative *La Grande Bouffe* in 1973 (written by M. Ferreri and R. Azcona); Henri Verneuil (1920–2002) French film director of popular super-productions harshly criticised by the New Wave; Jean Delannoy (1908–2008), French film director, whose heyday was in the 'Golden Age' of 1930s French cinema, a representative of what Truffaut and the New Wave condescendingly designated as 'French quality', a derogatory description of the 1950s avante-garde which Truffaut epitomised in his famous 1954 bombshell article 'Une Certaine Tendance du Cinema Français' in the *Cahiers du Cinema* (1954), 31 January 1954; Jean Renoir (1894–1979), French film director, hailed by the New Wave as one of the greatest French directors, see, for instance, F. Truffaut (1975), 'Jean Renoir', in *Les Films de Ma Vie*, Paris: Flammarion, pp. 53–67, which begins: 'This is not the result of a poll but a personal feeling: Jean Renoir is the greatest director in the world.' In his letter Godard puts thus back-to-back the directors he and his fellow New Wave critics had worked so hard to distinguish and contrast.

7 Extract from the letter from Godard to Truffaut, dated May 1973, in F. Truffaut, *Correspondance*, G. Jacob and C. De Givray (eds) (1988), Renens: Foma, 5 continents, pp. 479–480.

8 The fictional character of Antoine Doinel, played by Jean-Pierre Léaud, is the protagonist of a series of films directed by François Truffaut, *The 400 Blows*, in 1959 (written by F. Truffaut and M. Moussy, distributed by Cocinor), *Antoine and Colette* in 1962 (written by F. Truffaut, distributed by 20th Century Fox/Embassy), *Stolen Kisses* in 1968 (written by F. Truffaut, C. De Givray and B. Revon, distributed by United Artists), *Bed and Board* in 1970 (written by F. Truffaut, C. De Givray and B. Revon, distributed by Columbia Pictures) and *Love on the Run* in 1979 (written by F. Truffaut, M-F. Pisier, J. Aurel and S. Shiffman, distributed by AMLF/Gala). See Truffaut's own analysis of his 'ambiguous – ubiquitous' relationship as he calls it with Léaud as an alter ego in F. Truffaut (1970), 'Préface' of *Les Aventures d'Antoine Doinel*, Paris: Mercure de France.

9 From *Breathless*, written and directed by J-L. Godard, based on an original idea by F. Truffaut, from 1960 (distributed by UGC/Films Around the World). The dialogue is very famous and worth quoting in its original French, see J-L. Godard (1974), *A Bout de Souffle*, Nantes: Baland, Bibliothèque des Classiques du Cinema, pp. 189–191:

'Michel: C'est vraiment dégueulasse.
Patricia: Qu'est-ce qu'il a dit?
Policeman: Il a dit que vous êtes vraiment 'une dégueulasse'.
Patricia: Qu'est-ce que c'est 'dégueulasse'?'

10 A theme developed for example in conversation with the journalist Aline Desjardins in F. Truffaut (1996), *Entretiens avec Aline Desjardins*, Ramsay Poche Cinema, pp. 42–43.

11 George Pompidou (1911–1974), President of the French Republic from 1969 to 1974. Raymond Marcellin (1914–2004), Minister of the Interior from 1968 to 1974.

12 See on this episode, A. De Baecque and S. Toubiana (n. 1) at pp. 277–228.

13 *Wind from the East*, or *Le Vent d'Est* in French, is a film from 1969 made by the film cooperative Dziga Vertov Group, of which Jean-Luc Godard is an uncredited founding member. The script was written by S. Bazzini, D. Cohn-Bendit and J-L. Godard.

14 Ursula Andres, actress and model, was at the height of her fame at the time, former Bond girl in the 1962 *Dr No*, directed by T. Young, written by R. Maibaum, J. Harwood and B. Mather, distributed by United Artists.

15 Louis Chauvet (1906–1981) was a French film critic.

16 See n. 6.

17 In F. Truffaut, *Correspondance*, letters collected by G. Jacob and C. de Givray (1988), Renens: FOMA, 5 Continents. Translated by Ada Bronowski, with the kind permission of Eva, Laura and Josephine Truffaut.

18 Truffaut is referring to the motor accident in 1971 which deprived Marie Dedieu of the use of her legs (1945–2011), a French actress and feminist activist (affectionately nicknamed by Truffaut as 'la grande Marie'), who played a small role in Truffaut's *Bed and Board* in 1970 (written by F. Truffaut, C. De Givray and B. Revon, distributed by Columbia Pictures) and who was in a relationship at the time with J-P. Léaud. The tragedies in her life did not end there, as in 2011 she was kidnapped and murdered in Somalia, see M. Thomas (2017), *L'Histoire de la Grande Marie*, Paris: Arléa.

19 J-L. Godard's *Masculin Feminin* came out in 1966 (written and directed by J-L. Godard and distributed by Columbia Films SA).

20 J-L. Godard's *Breathless* came out in 1960 (written and directed by Godard, distributed by UGC/Films Around the World) and *All's Well* (*Tout Va Bien*) in 1972 (written and directed by J-L. Godard, distributed by Gaumont Film Company).

21 J-E Hallier (1936–1997) was a polemicist, a radical figure and *agent provocateur* on the French literary scene, a critic and author. Pierre Daninos (1913–2005) was a writer of light-hearted humoristic novels.

22 Jane Fonda is an American actress, born in 1937.

23 Henri-George Clouzot (1907–1977) was a French film director and screenwriter, excelling in the thriller genre.

24 Marin Karmitz (born in 1938) is a film director, producer and distributor, founder of MK2 productions in 1967; Bernard Paul (1930–1980) made a few militant socialist films.

25 Marco Ferreri (1928–1997), Italian film director, who made the extravagant *La Grande Bouffe* in 1973 (written by M. Ferreri and R. Azcona).

26 André Cayatte (1909–1989) French film director decried by the New Wave for the political correctness of his films, which the critics from the *Cahiers du Cinema* dubbed as 'thesis-films'. Yves Boisset (born in 1939) French film director whose films are mostly about historical miscarriages of justice. Michel Drach (1930–1990) French film director of mostly sentimental films.

27 See note 11.

28 Janine Bazin (1923–2003) was a TV and film producer, who was the wife of the legendary film critic André Bazin (1918–1958) who was a father figure for F. Truffaut, and spiritual mentor of the New Wave, who died tragically before Truffaut began filming his first feature film, *The 400 Blows*; Truffaut remained a close friend of the family.

29 Georges Kiejman (born in 1932) is a politician and lawyer specialising in media legislation and questions of freedom of speech. J. Bazin was the producer of a TV programme, *Vive le Cinema*, in one episode, Kiejman had been invited and was given free rein in the choice of topics, but the episode was censured.

30 In solidarity with the censorship J. Bazin had been subjected to with her programme, *Vive Le Cinema*, in July 1972, on Channel 2, Truffaut refused to appear in another TV programme on the same channel, *Les Dossiers de l'Ecran* also in July 1972, on the theme of freedom of thought, which had been planned after the TV screening of Truffaut's *Fahrenheit 451* from 1966, whose central theme is freedom of speech and thought.

31 Jean-Pierre Rassam (1941–1985) was a French film producer.

32 Patricia Finaly was J-L. Godard's secretary from 1963 to 1967. Helen Scott (1915–1987) was one of Truffaut's closest friends and the addressee of a great part of his correspondence. She was his liaison with the English-speaking world, assisting Truffaut in his book interview with Alfred Hitchcock: F. Truffaut, with the collaboration of H.G. Scott (1985), *Hitchcock*, New-York: Simon & Schuster.

33 Jacques Monod (1910–1970) was a French biochemist who won the Nobel Prize in medicine in 1965. He also published works in philosophy, in particular on necessity and determinism, within the philosophy of biology; Monod was also a relative of J-L. Godard from his mother's side, the Monod family, see A. De Baecque (2010), *Godard: Biographie*, Paris: Grasset, the chapter entitled 'Les Godards et Les Monods'.

34 Yves Montand and Jane Fonda starred in *Alls' Well* from 1972.

35 Pierre Messmer (1916–2007) was a French politician, Prime Minister from 1972 to 1974 under the presidency of G. Pompidou. The right to vote at 18 (lowered from 21 previously) was instituted in 1974.

36 Pierre Braunberger (1905–1990) was a French film producer who produced many of the New Wave films and short films of the 1960s, such as Truffaut's *Shoot the Piano Player* from 1960 (written by F. Truffaut and M. Moussy, distributed by Les Films du Carosse), or Godard's *My Life to Live* in 1962 (written and directed by J-L. Godard, distributed by Panthéon Distribution), amongst many others.

37 Louis Chauvet (1906–1981) was a French film critic, who wrote mostly for the *Figaro*.

38 Henri Verneuil (1920–2002) French film director of popular super-productions harshly criticised by the New Wave; Jean Renoir (1894–1979), French film director, adulated by the New Wave as one of the greatest French directors.

39 Anna Karina (born in 1940) is a Danish–French film actress, who starred in many of Godard's 1960s films, and was married to him from 1961 to 1965.

40 Liliane Dreyfus, (née David), (1937–2008) was a French actress, who had an on-off love affair with Truffaut from around 1959 to 1963, see A. De Baecque and S. Toubiana (1999), *Truffaut: A Biography*, C. Termerson (transl.), Berkeley: University of California Press, pp. 147–148. Marie Dubois

(1937–2014) was a French actress who starred in Truffaut's *Shoot the Piano Player* in 1960.

41 Jean Rouch (1917–2004) was a French film director, who harboured a lifelong passion for Africa. He was a pioneer of the '*cinema vérité*' movement, creating cinematic ethno-fiction, blurring documentary styles and fiction.

42 *Bebert et l'Omnibus* is a film directed by Yves Robert (1920–2002) from 1963 (written by F. Boyer and distributed by La Guéville).

43 Alberto Moravia (1907–1990), Italian novelist and journalist, wrote the novel *Contempt* in 1954 (translated in English by A. Davidson, 2004, NYRB Classics), on which Godard would base his film *Contempt* in 1963 starring Brigitte Bardot and Michel Piccoli (written and directed by J-L. Godard, distributed by Marceau-Cocinor/Interfilm/Embassy Pictures).

44 The actress Jeanne Moreau (1928–2017) star of Truffaut's *Jules and Jim* from 1962 (written by F. Truffaut and J. Gruault, distributed by Cinédis/Gala/Janus Films).

45 Jean-Pierre Melville (1917–1973) was a French film director who made *Léon Morin, Priest* in 1961 (written and directed by J-P. Melville, distributed by Lux Compagnie Cinématographique de France). He had made a guest appearance in Godard's *Breathless* in 1960.

46 *Eva* is a film by Joseph Losey from 1962 (written by H. Butler and E. Jones, distributed by Times Film Corporation).

47 Marie-France Pisier (1944–2011) was a French actress, who starred as Colette in F. Truffaut's Doinel series; around 1965, she was in a relationship with Robert Hossein (a film and theatre director and producer, born in 1927). She was politically engaged, especially in the 1960s and 1970s on issues of women's rights and was married between 1973 and 1979 to G. Kiejman, see n. 13.

48 Catherine Rebeiro (born in 1941) is a singer songwriter who also starred in Godard's *The Carabineers* on 1963, adapted by J-L. Godard, J. Gruault and R. Rossellini from the eponymous play by B. Jopollo.

49 Anne Wiazemsky (1947–2017) was an actress and writer, who made her explosive film debut in Robert Bresson's *Au Hasard Balthazar* from 1966, written and directed by R. Bresson, distributed by Cinema Ventures. She was romantically involved with Godard in the late 1960s and early 1970s, starring in several of his films from 1962 to 1967.

50 *Weekend* is a dark politico-anarchist comedy by J-L. Godard from 1967, starring Mireille Darc and Jean Yanne (written and directed by J-L. Godard, distributed by Athos Films).

51 Philippe Dussart (1928–2013) was a French film producer, who worked with many New Wave directors.

52 In June 1971, J-L. Godard had a motor accident which left him in a coma for a week, and he subsequently went through multiple operations.

53 *Wind from the East* is a film from 1969 made by the film cooperative Dziga Vertov Group, of which Jean-Luc Godard is an uncredited founding member.

54 François Cavanna (1923–2014) was a French journalist, novelist and cartoonist and one of the co-founders of the satirical journal, *Charlie Hebdo*.

55 Susan Sontag (1933–2004) was an American writer, critic and human rights activist. Bernardo Bertolucci (1941–2018) was an Italian film director whose films often tackle the great political struggles of the twentieth century. Richard Roud (1929–1989) was a New-York based film critic who founded the New York Film Festival in 1963 which introduced the New Wave cinema to America. Alain Jouffroy (1928–2015) was a French poet, writer and art critic, influenced by the surrealists and editor of *La Poésie de la Beat Generation*, Paris: Denoël, in 1965, introducing the Beat writers to France. Antoine Bourseiller (1930–2013) was a French actor and theatre director and a central figure in the post-war history of French theatre. Michel Cornot (1922–2007) was a film and theatre critic in *Le Monde*, who wrote and directed one film in 1968, *Les Gauloises Bleues*.

56 Henri Langlois (1914–1977) was the founder and director of the Cinémathèque Française in Paris.

57 See n.16.

58 Ursula Andress, actress and model, was the first ever Bond girl in the 1962 film *Dr No*, directed by T. Young (written by R. Maibaum, J. Harwood and B. Mather, distributed by United Artists).

59 From Robert Bresson's 1950 film *Diary of a Country Priest* (written and directed by R. Bresson, distributed by Brandon Films Inc.), based on the eponymous novel by George Bernanos, from 1934. The line is uttered by the priest who is the protagonist, towards the end of the film when he meets a friend from the old days in the seminary.

20 A Philosophy of Dance

1 M. Béjart (1991), *La Mort Subite*, Paris: Librairie Séguier.

2 Filmed versions of the dance, performed by some of the greatest dancers of the last quarter of a century are easily found on YouTube.

3 With the writer, artist, and Belgian politician Michel Robert in M. Robert (2000), *Conversations avec Maurice Béjart*, Tournai: Paroles d'Aube-La Renaissance du Livre; M. Robert (2006), *Ainsi Danse Zarathoustra*, Paris: Actes Sud; M. Robert, (2009) *Maurice Béjart: Une Vie, (derniers entretiens)*, Bruxelles: Luc Pire. As also with René Zahnd (2000), *Maurice Béjart- L'esprit Danse*, Lausanne: Bibliothèque des Arts.

4 Béjart's filmography can be found on the website of Fondation Maurice Béjart. Available at: at: www.maurice-bejart.ch/03_work_03.html.

5 At the Bayreuth Festival in 1961 where he created the Bacchanal dance to Wagner's *Tannhaüser* with the Ballet du XXe Siècle, as also a whole ballet devoted to the Ring cycle, entitled *Ring Um den Ring* (*Ring around the Ring*), in Berlin in 1990. On Béjart's relation to Wagner, see M-F. Christout, *Maurice Béjart*, Paris: Editions Chiron/Association-Danse-Sorbonne, pp. 160–162.
6 See Lucian, *Of Pantomime*, pp. 36–37, in *The Works of Lucian of Samosata*, H.W. Fowler and F.G. Fowler (trans.) (1905), Oxford, (repr. by Forgotten Books in 2007), vol 2. On Lucian, see Chapter 4 in this volume.
7 On Benjamin, see more in Chapter 18 in this volume.
8 M. Béjart (1979), *Un Instant dans la Vie d'Autrui*, Paris: Flammarion, p. 192.
9 In Maurice Béjart (2001), *Lettres à un jeune danseur*, Arles: Actes Sud, Letter 1. Translated by Ada Bronowski with the permission of the Foundation Béjart and Actes Sud editions.
10 A famous line which has acquired proverbial status from Nicolas Boileau's *Poetic Art* first published in 1674.
11 In M. Béjart (1979), *Un Instant dans la Vie d'Autrui: Mémoires I*, Paris: Flammarion.

INDEX

abstraction 98, 104, 113, 205
alienation 88, 153, 167, 174, 193
anatomists 66, 100–101, 160
animals 100, 114, 159, 184
aphorisms 21, 23, 77, 78, 93, 192, 196, 207
appearances 19, 43, 53, 128, 131, 200
Aristo of Chios 29, 31
Aristotle 10, 12, 101, 131, 141
art
    aesthetic theory 91, 93–94, 130, 137–138, 192, 202, 203
    creativity 86, 99, 112, 135, 141, 144, 163–164, 168, 179, 189, 203, 208
    history of 80, 91, 96, 202, 206
    vs real life 87, 114, 116–117, 139, 191, 192, 205, 207
atheism 75, 112
    see god(s)
atoms 8, 9, 10, 13, 175, 182
    swerve 13
awakening 2, 9, 22, 29, 33, 41, 104, 123
awareness 10, 11, 14, 18, 19, 21, 103, 129–130, 132, 154, 170

Balzac, Honoré de 181
Baudelaire, Charles 114, 201
beauty 3, 80, 92, 93, 94, 95, 112, 113, 117, 119, 128, 130, 140, 144, 184, 189, 203, 208
    its degradation 43, 148
    its snares 44, 116, 121, 125
Benjamin, Walter 173–185, 203
Berger, Gaston 201, 206

body
    bodily integrity 12, 49, 54, 160
    expressivity of 113, 136, 175, 202, 205
    sickness 66, 70, 82, 99, 107, 160, 196
    and soul 11–12, 23, 49, 50, 52, 53, 68, 112, 123, 141, 167, 203
bones 82
    intermaxillary, 100–101
Brod, Max 173, 179–183, 185
Byron, Lord 86, 109, 110

Caesar 27, 34, 82
capitalism
    critique of 121, 189–190, 192, 196, 199, 203
causes 16, 21, 43, 45, 50, 53, 67, 76, 122
    and effects 102, 105
chance 13, 18, 49, 100, 182
cinema 187–200
city-dwellers 9, 86, 114, 176, 177, 182
complaints 12, 30, 39, 41, 82, 143
    dissatisfaction with life 117, 121
consent 123, 136
consequentialism 13, 60, 114
consolation 11, 32, 168
contemplative life 12, 94, 144, 170
convention 38, 43, 122, 151, 174, 205
corruption
    of the body 82, 93
    of nations 76, 81, 128, 178, 183
cosmopolitans 85, 206
courage 17, 78, 82, 123, 137, 192

crisis 31, 35, 58, 146–147, 165, 174, 207
   war 81, 177, 183
cynicism 38, 42, 43
   Crates the Cynic 40

dance 81, 201–209
   and life 205, 207
de la Roza, Octavio 204
death 11, 13, 15, 21, 44, 46, 52, 116, 129, 166, 167, 170, 202, 207
   suicide 15–16, 87
Descartes, René 47–55, 61, 65, 67–68, 71
desires
   from a distance 94, 112, 113, 116
   to escape 110, 112, 122, 191
   to learn 29, 74, 95, 106, 111, 116, 153, 155, 158, 171, 188, 204, 206, 209
   measuring the one against the other 17, 53, 62, 115, 140
   to meet 79, 86, 99, 107, 200
   necessary and unnecessary 12, 16, 141, 145, 147
   to possess everything 44–45, 111, 133
   reduced 17, 40, 45, 153, 158
determinism 13, 18, 78, 100, 103
Diderot, Denis 75, 78
Don Quixote 112, 184
Donn, Jorge 202, 204
doubt
   of all dogmas 110, 166
   of oneself 31, 35, 67, 86, 117, 165, 168, 199

Eddington, Arthur Stanley 174–175, 177, 182
education 10, 14, 28, 30, 32, 65, 67, 92, 123, 143, 207–208
   self-educated 73, 109, 187
enlightenment, the 5, 74, 76–78, 87, 92, 95, 111
Epicurus 7–18, 20, 38, 41, 204
equality 37, 41, 44, 48, 82, 160, 192, 198

evil 14, 33, 50, 53, 110, 169–170
   pain 15–16, 42, 89, 116, 137, 144, 169
exile 86–87, 90, 112, 174
   castaway 178
experience 21, 31, 42, 51, 52, 77, 92, 95, 98, 100, 130, 140, 165, 171, 176, 202
   empiricism 101, 104

failure 13, 18, 59, 77, 104, 141–142, 148, 178, 184
   overcoming 50, 52, 137, 140
family 66, 79, 83, 85, 88, 135, 187
   mother 9, 85, 143, 146, 201
fear 3, 13, 14, 15, 17, 24, 42, 45, 52, 87, 90, 158, 166–167, 172, 183
fellowship
   in humanity 18, 20, 110, 119, 122
Finch, John 66, 68, 70
freedom 13, 16, 38, 49, 52, 86, 150, 153, 192
   free will 50
friendship 13, 19, 33, 42, 88, 92, 97, 99, 110, 113, 130–131, 156, 188
   confidences 111, 113, 115
food 13, 15, 40, 45, 140
fools 15, 16, 58, 107, 114, 139, 144, 180, 184
French
   influence 92
   language 74, 86, 88, 110
futility 16, 17, 19, 21, 42, 45, 114, 116, 128, 197, 208

Genet, Jean 188, 201
goal
   of life 17, 49, 123, 129, 143
god(s) 8, 13, 14, 18, 38, 41, 127, 129, 132, 159, 166, 169, 176
Godard, Jean-Luc 187–200, 201
Goethe, Johann Wolfgang, 91, 97, 100, 103, 201
ghosts 45, 116, 167, 168
Golden Age 38, 40, 132

240 INDEX

governing, the art of 33, 45, 61,
    76, 82
  see corruption, of nations
gratitude 14, 28, 29, 33, 66, 80, 127,
    129, 133
  absence of 147

habit 15, 17, 49–50, 62, 141, 148
happiness 16, 37, 40, 42, 49, 87,
    114–115, 116, 169
  as not suffering 113
help 11, 32, 49, 107, 131, 133, 171, 184,
    189, 192, 196, 199, 200
homoerotics 28, 93–94, 96, 135, 137,
    138, 140
hope 5, 16, 18, 41, 42, 89, 116, 178,
    184
human nature 28, 33, 49, 50, 77, 88,
    124, 139, 158, 190
humility 155, 159, 192, 200, 206
hybrid 3, 41, 206, 209
hypocrisy 43, 159, 178, 188, 189, 191

imagination 15, 50, 53, 110, 111–112,
    113, 116, 128, 146
  it's power 115, 130
independence 13, 17, 47, 120, 150
  what is up to us 13, 49, 53, 122,
    139
India 149–150, 153, 160, 208
inequality 39, 78, 121
  see equality
inner citadel, (with variations) 23, 30,
    50, 88, 111
introspection 30, 49, 137, 145, 165
inversion 24, 138, 139, 148, 166, 191
irrationality 44, 60, 77, 78, 177, 183
Italy 66, 87, 92, 94, 109, 198

Kafka, Franz 173, 175, 179–181, 183
Kant, Immanuel 98, 101, 103, 163
Kepler, Johannes 68, 71
Klee, Paul 183

language 205
  its shortcomings 175, 176

laughter 16, 32, 39, 120, 123, 206
  fun and games 17, 41, 43, 44, 81,
    107, 145
Léaud, Jean-Pierre 188, 190, 194, 196,
    198
letter, the
  as confession 139, 143
  as conversation 20, 48, 61, 79, 86,
    110, 117, 149, 151, 163, 168,
    173
  genre 8, 48, 76, 204
  its impact 34, 47, 65, 90, 91, 99,
    120, 123
    negative 151, 198
  as incriminating 135, 136, 173,
    198
  as a pledge of trustworthiness 8,
    19, 30, 37, 99, 115, 204
  postal service, the 39, 151, 155, 157
  read aloud 9, 79, 152, 171
  Republic of Letters, the 2, 47
  as soft power 74, 120
love 28, 87, 110, 111, 113, 116, 119,
    124, 136, 137, 167, 171
  bittersweet 137–138
Lucian of Samosata 37–46, 112, 203

materialism
  philosophy of 110
  in antiquity, see atoms
moderation 17, 76, 141, 145, 181
modernity 153–154, 157, 175, 176,
    177, 182, 203
money 13, 24, 39, 85, 146, 189
  generosity 42, 147
  luxury 13, 17, 42–43, 44, 147
  numismatics 92, 95
  ruin 146
  wealth 42, 52, 58, 86, 160, 199
monstrosity 39, 139, 148, 169
Montesquieu 73, 76–77
moral
  action 59, 60, 121, 130, 152
  immoral 34, 78, 136, 140, 191
  integrity 32, 48, 57, 61, 75, 120,
    123, 138, 140, 190, 192, 199

philosophy 7, 47, 60, 76, 78, 130
value 6, 29, 31, 77, 113, 119, 130, 138, 190
More, Henry 65–72
multitudes
   of people 14, 155, 177, 183, 192, 196
   of worlds 10
mysticism 123, 159, 169, 175, 176, 177, 181–182, 183

Napoleon 85
nature 12, 18, 22, 25, 60, 63, 82, 92, 98, 128, 132, 170
   endowments of 58, 127
   laws of 40, 102, 128, 182
Nietzsche, Friedrich 109, 163, 201
nightmares 8, 52
Non-Violence 150, 156, 158

optimism 24, 52

passions, the 50, 54, 60–61, 63, 159
   Cinephilia 188
Pater, Walter 141, 148
performance 107, 122, 124, 139, 145, 151, 170, 202, 206, 208
   its unrepeatability 203
pessimism 15, 88, 109, 116, 178, 195
Pessoa, Fernando 111, 112
Petitpa, Marius 206
philosophy
   as academic discipline 23, 163, 141, 174
   as derogatory 32
   its healing power 10, 14, 20, 32, 58, 61, 122
   as life-practice 122, 129, 150, 152, 165, 174
   philosopher, the 74–75, 78, 191
   as procuring fame 20
   its study 14, 31, 48, 105, 163
   theory and practice 48, 57, 101, 120, 192, 207
plants 40, 46, 98, 100
Plato 12, 74, 94, 112, 113, 138, 163, 181

pleasure 8, 13, 15–17, 50, 53–54, 110, 116, 141, 208
   its emptiness 45, 92, 115, 146
politics 61, 73, 78, 119, 150, 159, 189, 196
possibility 7, 10, 11, 17, 23, 39, 42, 43, 45, 59, 60, 62, 65, 87, 88, 102, 103, 105, 115, 117, 141, 168, 170, 175–176, 198, 202, 203
poverty 17, 43, 127, 131
   see money
prescience 80, 183
prison 135, 136, 139, 142, 149
privacy 7, 20, 27, 30, 47, 61, 66, 69, 93, 99, 119, 136, 153, 179
   pretence of 20, 79, 165

Realometer 128
reason 13, 49, 50, 58–59, 60, 101, 103, 123
   deficiencies 59
redemption 138
regret 53, 140, 188
   repentance 57, 59, 62
representation *vs* reality 50, 71, 111, 113, 116, 122, 139, 176–177, 180, 188, 199
reproof 29, 190
responsibility 30, 41, 43, 52, 53, 144, 190
revolution
   French 74, 76, 82, 85–86, 123
   May 1968 189, 196–197
   of the mind 69
   of society 40, 42, 122–123, 150
Rilke, Rainer Maria 3, 163–172, 201, 204
romantics 85, 87, 110–111, 112, 114
Rousseau, Jean-Jacques 78, 88, 92, 110, 111, 112

satire 38, 43, 76, 81–82
   tragic-comic 41, 177
Scholem, Gershom 173, 176
Schopenhauer, Arthur 109

science 18, 66, 69, 98, 100, 174, 177, 182, 206
experiments 68, 71, 152, 175
self 49, 52, 57, 85, 88, 98, 121, 150
self-knowledge 11, 139, 144
self-realisation 141, 150, 160, 205, 208
Seneca 19–26, 27, 39, 48–49, 50
senses, the 15, 67, 130, 140, 166, 175, 203
sight 92, 94, 98, 104, 148, 195
being a witness to 43, 46, 94, 130
sound 88, 127, 148, 177, 183
sensitivity 57, 63, 88, 94, 110–111, 113, 114, 116, 122
sex 17, 45, 46, 75, 91, 125, 136, 140, 198, 205
shallowness 111, 113, 116, 128, 141, 144
shame 29–30, 39, 137, 146, 146, 184
silence
of the organs 12, 16, 49
Socrates 11, 32, 43, 139, 181, 204–205, 207
soul
greatness of 125
as object of care 20, 85
as modified through perception 23, 67, 139, 141
with respect to the body, *see* body
Staël, Madame de 85–90, 111
Stoics, the 13, 21, 23, 32, 57, 59, 75
sublime, the 203
success 13, 18
Swaraj 150, 158
Switzerland 86, 88, 92, 94, 109, 187, 204

time
age 10, 14, 48, 75, 164, 202
fleeting 43
future, the 10, 14, 15, 16, 123, 128
past 117, 137, 201

posterity 20, 89, 140, 180
quantity of 43, 49, 50
speed 154, 157, 170
it's opposite 207
wasted 21, 25
Tolstoy, Leo 163, 166, 167, 171
traditions 11, 42, 76, 98, 122, 138, 153–154, 176, 178, 183–184, 202, 204, 206, 208
travels 87, 92, 110, 111, 120
of the mind 111–112
truth 29, 50, 75, 138, 150, 151, 193
between friends 131, 133, 138, 146, 173, 179, 189, 190, 194
and falsity 14, 37, 54, 92, 128, 139, 193–194

unions 120, 121, 122, 196
utopia 37, 40, 88, 114, 121, 122

value 13, 25, 30, 43, 50, 54, 88, 116, 127, 129, 191
vengeance 53–54
virtue(s) 17, 33–34, 49, 53, 59, 114, 127, 140–141, 160
void, that it exists 66, 69, 70, 175
Voltaire 73, 75, 110

Wagner, Richard 201, 202
Walden 127, 129
weather, the 70
in the soul 12, 16
as cultural atmosphere 88, 144
will-power 13, 31, 122, 147–148
wisdom 15, 18, 58, 117, 139, 183, 204
connoisseurship 93, 95, 144, 178
women 9, 47–48, 57, 65, 67, 73, 76, 85, 116, 119, 164, 198
emancipation 120–121, 124
feminism 122–123, 124
Woolf, Virginia 175

Youth, *see* time, age

www.ingramcontent.com/pod-product-compliance
Lightning Source LLC
Chambersburg PA
CBHW060948230426
43665CB00015B/2115